Ian W. Shaw is the author of seven books: *The Bloodbath*, *On Radji Beach*, *Glenrowan*, *The Ghosts of Roebuck Bay*, *The Rag Tag Fleet*, *Murder at Dusk* and *Operation Babylift*. *The Bloodbath* was nominated for a Victorian Premier's Literary Award and was shortlisted in the Local History category. Ian is a graduate of the University of Melbourne and holds postgraduate degrees from Monash University and the University of Michigan. After ten years as a secondary school teacher, Ian worked in the Commonwealth public service and private enterprise for three decades, and is an expert on security issues. He lives in Canberra.

OPERATION BABYLIFT

IAN W. SHAW

Published in Australia and New Zealand in 2019
by Hachette Australia
(an imprint of Hachette Australia Pty Limited)
Level 17, 207 Kent Street, Sydney NSW 2000
www.hachette.com.au

10 9 8 7 6 5 4 3 2 1

 A catalogue record for this
book is available from the
National Library of Australia

ISBN: 978 0 7336 4224 1 (paperback)

Cover design by Luke Causby, Blue Cork Design
Front cover photograph courtesy of the Australian War Memorial/Barrie Winston Farleigh Gillman
    (Ref: GIL/67/0485/VN). Back cover photograph: Robert Stinnett, Operation Babylift, April 12, 1975
    (H99.1.60). Gelatin Silver Print, 8x10 in. The Oakland Tribune Collection, the Oakland Museum of
    California, Gift of the Alameda Newspaper Group.
Text design by Bookhouse, Sydney
Typeset in 12/17.3 pt Simoncini Garamond by Bookhouse, Sydney
Printed and bound in Australia by McPherson's Printing Group

To my sister, Laraine Delia Talbot

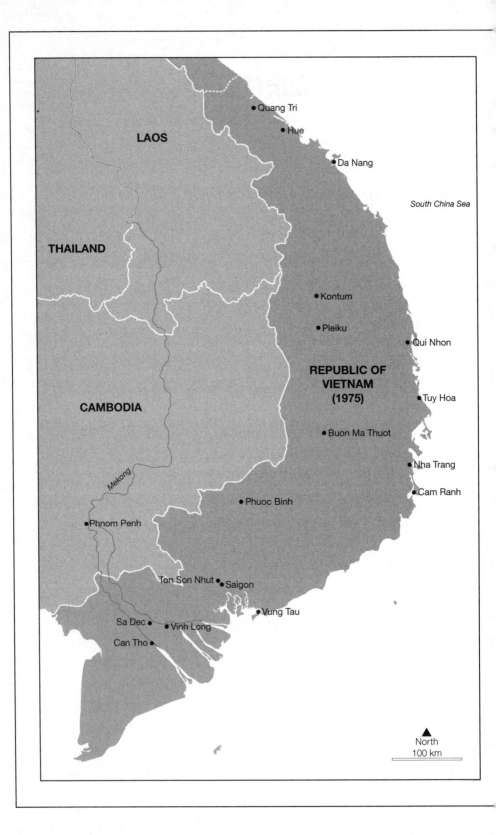

CONTENTS

PROLOGUE

DA NANG, FRIDAY 28 MARCH 1975

Ed Daly was not a man to be trifled with. He had started life with less than most of his countrymen, an orphan from the south side of Chicago, and had parlayed a lifetime of hard work, a healthy dose of rat cunning and monumental self-belief into the ownership of one of the world's most successful air transportation companies. When he bought that company, World Airways, in the early 1950s, it owned two old military aircraft that had first seen service a decade earlier during World War II, operating out of equally run-down facilities in New Jersey. Now, twenty years later, World Airways owned a fleet of modern passenger and cargo aircraft, and had a staff that numbered in the hundreds and a new, modern base at the Oakland International Airport in California. Much of the company's growth came from a series of US government contracts, most recently contracts for the movement of men and material into and out of the hotspots of Cambodia and South Vietnam. Now, though, it seemed to Ed Daly that he might be about to lose those contracts at the same time as the United States was losing its footholds in those two countries to the Communist forces sweeping through them both.

After thirty years of bitter fighting up and down the length of the country, an end to the conflict was in sight even though it was not the end the government in the south and its allies had envisioned.

The crunch had come just a few days earlier, in mid-March, in the northern reaches of South Vietnam when the old imperial capital of Hue was surrounded by North Vietnamese regular army units and cut off from the rest of the country. North Vietnamese and Vietcong forces were on the offensive throughout the south by late March and the fall of the country's whole northern section appeared imminent. As North Vietnamese forces closed in, nowhere was the collapse of government infrastructure more evident than in South Vietnam's second city, Da Nang. By then, Da Nang probably contained more than two million inhabitants, double its normal population, with most of the excess comprising refugees from the fighting to the north and west. It also contained many important civilian and military installations and personnel, and, as Da Nang's fate appeared increasingly problematic, the US Embassy in Saigon offered Ed Daly and World Airways a contract to fly twenty planeloads of refugees from Da Nang to Saigon.[1]

These evacuations commenced on Wednesday 26 March with two flights using Daly's Boeing 727 passenger aircraft, each carrying two hundred refugees; there were no problems either in the air or on the ground at Da Nang. The first evacuation the next day was not so smooth. The 727 landed at Da Nang without incident, but as it taxied towards the World Airways terminal people started rushing towards it. The pilot continued to the terminal where the aircraft stopped and lowered its rear passenger stairs. First down those stairs were two burly US Embassy security guards who happened to be on board. They

positioned themselves on either side at the bottom to regu-
late the passengers who were allowed on the flight. It worked
for a while and the aircraft slowly filled. As it did so, though,
those waiting realised that their chances of getting aboard were
decreasing rapidly, and they surged forward. The guards used
mace to keep them back, scrambling up the stairs as they were
raised. The aircraft taxied away from the terminal and took off
with considerably more people than the 131 it was authorised
to carry, but it had come very close to being a humanitarian
disaster.[2] Subsequent flights that afternoon proceeded without
any major problems.

The Thursday morning flight that was almost mobbed had
carried Ed Daly, who thus had first-hand experience of what
might happen if panic again set in among the refugees. The
presence of armed, deserting soldiers was a particular concern,
but the relative calm of the afternoon flights brought some
reassurance to Daly and his crews. That reassurance was not
shared in official circles and when the US Embassy heard of what
had occurred on the first flight on Thursday, US Ambassador
to South Vietnam Graham Martin immediately suspended all
evacuation flights to Da Nang. According to those who worked
with him, Daly was furious, believing that he was better placed
than anyone to assess the safety of his aircraft's operations. He
was able to arrange a brief meeting with South Vietnamese
President Thieu, who reassured him that Da Nang would remain
safe in the short term at least. The soldiers of the Army of the
Republic of South Vietnam (ARVN) would fight to the last if
they believed their families had been evacuated and were safe,
Thieu told Daly.[3]

Armed with this reassurance, Daly drove directly to the
embassy, where he demanded to see Ambassador Martin. What

followed was an extremely acrimonious meeting that ended with Daly calling Martin nothing more than a jumped-up used-car salesman and Martin responding by firstly cancelling World Airways' contract with the embassy and then warning Daly that if he attempted any more flights into Da Nang he would move to have his operating licence cancelled. Back at his suite in the Caravelle Hotel, Daly announced to his senior staff that his airline would be carrying out another evacuation mission to Da Nang the next day, and began making the necessary arrangements.[4]

•

The operation started early on the morning of Saturday 29 March, when Daly ordered his three available Boeing 727s to be fuelled and crewed for the flight to Da Nang. He would fly in the first with his chief pilot, Ken Healy;[5] co-pilot Glen Flansaas; flight engineer Charles Stewart; and three flight attendants, Jan Wollett, Val Witherspoon and 21-year-old Atsako Okuba. The second aircraft, flown by Dave Wanis, would follow, while the third, flown by Don McDaniel, would circle Nha Trang – about halfway between Saigon and Da Nang – until called into service. Also aboard Daly's aircraft would be American reporter Bruce Dunning and his camera team from CBS News, plus two reporters from United Press International and several World Airways ground staff. Each aircraft would carry a normal complement of cabin crew plus Vietnamese translators. Healy would land, they would load up with refugees and then depart, then both Wanis and McDaniel would complete the same process.

Daly's aircraft departed on the forty-five-minute flight to Da Nang around 8.30 a.m. The weather forecast was for fine and clear conditions all day, and the short flight up the country's east coast was uneventful, with cabin crew and journalists chatting in the main cabin until Ken Healy put the aircraft into a slow descent to Da Nang airport. The arrangements had been worked out: Healy would drop down for a flypast over the airport before attempting to land while the second aircraft, flown by Dave Wanis, would circle Da Nang. If it was safe to land, Healy would touch down and again taxi to the World Airways terminal. There, the rear stairway would be lowered for embarking passengers while Joe Hrezo, a World Airways ground controller from the Clark Air Base in the Philippines, would help load the aircraft before making his way to the control tower to act as an air traffic controller for the evacuation flights that day. Before then, he would assist Ed Daly to secure the stairs against a possible rush by panicked refugees; both men would be carrying pistols to help in this. The news crews would also exit the aircraft when it came to a halt to film the entire evacuation process.

The World Airways passenger jets were not the only American aircraft in the Da Nang area that morning. Two Air America helicopters were also circling Da Nang, flying low, searching for some Western diplomats who were stranded in the city and who had radioed for help. The crews of both helicopters knew that the situation at the airport was fraught with danger and when one of the pilots, Marius Bourke, spotted the approaching 727, he tried to send a radio message to it, warning the pilot not to land at Da Nang airport. There was no response. The pilot of the second helicopter, Tony Coalson, was closer to the airport than Bourke and could see the strikes of incoming shells and rockets. He could also see wisps of smoke rising from vehicles that had been burned out overnight, some destroyed by ground fire from the approaching communist forces and some simply abandoned and burnt by their owners. Coalson, too, radioed the approaching 727 with a warning that it might be too dangerous to land.[6] Coalson's radio message was also ignored.

While Wanis's aircraft circled high overhead, Ken Healy took his 727 down to two hundred metres and, with the engines throttled back, flew the length of one of the twin runways. With not a person in sight, the airport seemed completely deserted. Healy took his aircraft around again and this time, rather than overflying the runway, he adjusted the flaps, lowered the wheels and prepared to land. As he crossed the airport's perimeter fence, the entire facility burst into life as hundreds and then thousands of people suddenly appeared. They came from within, between and behind the buildings and bunkers that lined the airport's boundaries, hangars and sheds, and while most were on foot, others were on bicycles and motorbikes, or in cars, vans, jeeps and trucks. An armoured personnel carrier even appeared from somewhere, all headed towards the World Airways 727.

What had been a calm and peaceful scene soon turned into mayhem and chaos. As the 727 slowed down, a truck drew level with the cockpit and one of its passengers appeared to fire several shots at the aircraft from a pistol before disappearing. Ahead of them, another man also stood in the middle of the runway, aiming a pistol at the approaching aircraft. Healy turned towards him and that man also disappeared into the crowd. From somewhere between the buildings a shiny sports car, a Mustang, appeared and bounced across the infield driving towards the plane. The driver took it onto the runway where he stopped the car, jumped out and aimed a pistol directly at the window in front of the pilot. Healy ignored him: the windows were bulletproof.

Healy had lowered the rear passenger stairs when the aircraft touched down but raised them again when people streamed out onto the runway. Now he lowered them again as Ed Daly and

Joe Hrezo made their way to the rear of the aircraft. The plan was to slow down to walking pace, manoeuvre the aircraft across the taxiway to the World Airways terminal, turn around and, without stopping, collect a load of passengers, taxi back to the active runway and take off. As they approached the terminal and turned around, Daly and Hrezo would assist refugees aboard. When the aircraft was full one of the cabin crew would signal to Healy, who would power up the engines and take off.

It didn't quite work out like that. Slowing to a walking pace meant that people on the ground caught up with the aircraft. While Ed Daly remained on the stairs, Joe Hrezo and Tom Aspell, one of the television cameramen, made the mistake of stepping onto the tarmac and were immediately swallowed up by the crowd. The remaining newsmen opted to remain on the aircraft, one of them speaking into his small handheld tape recorder: 'The crew is scared. The mob is panic-stricken. There's a man with an M-16 pointed at us, trying to get us to stop . . . a jeep, a pick-up truck, just crumbled under an engine.'[7]

The first ten refugees onto the aircraft were deserting ARVN soldiers, one of whom was almost incoherent with panic and kept yelling about bombs and rockets. When the flow of those coming aboard decreased to a trickle the senior flight attendant, Jan Wollett, moved to the cabin's rear, looked into the stairwell and saw something that scared her out of her wits for a second. Near the bottom of the stairs, Ed Daly was hanging on with one hand and waving a pistol with the other. He was wild-eyed and shouting and it looked to Wollett as though part of his clothing had been torn off. As Daly attempted to prevent the crowd from storming the aircraft another flight attendant, Val Witherspoon, was trying to help refugees onto the stairs.

Wollett also moved onto the stairs to assist the other two. Near the front of the surge of people she saw a family of five – a mother with a baby in her arms, a father and two small children, running towards the base of the stairs. She reached out towards them and heard a sharp *crack, crack, crack, crack, crack* above the sound of the engines. A man with a pistol had shot the family from behind; they fell and were trampled by the crowd behind. The gunman forced his way onto the stairs and into the aircraft, brushing past Wollett as he did so; she thought she would have someone deal with him later.[8]

Still determined to help, Wollett turned back to the crowd and reached out towards another woman trying to climb onto the stairs. The two clasped hands briefly before a Vietnamese man grabbed the woman around the neck, pulled her from Wollett's grasp and threw her to the ground, climbing over her to reach the stairs. Ed Daly, who had seen the whole incident, smashed his pistol into the man's face, opening a large gash across his forehead and knocking him back into the crowd, where he was trampled underfoot and disappeared. With the aircraft now filling up rapidly, Wollett made her way back to the flight deck.

There, Ken Healy told her what was now going to happen. He had heard from Joe Hrezo, who was safe and who had made it to the control tower. Healy said that he would continue taxiing and would take the aircraft past the control tower and get as close to it as he safely could. As they passed the tower, Hrezo would sprint out and fight his way through the crowd and onto the stairs. Witherspoon would signal to Wollett from the aircraft's rear as soon as Hrezo was aboard and, when she did, Wollett was to immediately inform Healy, who would run up the engines, increasing speed and power, turn onto the runway from the taxiway and take off.

It worked well to begin with. Healy proceeded along the taxiway past the control tower and Hrezo ran as hard as he could towards the 727 and, using elbows and knees, was able to force his way onto the stairs. Val Witherspoon signalled to Jan Wollett, who called out to Healy that Hrezo was aboard. Healy immediately pushed the throttles forward, realising as he did so that there were several new problems he now had to solve. The first was an obvious one: the active runway and a second, parallel runway were both covered with people and a collection of moving and abandoned vehicles, meaning the only take-off route now available was the much shorter taxiway. Powering up the jet engines also sent a signal to the crowd that the aircraft was going to take off, sending some of them into a frenzy.

In the main cabin, an increasingly nervous reporter continued talking into his tape recorder, his voice rising and becoming increasingly shrill.

> People are storming aboard, shouting, pushing, soldiers, civilians. People are climbing up on the wings . . . They're falling off. Soldiers are firing into the air to scare others away . . . Women and children are lying on the ground. Some are trying to lie in front of the wheels.[9]

He was reporting just what he could see; out of his purview much more was happening. Those who could scrambled into any opening on the underside of the aircraft, hoping to find refuge in its cargo hold, while others vented their frustration by screaming abuse and throwing objects at the 727 as it began to pick up speed. Some soldiers shot at it and one threw a hand grenade that exploded beneath the left wing, causing quite a bit of damage. The real drama, though, remained at the rear passenger stairs.

There, several people were caught on those stairs as the aircraft gathered enough speed to outpace those who had been running to try to clamber aboard. The main issue was that the man at the top of the stairs had been caught in the crush and had suffered a badly broken leg. Even worse, he was trapped in a way that meant the door at the top of the stairwell could not be closed, while efforts to both comfort and free the man prevented at least half a dozen others below him on the stairs from entering the main cabin. To complicate matters further, the weight and the pressure on the stairs had twisted them and Ed Daly, still there, believed that it would be impossible to retract the stairs and so seal the stairwell. He, Joe Hrezo and Val Witherspoon worked quickly and carefully to free the injured man and were eventually successful. By then, the aircraft had left the ground.

On the flight deck, Ken Healy focused solely on getting his aircraft off the ground before it was destroyed by the mob clamouring to be saved. He pushed the engines to full power, partly to scare off anyone who sought to get close to the 727, but mainly to gain enough ground speed for what would be a very difficult take-off. There was not enough concrete taxiway so the take-off would have to be from a grass surface, but Healy believed it was possible. As the 727 picked up speed the wings smashed through several small sheds and Healy struggled with the controls, which seemed to resist his attempts to move them, while warning lights began to flash on the aircraft's control panel.[10]

The 727 continued to gather speed along the taxiway and over the grass and, just when it seemed about to crash into the airport's perimeter fence, Healy hauled back on the controls and the aircraft slowly lifted into the air. As it did so, the undercarriage smashed into an abandoned vehicle and through a fence pole and fence, tearing through the concertina wire, which caught and trailed sixty metres behind and below the aircraft. The plane just cleared a large pile of rocks at the edge of Da Nang harbour before slowly, ever so slowly, clawing its way into the sky.

In the main cabin a cameraman named Mike Marriott had been filming the evacuation and, as the 727 gathered speed before take-off, he had moved back towards the rear stairs to see if he could shoot any footage looking out and down as they departed Da Nang. He arrived at the stairwell just as Daly, Hrezo and Witherspoon moved the injured refugee back and away from the stairs; suddenly, Marriott found that he was unable to film, struggling just to hold onto a rail and stare at what was happening. There had been five other refugees behind the man with the broken leg and now they were all in a life and death struggle. The out-of-shape stairs, the aircraft's speed and angle of ascent, plus gravity all conspired against them, and as a horrified Marriott looked on from just a few metres away the Vietnamese began to lose their grip on the railings and fell off, one by one. Marriott guessed they were several hundred metres in the air when the last one fell.

Mike Marriott turned away and walked back through the main cabin, filming rows of traumatised soldiers and civilians, and charting the aircraft's progress by filming through the cabin's windows. He would never forget what he had seen in the stairwell, but now he was filming history hoping that someone, someday might be able to make sense out of what he had just witnessed. Marriott, Daly, Wollett and many others aboard were also struggling with a greater issue: if what they had just seen represented the response of the people in and around Da Nang to the imminent arrival of communist forces, what would happen when there was a requirement to evacuate women and children from Saigon, a city already full of refugees and likely to contain five million people by the middle of April?

PART I

THE WAIFS OF WAR

BUILDING A WARM NEST

In late March 1975, at the same time as Ed Daly's battered 727 was flying back to Saigon, a small group of women in that city were grappling with an issue similar to that which Marriott and the others were now considering. Their problem was not so much with trying to evacuate refugees ahead of the advancing communist forces – there were far too many in the city for that to be a viable option – but with the future of hundreds of orphans who were now their responsibility. It was a problem they had been grappling with since the beginning of the year, and while they had at times seemed to have found a solution, that solution was now as far away as it had ever been. They were anything but ordinary women, though, and all had been in comparable situations before. They had always found solutions, sometimes in the most unlikely places, and they all had faith in themselves and in one another.

•

On the evening of Thursday 2 October 1941, several prominent local figures organised a bridge night at the Mount Barker Hotel, one of the older buildings in the small country town. Mount Barker was and is in Western Australia's Great Southern agricultural district, some fifty kilometres to the north of the larger coastal town of Albany, and its premier hotel had hosted many similar nights in recent years to both provide some entertainment for the locals and to raise funds for the war effort that was now the focus of most public and private enterprises in Australia. This night would be a bit special, though, because it would also serve as a farewell ceremony for one of the district's local sons, Edward George 'Ted' Moir, who was going off to do his part in that war.[1]

Ted Moir was in his hometown on pre-embarkation leave. Part of the irony of that was if he had chosen to remain at home he could have avoided military service completely. At thirty years of age, married with three small children and self-employed on his own farm, Ted had more than enough reason to stay at home to do his bit – but the Moirs were pioneers of the Mount Barker district and there was family pride and family history to consider. In August, Ted had travelled to the Perth suburb of Claremont to enlist and now, just two months later, he was on his final leave before heading off to who knew where to fight the good fight. He needed to be back at camp on 4 October, so the bridge night was one of his last home duties. That and, of course, catching up with his young family.

The Moirs were a close-knit group: Ted and Clarabelle and their three children, seven-year-old Vivienne Jean, six-year-old Elaine and Bryan George, at five years the adored little brother. Not many memories would remain of Ted's pre-embarkation leave. Elaine would recollect a smiling man handing her a teddy bear, which she loved with all the passion she could muster. She hung on to the little bear tightly as she waved her father goodbye.

Ted Moir had become a machine-gunner, a private in the 2/4th Machine Gun Battalion, a proudly Western Australian unit that would be regarded as one of the fittest and most cohesive units to ever leave Australian shores. Japan's entry into the war in early December 1941 saw the 2/4th sent first from Perth to Darwin, and then to Singapore when the threat to the island bastion from Japanese forces moving down the Malay Peninsula became manifest. Ted and his mates arrived in Singapore just in time to dig in on the island's northern coast where they bore the brunt of the Japanese landing on the night of 8 February 1942.

The machine-gunners' war was over almost before it began. Just over a week later, Ted Moir was one of almost fifteen thousand Australian troops who surrendered to Japanese forces alongside another eighty thousand British and Indian Army soldiers, joining them on the long march out to the old British barracks at Changi. Ted's war didn't end in Changi either. Just over a year later he became part of D Force, a mixed task force of Allied labourers, one of 2200 Australians who were sent north from Changi to work on a project somewhere in the interior of Thailand. They departed Changi during March 1943 and just over six months later, on 1 October 1943, Ted Moir died from cerebral malaria at the hellhole known as Number Six Camp on the Burma–Thailand Railway.[2]

The tragedy of losing a father – even if the children did not know that this was what had happened – was followed very shortly afterwards by the loss of their mother, Clarabelle, on 9 February 1944. With both parents gone, the children's guardianship was assumed by their maternal grandparents, Andrew and Elizabeth Lilford of Narrikup, an even smaller town than

Mount Barker and located halfway between their home and Albany. Vivienne, Elaine and George did not live with their grandparents for long, being sent to boarding school in Albany where they grew up quickly and close.

•

At St Joseph's Convent in Albany, where she lived from the age of six, Elaine Moir grew into a determined young woman. As soon as she finished her secondary education she moved to the bright lights of Perth and met another student named Chai, a Thai national with a family connection to the Thai royal family. The couple fell in love and married, and in 1963 moved back to Thailand, the land where Elaine's father had died. There they had two children, Kim and Mali, but by 1965 the marriage was struggling and the couple decided to separate, and later divorce. In the beginning, at least, there was little acrimony. Elaine wanted – needed – some time and space, and while her soon-to-be former husband looked after the children in Thailand, she moved across to Vietnam, where she believed so much was happening that living there would be like living on the doorstep of history.

Basing herself in Saigon, Elaine worked as a photojournalist for the sometimes sensationalist Australian magazine *Everybody's*.[3] She lived in a small bungalow near Saigon's airport, Tan Son Nhut, on the city's northern outskirts and some five kilometres from downtown Saigon. Her bungalow was located down a rabbit warren of small alleys and behind a high bamboo fence. In Saigon she mingled with other expatriates, and it was these connections that gave Elaine entrée into a world she would never really leave.

A Scandinavian couple Elaine knew were in the process of adopting two Vietnamese children, and one day Elaine accompanied them to the orphanage where the children were living. There, she was shocked and confronted by the reality of Vietnamese orphanages. One orphan at ten years old was a lot older and darker than the others, allegedly fathered by an American soldier. She rarely spoke and never smiled. Afterwards, Elaine found that she could not forget the girl and wrote a short article for an American magazine and in it offered to pay both travel costs and medical expenses if there were any Americans prepared to adopt her. The magazine declined to publish.

In 1966, following her burgeoning interest in orphans, Elaine visited Saigon's largest orphanage, Vo Gap. She would never forget what she saw there.

> There was a child of about two years, sitting in a basket next to a stone pillar on a veranda. He was beating his head with slow deliberation against the stone pillar in a trance-like movement. I rushed to move him away from the pillar as his forehead was swollen and absolutely black with bruises, but the girl in charge moved him back and I was told that he liked to hit his head.[4]

That year Elaine met another expatriate and adventuress named Rena Briand, who was also captivated by Vietnam and distraught at what that country was allowing to happen to its orphans. The two young women pledged to do something about what they saw around them.

After eighteen months in South Vietnam, Elaine had seen and felt enough and wanted to return, with her children, to Australia. In Bangkok, after collecting Kim and Mali with her husband's agreement, Elaine went to the Australian Embassy to apply for a new passport. She had a rude awakening when told that she had forfeited her citizenship through marriage to a citizen of another country. Using their Thai passports, Elaine and the children then travelled through India, Nepal, Iran and Turkey to Greece, where she again applied for an Australian passport.

Confronted once more by stubborn bureaucracy, Elaine simply took things into her own hands, booking tickets for them all and flying direct to Sydney, where she demanded that they all be granted entry. After confrontations and threats on both sides – and some kind of naturalisation ceremony – Elaine and her children were again Australian. The family moved to Melbourne, not far from where her sister, Vivienne, had made her family home and also looked to settle down and make a life for herself and her children. She could never, though, forget what she had seen in Vietnam.

•

Rena Briand was also in Vietnam because of a failed marriage, although her circumstances were far different from Elaine's. Rena was born in Germany in 1936 but had left her homeland for Canada and married a Frenchman, Jean-Henri Briand,[5] in 1954. During the first three years of their marriage the couple travelled extensively throughout North America while Jean-Henri tried to set up business enterprises that ultimately failed. While he was trying to become a successful entrepreneur, Rena worked as a hostess – a Bunny – at the Gaslight Restaurant in Toronto, taught French in Acapulco, worked in a gift shop in Las Vegas's Flamingo Hotel and again as a Bunny at the Fairmont Hotel in San Francisco.[6]

In 1965, after several years in San Francisco, Jean-Henri was offered a senior position with a construction company in Saigon and flew out straightaway to begin work; Rena followed by boat several weeks later. Like Elaine Moir, Rena fell in love with both

Saigon and Vietnam, sensing that something very significant was happening in South-East Asia and that Saigon would be the centre of whatever it was. Her first impressions of Saigon were that it was like a disturbed ant's nest and that individuals within the city had to struggle most days for their very existence:

> the streets just teemed with hundreds of thousands of bone-poor, stunned, hopeless-looking Vietnamese refugees who had fled from the battle zones and swarmed into Saigon with their few belongings to set up houses in some old discarded packing cases or simply on a vacant patch of sidewalk.[7]

Rena would have a lot of time to explore those streets. Just a few weeks after arriving in Saigon she returned home to their small apartment in a residential part of town to find a note from Jean-Henri. In it he announced that their marriage was over. Jean-Henri disappeared into the fog of history, leaving Rena to make her own way in the world.[8] It proved to be relatively easy for her. She had a good camera and was a keen photographer; she also spoke several languages and had, some years earlier, completed a six-month nursing course. With these qualifications, and with an attitude that anything was possible, Rena soon found work as a war photographer.

It was 1965, and a decade after sporadic fighting broke out in South Vietnam following the division of the country into two parts following the departure of the French colonial power, the broad outline of the Vietnam War was taking shape. North Vietnamese and Vietcong forces were confronting the American and Allied forces pouring into South Vietnam to assist the Army of the Republic of South Vietnam (ARVN), which was sorely pressed to maintain control across most provinces in the south in the face of growing northern support for local anti-government forces. The conflict was capturing the world's attention and there was a growing public, international interest in what was happening both in the war and in the country. It was an opportunity Rena was determined to grasp.

Working with both the ARVN and the US forces increasingly engaged in the conflict, she travelled into the back-country, the hinterland that surrounded Saigon, documenting little fire-fights and clashes that would not make the evening news in America, which was her main market. Looking for a niche, and using her camera while honing her writing skills, Rena began writing illustrated essays for hometown papers across the United States, trying to tell the story of what the young soldiers were doing in South Vietnam.

It was work that also took her behind the lines to those places where the other victims of war – the orphans of those who had died or were incapacitated in the fighting – were sent when there was nowhere else for them to go. In one of those places, Rena met Elaine and the two young women found they were kindred spirits in their despair at what they saw of the orphaned children of Vietnam. Rena had an experience very like Elaine's at Vo Gap after visiting several orphanages as research for a photo essay. Among the sights that greeted her were:

> orphanages where up to five babies were crammed into one cot, lying in their filth; twenty-five children in one room with a single doll enthroned on a shelf to be looked at but not touched. Toddlers rocking monotonously for hours, some bashing their heads against the cot's rails, others plucking at their fingers or fidgeting with their ears until the skin wore off.[9]

For Rena it was particularly distressing as she had suffered two miscarriages early in her marriage to Jean-Henri.

Rena became a well-known figure in expatriate and media circles in Saigon, and questions began to be raised about what she had done to gain access to senior military and political figures. As they were, rumours that she was working undercover for one side or the other also began to circulate, as did stories that she was being marked for some form of special treatment. Rena, learning of all the rumours, decided that her future as a photojournalist in Saigon was limited and that she might be better off somewhere else. After lying low at a convent, Rena Briand left South Vietnam for Canada shortly before Christmas in 1967. She vowed she would return and, when she did, she would do something to help the orphans of war.

•

Earlier that year another young woman had arrived in South Vietnam, one whose life would become intertwined with those of many Vietnamese war orphans. Rosemary Taylor, a young former nun from Adelaide, had, like Elaine and Rena, taken a long and circuitous journey to Saigon.

Born in Adelaide in 1938, Rosemary was one of five Taylor children in a close-knit and staunchly Catholic family. She completed her secondary education at St Aloysius College, a Sisters of Mercy school in the heart of Adelaide. There, she would commit to the Sisters of Mercy as a novitiate and then a nun. After school, Rosemary went on to the University of Adelaide, earning a Bachelor of Arts and completing teacher training.

Rosemary then moved to Sydney in the early 1960s, teaching for a while at St Vincent's College, Potts Point,[10] all the while trying to deal with a crisis of faith. She was unsure about the direction of her religious calling and thought that time spent in a more contemplative and closed order than the socially committed Sisters of Mercy would help her decide. With that in mind, she resigned all roles with the Sisters of Mercy and travelled to the United Kingdom, where she knew there were several orders that might meet her needs. There were no immediate prospects for her when she arrived in London, as the Carmelite order in Wales she had sought to enter would have no vacancy for eighteen months. In the interim, Rosemary sought employment and waited.

She had several jobs in the succeeding months, including as a researcher at a large psychiatric hospital, where she learned of the possibility of working as a missionary in Alaska. The idea of such work was attractive and prompted Rosemary to again rethink her future. Realising that she could make a major contribution as an individual rather than as part of an order, Rosemary resigned from all religious affiliations and set about exploring all the possibilities of missionary work as a layperson.

Rosemary made it to Alaska as a deaconess at a Russian Orthodox church at the remote settlement of Dillingham, a position that required her to learn Slavonic, a centuries-old language rarely used outside the church. Unfortunately, her work at Dillingham was cut short after seven months. It was the height of the Cold War, she was a foreign national working for a Russian institution, and there were sensitive early-warning radar sites near Dillingham. The FBI called and escorted her out of the country. Twelve months later, Rosemary returned to Alaska and for a year worked at a Jesuit mission at the even more remote settlement of Bethel.

This time, Rosemary had a twelve-month visa and when it expired she returned to Australia, exiting the aircraft in Adelaide wearing a braid and a fur-trimmed Inuit dress. Before long she had set her sights on another part of the world with pressing problems: South Vietnam. In September 1966, through the Australian Council of Churches (ACC), Rosemary applied to be a volunteer with the Division of Inter-Church Aid, Refugee and World Service, which was part of the World Council of Churches, and was accepted.

Rosemary was to become part of an aid team, working as an 'educational social worker' at a major refugee camp at Tuy Hoa, on the coast some four hundred kilometres north-east of Saigon. There were two refugee camps outside the town, whose occupants were living depressed lives some distance away from their traditional homes. Rosemary's main job at Tuy Hoa would be to work with the children and she was informed that there were likely to be at least two thousand of them in the camps. She was also told that these camps comprised mainly corrugated iron shacks, but that there was an elementary medical clinic onsite and the construction of a school building had commenced. Access to the camp was by air and sea only.

Rosemary joined a team with a doctor, John Whitehall, his wife, the camp's other teacher and a draftsman, Guy Brehon. Rosemary, the first Catholic aid worker to be sent overseas by the ACC, was in the company of two Baptists and a Methodist. Five volunteers were already there, having arrived at Tuy Hoa in late 1966. The publicity around the mission stressed that it existed to provide medical services, work and community programs, and classes for the children. It also pointed out that the nine-person team was expected to cost A$37 500 to maintain throughout 1967 and that contributions to the ACC to defray these costs would be welcome.[11]

Before the members of the group departed Australia, they were given a briefing about mission conditions. There would be few able-bodied men in the camp, they were told, because all the men of military age had either been killed or incapacitated in some way, or were fighting – willingly or unwillingly – with either the ARVN or the Vietcong. While the refugee camps were considered safe areas during the day, they were not at night, so all Western volunteers would have to be out by 5 p.m. every day. Overwhelmingly, those who lived in the camp had been displaced from their homes and their lives were now very basic, with little real hope of improvement in the short term. The men and women who were able to do so would work their fields during the day, usually with armed guards somewhere nearby, but they would start later and finish earlier than had been the norm in their previous lives. Those left in the camp would have little to do but look after their small huts and watch over those children who were not attending some form of classroom. It was a rootless, listless life.

Prior to her departure, Rosemary made several personal preparations based on what she had learned in her months in the far reaches of Alaska. She bought a sturdy pair of jungle boots, an ankle-length raincoat and a rain hat from a military surplus store, and packed only those items she thought would be essential in the steamy heat of South Vietnam. She also bought a good guitar to teach a few simple songs to the Vietnamese children she would be working with, as well as a Vietnamese phrase book that she began working through before her departure. On 17 February 1967, the small group of people came together at Sydney Airport for their great adventure.

•

The members of the aid team flew from Sydney to Saigon via Singapore and, once settled into their accommodation in Saigon, commenced six weeks of intensive Vietnamese language training and acclimatisation. Rosemary would later remember those six weeks as a balancing act between books and the bathroom. As her brain struggled to learn basic Vietnamese her body was trying to cope with chronic dysentery. This was another reason why she would never recall the period with anything but distaste.

At the heart of Rosemary's commitment to humanity, whether it was Inuit in Alaska or refugees in South Vietnam, was her innate belief in the sanctity of life and the almost unlimited potential of all human beings. Part of her role in life, as she saw it, was to both nurture those other lives and provide them with the possibility of achieving whatever destiny God had planned for them. As such, she was a servant of a greater purpose and had no trouble accepting that role for herself. While Rosemary did not expect everyone else to share her vision or her self-lessness, she did expect those in comfortably accommodated positions within caring organisations to try to at least live by the principles those organisations espoused. That was not what she found in Saigon.

The aid project had a team leader, a Burmese national, who lived with his wife in a substantial villa in Saigon. Rosemary found the conditions there repugnant to her sense of service and, after thinking long and hard about what she could do, penned a letter to the ACC in which she shared her feelings about what she had found in Saigon.

> Would you believe that in this time of war when everything is upside down, when the servants themselves sleep in the garage and eat off packing cases in our backyard . . . the Director and his wife complain because our cook never serves hors d'oeuvres . . . [12]

The response was swift. The first six weeks of the mission to
Tuy Hoa were spent in learning the language and culture of the
country where the group was to spend two years. The next week
was spent preparing for the move up-country. After seven weeks,
and a formal complaint about the program's director, Rosemary
was informed that her services were no longer required. The
29-year-old former nun found herself in a strange country without
anywhere to live and anything to do. She relished the opportunity
that her circumstances provided.

•

Rosemary Taylor was not the kind of person to either feel sorry for
herself or sit around waiting for something to come her way. She
knew what she wanted to do – contribute to the wellbeing and
welfare of those who had so little – and she had a starting point
for the work. That starting point was a Saigon institution known
as Phu My. Run by the Sisters of St Paul de Chartres, Phu My
was a combination of orphanage, hospital and nursery.[13] The
complex of buildings in central Saigon housed some fifteen
hundred people including the homeless, destitute, terminally
ill and those suffering from a variety of mental illnesses. It also
included a centre for children with polio. Though obviously a
Catholic institution, Phu My was completely non-denominational
in its admission policy, also allowing its residents to follow the
religion of their choice. As well as its own residents, Phu My
catered for the children of poor families in the neighbourhood.

Rosemary practically walked straight from the Australian aid
team and into Phu My. After she approached the administrators
there to see if she could be of any assistance she was offered a
position, one that provided food and board. A small room that
was part of the complex's outer wall would become her home

for most of the following eight years. The mission occupied almost four hectares in inner Saigon and was supported and sponsored by several organisations and congregations in France, Switzerland, Germany and Australia whose contributions paid for the facility's upkeep and the provision of its welfare, medical and educational programs. For its part, the St Paul de Chartres operation gained a committed worker and caring human being. When she joined in April 1967, Rosemary was the only native English speaker at Phu My; her fluency in French and growing knowledge of Vietnamese were added advantages.

Very quickly she learned that the war was creating immense social problems across the entire country of South Vietnam, and that orphans and orphanages were some way down the government's list of priorities. Orphans appeared almost overnight on the doorstep at Phu My for many reasons, one of the most common being that mothers believed their babies would have a much better chance at life in an orphanage than with them. Single mothers, and mothers whose children were not fathered by a husband, could expect to be treated with disdain at the very least and forced from the family and village at the worst. Their children would have no recognition or status and would be outcasts. Those whose husbands had been killed in the fighting, or who had run away to avoid it, would be marginally better off, but life would be a struggle for them and their children. In such cases, orphanages were a popular alternative. This was usually a misguided perception. One casualty of the war was South Vietnam's medical system. At the time Rosemary commenced at Phu My, there were only two hundred civilian doctors in the entire country; another two hundred had been refused registration, but many of them continued to practise.[14]

With extremely limited access to qualified medical practitioners, most orphanages relied on their nursing staff and the goodwill of those providing healthy foods, milk and medicine. Even that was rarely enough: an American aid official at the time estimated that at the best orphanages in the larger cities, the death rate among orphans was around 30 per cent. In the poorer country establishments, that figure could reach as high as 85 per cent.[15]

•

At the Phu My orphanage, unlike most orphanages in South Vietnam, the children were at the centre of its organisation and functioning, and their welfare was central to all the processes and procedures it embraced. For instance, Rosemary was surprised to learn that the babies were all held for feeding rather than being propped up in a cot with a bottle. This was possible because the older children were involved in looking after the younger ones. From six years of age each child was responsible for feeding one of the babies; the underprivileged children joined the orphans in walking to the local school, also run by the sisters; while the children who had suffered polio, unable to negotiate the staircases at the local school, were bussed each day to a special school in Saigon.

Phu My was almost self-sufficient. It contained within its walls its own small farm where both pigs and rabbits were bred. Its garden produced a wide range of fruit and vegetables for its residents, while any excess was sold at a local market. The adults at Phu My were involved in the everyday work and chores, including food preparation, laundry, gardening, cleaning, guard duty and helping in the nursery and orphanage. Those who were able to do so also undertook small handicraft activities, making toys and novelties to sell at local markets.

If any children at Phu My exhibited signs of delayed physical or mental development they would be removed from the nursery section and placed in the care of an adult resident. Generally, the elderly, indigent carers treated them as they would their own children or grandchildren[16] and the practice clearly had positive benefits for both the caregiver and the affected child.

When Rosemary started at Phu My she worked in the children's orphanage and quickly fell in love with both the work and the children. She also became involved in overseas adoptions. The process was organised by Terre des Hommes, a Swiss-based children's humanitarian relief agency founded in 1960 in Lausanne. The agency had been heavily involved in supporting Phu My for several years and, some time during that period, it facilitated the adoption of several Vietnamese orphans by European families. The success of those adoptions had created its own demand and Terre des Hommes regularly received requests for adoptions from Switzerland, Germany and France, countries where it was then represented.

For Phu My, the process could be quite complicated. There was never a shortage of orphans, but because the requests were sometimes specific in terms of age and sex, there was often some kind of search necessary. From Phu My, nurses or aid workers would regularly visit orphanages in the provinces outside Saigon and on those visits would take notes on the orphanage occupants. Thus, if there were no suitable adoptees at Phu My, they would know just where they could find a suitable adoptee. Those visits to the provinces also led to orphans being brought back to Phu My, especially if the up-country orphanage was overcrowded or if any of the orphans needed the specialised medical treatment that could only be found in Saigon.

Rosemary quickly learned, too, that adoptions in South Vietnam, especially intercountry adoptions, were subject to an involved bureaucracy. South Vietnam had inherited adoption procedures from the French colonial administrators that were complicated, time consuming and costly, with a two-year timeline being typical; at times it took four years to complete. For overseas adoptions, a child first had to be formally adopted in South Vietnam. The adoptive parents were required to be either physically present or represented by a proxy in a process that involved a judge and that could only be waived with presidential approval.[17]

•

Rosemary was soon making trips out into the countryside, to the provinces and the provincial capitals, where she met dozens of hardworking nuns and hundreds of orphans. Transport could be problematic, but she found that the work in which she was engaged would almost guarantee a lift with both civilian and military carriers. There was a war being fought throughout the country and, while she often saw signs of that war, burnt-out vehicles and buildings and craters in the roads, she was never caught up in it herself. The skills she brought to the job also guaranteed that Rosemary became an integral part of the process. In a short time she was being asked to accompany adoptees on their flights to Europe, where she was assisting in the handover of the orphans to their adoptive parents.

In late 1967, two important events took place. First, the Swiss nurse who had been handling all the adoptions for Terre des Hommes returned to Europe and the agency asked Rosemary to take over the entire process. To confirm the appointment, the organisation sent her an official 'Order of Mission', asking her to represent its interests in Saigon on a voluntary basis, and Rosemary immediately agreed. Then, while escorting a group of adoptees to Europe, she met a Spanish nurse named Rosa Tintore.

Rosa was from Barcelona but had travelled far and wide since growing up there. When she met Rosemary in late 1967, Rosa was employed by Terre des Hommes and was preparing to be posted to South Vietnam sometime around the middle of 1968. Rosa was also a highly qualified nurse with tertiary nursing qualifications from Spain, Switzerland and Belgium, and a specialist in public health and tropical diseases. She had also worked for several years in developing countries. Most importantly, though, both young women shared a vision of what orphanages could really do for their orphans. It was a vision that flowed from another shared conviction, that every life was unique and that, whatever the circumstances, every child had the potential to become something special in the wider tapestry of humanity.

•

Rosemary would always view herself as being separate from the politics of Vietnam and the Vietnam War, but early in 1968 she found herself caught up in it all. In the early hours of 30 January, coinciding with Tet, the Vietnamese lunar new year, North Vietnamese and Vietcong forces staged a number of attacks on government and American facilities in central Vietnam. Within twenty-four hours the attacks had spread across the country to over one hundred cities, towns and hamlets, including several attacks in Saigon, where six major targets were struck, including the American Embassy. The attacks, aggregated into what was then called the Tet Offensive, were designed to create conditions suitable for a general uprising in South Vietnam and, in doing so, put such pressure on the United States that the Americans, realising they were fighting a war they could never win, would be forced to reconsider their commitment to South Vietnam.

One of the immediate effects of the offensive in Saigon was the imposition of a dusk-to-dawn curfew, trapping Rosemary and many others in the city. No longer able to travel out to the provinces to collect orphans, she remained at home at Phu My overnight but during the day volunteered at the large US Army 3rd Field Hospital alongside Saigon's Tan Son Nhut airport, which itself had been a target for communist forces. Ask as she might, Rosemary was never able to get any form of military escort for her journeys from Phu My to the hospital, her requests being met with a categorical statement that the streets were too dangerous for any form of non-military travel. So she would ride her bicycle through deserted streets to work with the wounded each day and prepare travel documentation for Vietnamese orphans during the night.

While there would be sporadic fighting for some time to come, the bulk of the action within Saigon was over in just a few days, and a week after the opening clashes the city was declared safe and the curfew lifted. The Vietcong, who bore the brunt of the fighting in Saigon, were unable to generate a popular uprising, and retreated to the countryside. Whole neighbourhoods had been partially destroyed by one side or the other and some 300 000 residents had been made homeless. It was relatively safe to travel, though, and Rosemary set off by bus to the provinces as soon as she could organise it.

Her first destination was Vinh Long, a provincial capital in the Mekong Delta, 160 kilometres and three hours to the south-west of Saigon. There, the Good Shepherd Convent and orphanage[18] had a close relationship with Phu My and had provided several orphans who were subsequently adopted by European families through Terre des Hommes.

Rosemary found that much of Vinh Long had been destroyed in local fighting. The convent, school and orphanage complex had been caught up in much of that fighting as it bordered the main American air base in the province. She found that the orphanage itself had been badly shot up, its walls pockmarked by bullets and shrapnel from exploding shells. Several of its babies had died, some from malnutrition, while others seemed to have been so traumatised from the fighting going on around them that they had succumbed to shock. Some local staff fled at the outbreak of fighting and the mother superior, Sister Mary Hayden, was distraught at the destruction visited upon her institution.

The nuns there were all safe and for that Rosemary was especially thankful. She had come to enjoy a good friendship with the nun responsible for the orphanage, the Malaysian-born Sister Ursula Lee, and she was happy to learn her friend and the others had come through unscathed. They also had some orphans for Rosemary to take back to Phu My, but the fighting had left the local infrastructure in tatters. Rosemary took them all by bike to the American air base, where she cajoled the airport commander into flying the small group back to Tan Son Nhut.

Not long afterwards, she was on another mission to bring back orphans from the Providence Orphanage at Sa Dec, an important river port on a waterway linking the two major branches of the Mekong River. She travelled the 140 kilometres to the town by bus but the roads were cut by fighting shortly after she arrived and it appeared she might be trapped there with the children. Sa Dec was an important base for an American patrol boat operation, and when their commander heard of Rosemary's plight he arranged for her to be taken to Vinh Long on one of his boats. Rosemary and her two orphans made it safely home from there.

Rosemary was once more urgently summoned back to Sa Dec to collect orphans before the fighting along the roads ended. Again, uncertain about how to proceed, she called on some contacts she had made in earlier missions into the provinces. Out of the blue, an ARVN officer contacted her to say that his general would make his personal helicopter and pilot available for the rescue mission. She met the pilot at Tan Son Nhut and was flown directly to Sa Dec, where she was deposited at a landing pad in the town. The helicopter immediately took off again to avoid attracting mortar fire, returning a few hours later to fly Rosemary and two more small orphans back to Saigon.

•

Almost before Rosemary realised it, the calendar had rolled over to June 1968 and Rose Tintore arrived in Saigon to help her with her activities on behalf of Terre des Hommes. They had stayed in touch since meeting in Europe the previous year and had come to a broad consensus on the problems they were facing in Vietnam, as well the possible solutions to the most significant of them.

To begin with, they were convinced that the orphanage system in Vietnam was nothing more than a temporary solution to a permanent problem. What was worse, the mortality rates in most of the country's orphanages meant that the system – such as it was – destroyed the futures of most of the orphans who were brought into it. At a national level, there was very little that could be done about these problems, as orphaned children were well down the scale of concerns the small nation faced.

The half-million or more refugees from the fighting in the countryside were considered a more immediate and pressing issue.

The South Vietnamese government actively tried to limit the growth in orphanage numbers, suspecting – with some justification – that many of the children they contained were not orphans at all but simply children who were 'inconvenient' for some reason. As well, adoption – especially overseas adoption – was frowned upon. In 1967, the official policy was that the South Vietnamese government would do everything it could to keep its children in their homeland so that they might later contribute to its reconstruction.

The reality of life in South Vietnamese religious orphanages was brought home to Rosemary early in her time there when she was on a collection trip to one of the provincial orphanages she would come to know well. After she arrived, she sat down with the orphanage administrator and asked how they coped with the number of incoming children, which was between twenty and thirty each month.

> They were relieved to inform us that God was good, and that since the mortality rate each month was about the same as the admission rate, the orphanage did not become impossibly overcrowded. They thanked God for the justice of this arrangement.[19]

Rosemary believed they were very sincere in this assessment.

Rosemary and Rosa chose to create a new paradigm for what they hoped to build. They could not save every orphan in South Vietnam so they would narrow their focus. What both considered most important was an intensive care facility for abandoned newborn babies, one where the standards of health care and hygiene were such that the admission of malnourished and often-diseased babies was not necessarily a death sentence. In their nursery, they would firstly save the lives of those abandoned children and then restore them back to health before sending them to adoptive homes in Western countries. They were not interested in keeping their children in South Vietnam and saw no political will to improve the conditions in the country's orphanages, so they would use their nursery to give each child their best possible chance to survive and thrive.

They even had a name for the facility they would create, To Am, a Vietnamese term that translated into English as 'Warm Nest'.

•

To Am was officially opened in August 1968. It began operations in a single room in a dilapidated house that Rosemary and Rosa had rented in a dingy alley in a run-down part of Saigon. Terre des Hommes paid the rent to the building's owner, an expatriate who now lived somewhere in Europe. Rosa volunteered to take complete charge of all the administrative aspects of the nursery's operation, leaving Rosemary free to look after the networking and favour-calling that needed to be done, a task at which she proved to be more than adept.

Within just a few weeks, To Am had thirty-five beds courtesy of the Australian Army. Somehow, she convinced the US Navy to donate a refrigerator and, not to be outdone, the US Army provided a regular supply of bottled fresh water and subsequently installed a reticulated fresh water system. Individual servicemen took it upon themselves to regularly call in with gifts to make the orphans' and their nurses' lives that little bit easier. Rosa, petite, vivacious and outgoing, was an instant success with the servicemen and Rosemary sometimes wondered whether the babies or the nurse were the main attractions at the nursery.

Packages from friends abroad supplied most of the linen and utensils needed, and Rosemary would be forever grateful for the Australian Army's parcel post scheme that allowed those donations to be brought from Australia to To Am without cost. Medical aid was also forthcoming from the military. Rosemary and Rosa were offered assistance by the US Army's 3rd Field Military Hospital at Tan Son Nhut, the Australian Army clinic based at the Free World centre in downtown Saigon, and the British medical team based at the Nhi Dong Children's Hospital.

Within a few weeks, the nursery was accepting orphans from the provinces and from Phu My. The only question was whether, as the orphans kept arriving, some form of international adoption scheme could also be implemented.

2

WARM NEST TO ALLAMBIE

For Rosemary and Rosa, the twelve months after the opening of To Am in 1968 were both exciting and exacting. Exciting because they were building something new and full of possibilities, a combination nursery and orphanage where they would nurse and nurture South Vietnam's forgotten ones, the little children who no one seemed to want and whose care had often been haphazard at best. They would nurse those children back to full health and nurture their bodies and souls in a safe, clean and caring environment before handing them over to a new family who would allow them to grow and develop in a way and in a place that would not be available to most Vietnamese children.

Exciting, yes, but exacting as well, for they would be building from the ground up. They would also do so without any official or formal backing, relying on the generosity of sponsors and the kindness of people they either knew or who knew what they were trying to achieve. They were fortunate in both regards. They were assisted by Terre des Hommes right from the start. As well as its Swiss headquarters providing Rosa Tintore's time and expertise, the organisation's French branch sent a car and a regular supply of baby formula while the German branch sent regular shipments of medical supplies. An Australian rubber company donated enough mattresses to furnish every cot they had been given by the Australian Army, but it was individuals and small groups scattered across the globe who underpinned To Am's operations in its first two years.

These individuals and small groups came from the United Kingdom and several European countries, from the United States, Canada and New Zealand, but it was those from Australia of whom Rosemary was most proud, in part because many were family and friends. Some came from the schools where Rosemary had a personal connection, and those groups were particularly important in collecting and forwarding Farex baby cereal and Lactogen milk powder, which would be sent to Saigon through the Australian Army parcel post system. One especially loyal and hardworking supporter in Adelaide volunteered on behalf of Rosemary's nursery for several years. A public servant with the Taxation Department, she would take up a collection from her colleagues each payday. The following weekend she would shop for specials at her local supermarket, which she would then forward to Saigon.

A particularly important support group formed around Elaine Moir in Melbourne. Elaine was tireless. Soon after her return from Vietnam via Europe she organised two groups in her new hometown, Vietnam Sponsors and the Vietnamese Orphans Medical Fund. While both groups collected supplies for Rosemary's Vietnamese operations, the latter also raised funds for orthopaedic and eye surgery for orphans in need of such remediation. When that need was identified, a surgeon was flown to Vietnam to undertake the surgery or, if more appropriate, the child would be flown to Australia. When not seeking donations for such special projects, Elaine and her team concentrated on stockpiling and forwarding baby food, cereal, linen and toiletries. Elaine's fundraising focused on private donors and, in seeking their support, she not only created several informal networks, but also raised Rosemary's profile and her work with Vietnamese orphans.

Many orphans who made their way to To Am travelled there via provincial orphanages. Rosemary's previous work on behalf of Terre des Hommes and Phu My had given her a good feel for the types of orphanages that operated outside Saigon, and she had been very unimpressed by some of them. Most of those she visited were either Buddhist or Catholic-based institutions and, for Rosemary, there could be a very wide gap between the religious values they espoused and the reality of the conditions in which the orphans lived.

While she found Buddhists and their orphanages relatively cut off from Western ideas of health, hygiene, education and rehabilitation, it was their seeming indifference to life and death that she found to be most baffling. She also found it especially jarring to find similar attitudes in some of the Catholic institutions. At one large Catholic orphanage, the mother superior had told Rosemary that she preferred the orphans to die *Dans le bon Dieu* (In the good Lord) than be sent abroad for adoption or raised in a non-Catholic home. Rosemary gave the comment the silence she thought it deserved.

She also found that most of the orphanages, irrespective of their religious or secular leaning, wanted to keep their children in their orphanage and raise them there rather than allow them to be adopted by families overseas. Many, perhaps most, would cling to this belief despite declining living conditions and rising mortality rates. Over time, though, many of the Catholic-run orphanages would come to accept Rosemary's argument that it was better for a child to be alive in someone else's country than dead in their own. The nuns running the orphanages came to identify, in association with To Am, orphans suitable for adoption who were then forwarded to Rosemary in Saigon.[1]

In the early days of To Am, Rosemary travelled often and alone to the provincial orphanages she knew, irrespective of the state of the fighting between South Vietnamese and communist forces. She drove if necessary but preferred larger civilian or military vehicles. Once, in central Vietnam, she even travelled in a helicopter at high speed and at treetop height. She was with a small group of children, one of whom – a small girl – was in the midst of a full-blown typhoid crisis. They needed to get her to hospital in Saigon or she would die. Rosemary was successful this time, but that would not always be the case.[2]

In those early days there were times when Rosemary arrived back in Saigon with more children than she had expected to bring back, with the knowledge that To Am was not yet ready to receive them. In such circumstances she would contact a friend, the assistant defence attaché at the British Embassy, Lieutenant Colonel Peter Trueman. Trueman and his wife were great supporters of Rosemary's and Rosa's work and offered their home to the infants temporarily. If they were babies, the Truemans would use their cupboard drawers as cribs. 'We made a temporary mattress by crumpling up airmail copies of the "London Times." At least it was a respectable newspaper.'[3]

The requests for adoptions surpassed Rosemary's and Rosa's early expectations, as did the number of orphans they welcomed. They interviewed and hired Vietnamese locals as childcare workers to help, young women all, and called them mother-care nurses. In line with their own philosophy, they employed one mothercare nurse for every five children in To Am; when children also required medical assistance, they hired additional mothercare nurses to achieve a one-to-one ratio.[4]

Their objective in establishing To Am was always, however, to place their orphans with adoptive families overseas and, when they did, it was heartbreaking for all at the nursery. The number they placed far exceeded their expectations. In 1968, Rosemary and Rosa placed 150 children from To Am with adoptive families overseas. While Europe remained the destination for the majority of the children, in November that year they placed their first orphans, two boys, with families in the United States, and the following month they placed their first orphan with an English family.[5]

The 'salvage operation', as both women referred to their work, was successful from the start – so successful, in fact, that within twelve months they began to look for larger and more appropriate accommodation, outgrowing their run-down little house in the run-down little neighbourhood. The search, begun in October 1969, was completed on 23 July 1970 when Rosemary signed the lease on a new property with a clean and regular water supply and reliable electricity in the far more salubrious (and healthy) Saigon locale of Nhat Linh. A year's rent, US$3600, was payable in advance.

It was a home that Rosemary fell in love with from the moment she set eyes on it. The main building had three storeys; the third floor consisted of one large, airy room that would become a nursery with a small pharmacy and bathroom attached. A staircase led to the roof where the babies could be put to sunbathe in the morning before the heat became too fierce. The three smaller rooms on the second floor served as bedrooms for the expatriate staff and as isolation rooms for premature, newborn and ill babies. The ground floor contained a large living room and pantry, while behind the main building there was another block with five bedrooms upstairs and, on the ground floor, a kitchen, storeroom and laundry, plus a bedroom for older children.[6]

When they left the old building behind, among the things they took with them was the name: the new nursery would also be known as To Am.

•

All this was done against a background of declining confidence in the ability of the United States, South Vietnam and their allies to win the war. The Tet Offensive in 1968 had rocked the US military and political establishments, which were shocked to discover that an enemy they had claimed was teetering on the edge of defeat was actually capable of launching multiple coordinated attacks across the length and breadth of South Vietnam. There were both military and geopolitical implications to Tet, issues that would simmer for several years, but these were of limited interest to the volunteers and staff at To Am. Their concerns were more immediate. In the aftermath of the offensive, the South Vietnam countryside emptied and refugees again streamed into the country's main urban centres. By the beginning of 1969, Saigon's population had swollen to three million, and half of the more than one million refugees now living in the city had no permanent shelter. Many of the new slums they formed lacked both fresh water and a sewage system and, as a direct result, thousands of people would die from cholera and typhoid – both preventable diseases.

Another consequence was the influx of thousands of children into Saigon, a significant proportion of whom were, or would become, orphans. One estimate put the number of refugee children at 150 000.[7] Many of them would live and grow up on the streets, begging, scavenging, searching for non-existent homes and work, looking for somewhere to sleep and something to eat. It was the war within the war and it broke the hearts of the young women at To Am.

•

Rosa Tintore was not there to move into the new To Am nursery, as she had returned to Europe to work with Terre des Hommes in February 1970 after eighteen months with Rosemary in Saigon. She handed over her responsibilities to her replacement, a French nurse named Yvette Charamont, while Terre des Hommes would send a second nurse several months later to help with the ever-increasing workload.

The increasing number of both expatriate and locally engaged staff allowed Rosemary to grow the services that To Am provided. Now on their regular visits to orphanages in the Mekong Delta they would take supplies for those orphanages with them. They immunised children who were there for a short-term stay and took clothing and food with them as well. There were always newly abandoned children to care for, so Rosemary or one of her nurses prepared and placed articles in the local newspaper describing them, asking for relatives to contact the orphanage. If no contact was made, that child would be considered for adoption. Adoption was, and would remain, the ultimate aim of almost all of Rosemary's activities.

•

By then, Rena Briand had also decided to adopt a baby, feeling that at last it might be time to settle down. Rena had returned to Vietnam in 1968 and, for a while at least, had continued working as a photojournalist. Two things eventually drew her away from that career, though. The first was the sense that the war had created a seemingly insurmountable problem, with an increasing number of war orphans outstripping South Vietnam's capacity to deal with them. The plight of these children, whom Rena referred to as waifs, grew increasingly central to her photojournalism, and to her life. The second was an affair of the heart. While working from Saigon in 1967, Rena met an Australian Army officer serving with the Australian Task Force based at Nui Dat, just outside Saigon. They fell in love, embarking on a passionate, if doomed, love affair. That affair ended when the soldier returned to Australia at the end of his posting. Rena, too, travelled to Australia, perhaps hoping to rekindle the affair, and settled in the Melbourne suburb of Essendon. The old flame was not rekindled but Rena found somewhere she could call home. To complete that home, she wanted a child.

While in Vietnam, Rena had met and become familiar with the activities of a number of those working in the area of orphan welfare, including Rosemary, Rosa and the staff at Phu My orphanage. She also met a remarkable US Army chaplain, Father Joe Turner. Turner knew more than most about orphans and orphanages. He was the only child of a couple who had separated before his birth and his father died when Joe was two. His mother was too poor to raise him, so Joe grew up in an orphanage in Philadelphia. As an adult, he became a Salvatorian priest – a member of Order of the Divine Saviour – and was serving in a Catholic church on the outskirts of Milwaukee when he became a US Army chaplain in 1966.

Father Turner completed two tours of duty in Vietnam, in 1968 and 1970. He worked with orphanages in his spare time during those tours, placing twelve orphans with American families. During his first tour he met Rena Briand; during his second tour she contacted him again. Rena wanted to financially support a Phu My orphan and asked Father Turner to nominate a suitable child. He selected Tuyen, a Vietnamese-American girl abandoned at Phu My, about thirteen months old, malnourished and covered with sores.

Once Father Turner had identified Tuyen, Rena began sending money to Phu My regularly to support her. Rena quickly realised that adopting the little girl and bringing her back to Australia would give her a better life than would be possible in Vietnam. She negotiated Tuyen's adoption through a French lawyer in Saigon, a process that eventually cost her A$165. In December 1970, Rena flew to Bangkok to collect Tuyen, who had been taken there by another of Rena's friends in Vietnam.

Their return to Australia was facilitated by the Australian Embassy in Bangkok without any issues. Rena had hoped and expected to be granted a six-month temporary entry visa for Tuyen, whom she named Tuyen Bettina Briand, and was pleasantly surprised when she was granted a migration visa instead. That proved to be the easiest part of the journey. To save money, Rena had decided to travel by train rather than fly from Bangkok to Singapore, and during that train journey her handbag was stolen. In it were money and jewellery valued at A$800, Rena's Canadian passport and Tuyen's immigration documents. Both Canadian and Australian authorities came to her assistance, issuing a new set of travel and immigration documents. Rena and her daughter arrived back in Australia in mid-January 1971.

Shortly after she returned to Australia, Rena was interviewed by a journalist and told him that she was keen for others do what she had done.

The worst of conditions in Australia would be better than in any Vietnamese orphanage. All half-caste children are stigmatised, and the girls face the prospect of being forced into prostitution by the age of thirteen. The Australian government has been so marvellous about Tuyen's entry that I am sure other people would have no trouble either.[8]

Then Immigration Minister Phillip Lynch appeared to agree, saying that there was no government objection to individual adoptions, but stressed that there would need to be appropriate investigations and support at both ends of the process. He added that child welfare authorities would also have to be involved.

The same newspaper printed a follow-up the next day, announcing that little Tuyen Bettina Briand was only the fifth Vietnamese orphan to be officially adopted by Australians. That statistic pointed to the implicit and explicit barriers to Asian intercountry adoption in Australia. It also indicated what problems lay in wait for those who, like Rosemary Taylor and Elaine Moir, believed that there was a place for Vietnamese orphans in Australian homes and hearts.

●

Australia was not a major destination for Vietnamese orphans because of a unique combination of bureaucratic and historic social issues. Under the Constitution the bureaucratic obstacles to intercountry adoption were formidable. In Australia adoption was the responsibility of the individual states and territories, and was handled by child or social welfare authorities, or sometimes both. Intercountry adoptions added another layer of bureaucracy at a federal level and sometimes involved the departments of Prime Minister and Cabinet, Labour and Immigration or Foreign Affairs.

Although they were rarely invoked, immigration regulations and protocols formed around the White Australia Policy[9] were still on the books when Rosemary Taylor began To Am and, combined with a form of institutionalised racism, acted to obstruct intercountry adoptions from non-European nations.

In March 1967, a spokesman for the Department of Labour and Immigration addressed the question of the adoption of Vietnamese orphans. He said such orphans might be admitted if several conditions were met. To begin with, it would have to be in the child's best interests. His department would not be the only body concerned in the process, either: child welfare authorities in South Vietnam and Australia would also need to be consulted. It was a conservative government's response and, surprisingly, that conservative government's barricade was first breached by an organisation regarded by many as even more conservative.[10]

Two years earlier, conservative Catholic commentator and political activist B. A. Santamaria was the first prominent figure to call for Australians to adopt and accept Vietnamese orphans. Speaking on his weekly television program in early September 1965, Santamaria said, 'There are up to one million refugees from Vietcong terrorism in the relatively safe parts of South Vietnam, living in indescribable conditions of human degradation.'[11] Santamaria argued that Australia had a moral and political duty to address the refugee issue. It would show, he reasoned, that Australia's concern for human beings was not limited to just those with white skin and would recognise publicly that Australia's future was interwoven with that of Asia. He closed a powerful appeal to the public and the body politic by saying that Australia's responsibility to South Vietnam was not limited to military and economic aid.

It took eighteen months for various hurdles at state level to be cleared and it wasn't until July 1967 that the first two applications for entry visas for Vietnamese adoptees were lodged with the Department of Labour and Immigration. The two sets of adoptive parents were John and Maree Hoare of Glenorchy in Tasmania and Senior Constable Allen Donnelly and his wife, of Forbes in the central west of New South Wales. John Hoare, the Tasmanian president of Santamaria's National Civic Council, later explained to a reporter that adopting a Vietnamese orphan 'was his family's way of lending a hand to Australia's war effort in Vietnam'.[12] It would take another six months for the orphans, two little girls named Cao Thi Phuong and Pham Thi Nguyet, to arrive in Australia to meet their new families.[13] In the next four years they would be followed by just three more Vietnamese orphans.

•

By the end of 1970, the new To Am was almost full and was costing Rosemary around US$1500 a month to run. That sum covered staff salaries, the cost of utilities and services, fresh vegetables and rice, and nursery and kitchen equipment. For consumables like milk and baby cereal, and for ongoing supplies of toiletries, clothes, linen and disposable nappies, To Am was dependent on donations generated primarily through individuals and small support groups around the world. Financially, they didn't depend on any single organisation, which enabled them to retain their independence.[14] The model did have its drawbacks, though, as limited available finances hindered possibilities for growth and expansion. In March 1971, Rosemary returned to Australia to thank those who were supporting To Am and to seek volunteers to allow its work to continue and develop.

Arriving in Adelaide she hoped, above all else, to convince an old schoolfriend from St Aloysius, a young woman named Margaret Moses, to join her in Vietnam. The two had maintained contact since their schooldays, and Rosemary knew that Margaret would be an invaluable asset in Saigon. Rosemary had long admired Margaret's intellectual prowess and organisational talents as much as her friend's humour and eloquence. Her excellent French would also be an asset but, most important of all, Rosemary had a close rapport with Margaret and knew that she could always rely on her.

Margaret Moses had always put a lot of herself into everything she did. Born in Launceston, Tasmania, in February 1940, Margaret was the second of seven children born to schoolteacher parents who separated when she was still a child. Following that separation, her mother took the children to Adelaide, where Margaret completed her education at St Aloysius College and met Rosemary Taylor. In 1957, Margaret followed Rosemary into the Sisters of Mercy order, professing in 1960 and taking the religious name 'Miriam'. After completing an Arts degree at the University of Adelaide, Margaret was posted to Mater Christi College at Mount Gambier in south-eastern South Australia.

Margaret proved to be a very gifted teacher, able to both inspire and lead her students. However, her passion came with a cost and in 1968, worn out from the combination of educational and religious responsibilities and obligations, Margaret left the order. She remained in teaching, though, switching from the Catholic to the state system and from 1968 until 1970 she was a teacher at the Port Adelaide Girls Technical High School. There, her educational expertise was recognised when, in 1970, she was appointed to two South Australian Public Examination Board subject committees, charged with developing an English syllabus attuned to contemporary society and focusing on contemporary issues.

Margaret's strong sense of social justice, her commitment to a style of teaching that both involved and engaged students, and the innate conservatism of the South Australian educational establishment were a mix guaranteed to strike sparks. Small disagreements led to large disagreements, ultimately resulting in a loss of trust on both sides. Tired of arguments and frustrated by a lack of progress, Margaret resigned when a better opportunity came along. That opportunity was provided by Rosemary Taylor.

•

Together, Rosemary and Margaret would make a formidable team. They shared a vision of doing all they could to provide the orphaned and abandoned, underprivileged and powerless children of South Vietnam with the opportunity to live and thrive, and then achieve the potential they believed all children had. Both young women felt that governments who failed to protect their most vulnerable children had lost any responsibility for their future. Volunteers who stepped into the vacuum created by such government inaction could therefore assume the rights and roles elsewhere exercised by the children's parents. They had the moral and ethical right to make decisions in the best interests of each child, and if those decisions included placing a child in an adoptive family overseas, then so be it.

Rosemary and Margaret shared that vision and the values that underpinned it, and had led lives devoted to the service of others; however, they had very different personalities and interpersonal skills. Rosemary was strong and focused; her considerable intellect always sought out potential problems and solutions long before they became apparent to anyone else and, when they were identified, she would brook no opposition in forging the way ahead. She set very high standards for herself, and standards almost as high for others. At one point, she let almost half of her locally engaged staff go because she felt they were concerned about their own welfare above that of the orphans. Rosemary's colleagues and staff loved her, but it was a love sometimes tinged with fear of her single-mindedness.

They would come to love Margaret as well. On an intellectual level, Margaret was Rosemary's equal, but she possessed a softer, more empathetic personality. Margaret possessed what used to be called *the common touch*, the ability to be able to connect with people of all types at all levels. While she could be outspoken, Margaret was that only when she felt it would help her to achieve something for the nursery or the orphans. Where Rosemary could seem stand-offish, Margaret was always very inclusive and seemed to need people very much more than her friend. While Rosemary appeared to be hard as nails, many felt that Margaret had an inner softness and even an inner sadness. An American colleague who came to know them both well believed each had committed herself totally to their work in Vietnam, but for very different reasons: 'While Rosemary was fighting for justice, Margaret was trying to save her soul.'[15]

•

When Rosemary asked Margaret to join her at To Am, Margaret resigned from all her positions with the South Australian Education Department and began planning to join her friend in South Vietnam. Before her own return, Rosemary also managed to recruit another two volunteers, Carmel Curtain, a mother-craft nurse from Melbourne, and Judy Soward, a registered nurse from Adelaide. Then, shortly after her return to Saigon, a German nurse, Ilse Ewald, appeared unannounced. Ilse had been sent by Terre des Hommes in Germany to replace the recently departed Yvette Charamont. She had previously worked aboard the German hospital ship *Helgoland* based at Da Nang and so was already familiar with Vietnamese conditions. When Margaret arrived in April, the new team was complete.

With that team assembled at To Am, Rosemary, with renewed enthusiasm, set out to take her little operation forward. While she remained the titular head of that operation, Rosemary was more than willing to share some of the burden she had been carrying. Ilse Ewald was made Chief Nurse and Medical Administrator, responsible for all the medical and public health decisions relevant to To Am's operations. She also took over responsibility for the regular ambulance circuit through the Mekong Delta provinces, collecting babies and infants from the orphanages there. When the team at To Am learned of Ilse's skills as a carpenter, mechanic, electrician and photographer, several other tasks also devolved to her. When she arrived, Margaret Moses was given, among other roles, responsibility for maintaining the nursery facilities in Saigon – facilities plural as To Am was about to expand its operations.

Even before she went back to Australia, two issues had been weighing on Rosemary's mind. The first was the chronic overcrowding at To Am. No matter how many children were taken to new families overseas, there were always more than enough replacements for them. The second issue was an ever-present one – the Vietnamese orphanages and their continuing haphazard approach to the children in their care. Rosemary, and now Margaret and Ilse, felt that they could do more for more children if they had an additional facility. When another villa not too far away became available, they seized the opportunity. It was not as large or as modern as To Am, but they could easily turn it into a nursery home for their older children. It, too, had to have a name and so they called it 'Allambie', Aboriginal for 'rest a while'.

•

Several important events occurred in 1971 that would have a significant impact on the operations of To Am and Allambie, and the course that Rosemary and her staff would follow. The first happened a long way from Saigon, in the US city of Denver, Colorado, where a group of concerned social activists formed the Friends of the Children of Vietnam (FCVN). One of the driving forces behind that organisation was a woman named Wende Grant, who, with her husband, Duane, was one of the first Americans to adopt a Vietnamese child, a little girl, in April 1965. FCVN was established to funnel voluntary aid to orphanages in South Vietnam and, with Wende Grant on its first board of directors, the possibility of intercountry adoptions was soon part of FCVN's agenda. The welfare and adoption aspects of FCVN's work almost immediately led them to contact Rosemary, and the organisation soon became one of her major sponsors.

The second was a determined effort to open Australia's doors to significant numbers of Vietnamese orphans. One of the three Australian adoptions between 1968 and 1972 was especially significant. In early 1971, the Deputy Leader of the Federal Opposition, the Tasmanian ALP member Lance Barnard, and his wife adopted a Vietnamese baby they named Amanda Louise Barnard. The adoption, undertaken by proxy in Saigon, was organised through negotiations with and through the Tasmanian Social Welfare Department and the South Vietnamese Ministry for Foreign Affairs. The Barnards attempted to keep their adoption out of the public eye to avoid politicising the issue and to protect both Amanda and their other children. Given Lance Barnard's position in public life, this was always going to be difficult and became impossible when little Amanda, just eight weeks old, died from a chest infection shortly after arriving in Tasmania.

One person in particular, Elaine Moir, was determined that the publicity and public sympathy for Amanda Barnard would not be allowed to dissipate. In 1971, Elaine was a 34-year-old secretary, a single mother with two children living in a flat in the Melbourne suburb of Glen Iris, where all spare space was stacked high with goods destined for Allambie and Phu My. Her passion for Vietnam and its orphans had never dimmed. As well as being a prospective adoptive parent herself, Elaine was now acting as both an adviser to and an advocate for the growing number of Australian families hoping to adopt a Vietnamese orphan.

In this capacity, in mid-1971, Elaine spent six weeks in Saigon sourcing orphans for a small group of Australian families and commencing their adoption processes. The orphans were chosen in conjunction with an Australian medical team and with the cooperation of World Vision, which also checked the proposed adoptive parents. All the applications Elaine lodged in Saigon were approved by South Vietnamese courts between November 1971 and March 1972, but there appeared to be no progress at home. The prospective adoptees were refused entry into Australia by Commonwealth Immigration authorities, while in Victoria – where four of the five orphans were headed – the Social Welfare Minister, Ian Smith, who was becoming a particularly obstructive conservative politician, refused to allow his department to process any settlement documents. To Elaine, the whole system had descended into low farce. Prompted by the imminent expiry of an exit visa for one of the orphans, and with the approval of the other parents, Elaine decided to act.

On 21 May 1972, she flew to Saigon to complete all travel arrangements and collect the children. Three days later her friends in Saigon tried to increase the pressure. Margaret Moses went to the Australian Embassy and spoke to one of the officials about the five Vietnamese orphans Elaine had flown up to collect. Margaret said she felt compelled to point out that the five children had all been legally adopted under Vietnamese law and all held valid Vietnamese passports and exit visas, adding that those visas were due to expire in early June. She also pointed out that several of the adoptive families in Australia had moved interstate to comply with adoption laws and that there would be problems for the children if their adoption did not proceed. There were no readoption processes in South Vietnam and further hold-ups would leave the children in legal limbo.

The conversation with Margaret Moses was duly summarised and transmitted back to Australia in a cablegram that was classified 'Restricted'. The anonymous author of that cable noted that there was now a lot of emotion tied up with the adoption of Vietnamese orphans by Australian families, and that accusations of Australian government indifference to the fate of these orphans were now being aired. He did note reasonable fears that children adopted by proxy in South Vietnam might be flown to somewhere like Singapore before being taken to Australia to circumvent existing regulations. It was a cable that would be filed somewhere along with hundreds of others, cataloguing a government and a bureaucracy struggling to either introduce or implement both national and international protocols for cross-border adoptions.[16]

Elaine Moir didn't care for most protocols. At noon on Saturday 27 May she and the five orphans departed Saigon on the short flight down to Singapore, where they boarded a British Overseas Airways Corporation (now British Airways) jet for the twenty-hour long-haul flight to Sydney, via Perth.[17] The circus began, as Elaine knew it would, when her aircraft touched down in Perth. After it had taxied to the terminal, passengers were informed that local health and immigration officials had decided that the jet would be cleared for what they termed a 'routine inspection'. Elaine suspected that it was anything but that and refused to leave the aircraft. She would stay on board with the children until they reached Sydney, where the adoptive parents – and several reporters and photo-graphers – would be waiting.

She told the crew that if any Australian officials wanted to talk to her they would have to come to the plane. They did. Several Immigration officials arrived and in the stand-off that followed, Elaine insisted on staying aboard the aircraft, warning that any efforts to remove herself and the children would require at least five nurses and would involve crying babies, dirty nappies and one very angry woman. Certainly wanting to avoid a confront-ation, and possibly wanting to transfer the problem to someone and somewhere else, the officials asked if they could see all the travel documentation Elaine carried for herself and the orphans. They examined it all and cleared it, and after the other passengers had been reboarded the aircraft departed for Sydney.

When the plane landed in Sydney, Elaine and the orphans were helped off and taken to a secure immigration area. After a two-hour interview, interrupted by several phone calls between officials at the airport and officials in Canberra, Elaine was told that while she had not committed any major immigration offences, the children she had brought with her had entered the country illegally – but for the time being, nothing would be done about that breach. As four of the five children had been adopted by Victorian families the matter would be referred to the Victorian Social Welfare Department. The children were then all issued with thirty-day visas.

There would be celebrations and recriminations afterwards, accusations of unsportsmanlike behaviour would be levelled by both sides, but all those claims became irrelevant as the orphans would join their new families and later be given permanent migration visas. The breach in the immigration barricade was now a little bit wider.

●

Another very significant event that year was the winding-down of the war. This did not happen overnight, but gradually over a period of months. In Australia, as in the United States, the Vietnam War had become increasingly unpopular and that unpopularity had reached a level where it was able to affect the outcome of national elections. With the war looking increasingly unwinnable on the ground, Australian and American combat forces were slowly scaled back and brought home, a process commencing in 1970. Although no peace treaties were signed, there was a general belief that one would be negotiated, and that this would occur sooner rather than later.

The Australian forces were withdrawn from South Vietnam between December 1971 and March 1972, and there was an immediate impact at To Am. The Australian Army visitors and their little gifts stopped arriving and, more importantly, access to the army's parcel post also ceased. This meant increased costs and slower delivery times for the donations that were collected in and dispatched from Australia. Potentially, the greatest issue would be with Lactogen and other milk products, even though before the Australians departed Vietnam they flew in a six-month supply of milk products.

The nursery and adoption operations continued to grow, and grow efficiently, throughout 1972, and in November a third nursery, Newhaven, was opened. The new facility would take the older babies and toddlers from To Am and would also be used to relieve the periodic overcrowding at Allambie. To assist with the financing of the new nursery, the French branch of Terre des Hommes agreed to assume part of the monthly rent as well as contribute to Newhaven's upkeep.

By November 1972 Rosemary expected their stockpile of milk products to be exhausted, but, fortunately, she had taken steps early to address the looming shortfall. An appeal to the manufacturer, Nestlé, for cost-free supplies received no positive response, so Rosemary called on Elaine Moir for assistance. In the run-up to that year's Melbourne Cup carnival, Elaine put an article in several Melbourne newspapers asking punters to donate to Nestlé 5 per cent of what they were planning to bet to buy milk products for Vietnamese orphans. Within three days, the company complained that it was now holding donations of $25 000 and asked for the donations to stop. Nestlé also asked for a dedicated account to be established for the specific purpose of the Vietnamese orphans appeal. It was, and the funds raised would underwrite the supply of milk products to all of Rosemary's nurseries until February 1974.

By the end of the year, Rosemary and her team had achieved a lot to be proud of. That team had grown to a permanent foreign volunteer staff of six, plus almost a hundred locally engaged staff, including mothercare nurses, cooks and cleaners. That staff ran three large nurseries in inner-city Saigon and supported several provincial orphanages as well. In 1972 they had placed around five hundred orphans with adoptive families, bringing the total number of placements since To Am opened in 1968 to 1132. That figure represented the overwhelming majority of all intercountry adoptions from Vietnam.[18]

While they would continue to work with Terre des Hommes, the new relationship with FCVN opened opportunities for placements in North America. It was a relationship cemented in September of that year when Wende Grant and another FCVN board member visited Saigon; Rosemary and Wende became firm and close friends. Theirs became the only significant adoption program operating in South Vietnam and Rosemary's experiences over the previous five years had now given her both expertise in the area and a reputation as an authority on adoption policy. US Embassy officials sometimes sought her advice when developing their own policies.

There were high hopes for peace, too. Richard Nixon, re-elected as US president, had promised to end the American involvement in conflict in South-East Asia and talks in Paris were slowly moving towards that conclusion. There were some clouds on the horizon, though, and one of them was in Rosemary's homeland, Australia, where intercountry adoption was still a matter of some controversy.

3

FROM NEWHAVEN TO RATHAVEN

In Australia, the repatriation of the last Australian combat troops from South Vietnam in March 1972 and the obvious de-escalation of the fighting in that country contributed to a growing sense of hope and optimism that something positive could and would be done to assist in the rebuilding of a nation and a society brought to their knees by thirty years of nonstop warfare. It was a sense heightened by the idea that after twenty-three years of conservative rule, the much more progressive Australian Labor Party might be elected to power in the federal elections to be held on 2 December that year.

•

Elaine Moir's direct action in bringing five Vietnamese orphans to Australia in May 1972, and challenging authorities to send them back to an uncertain future, had several consequences, at least one of which was totally unexpected. A benefactor who was never identified developed an interest in the plight of orphans in South Vietnam. That benefactor wanted to both learn more about what was happening there and also do something about it by highlighting the extent of the problem for the broader Australian public. To do so, he paid for a study trip to South Vietnam by two prominent Australian social activists, the lawyer and senior Red Cross board member (and future Australian Governor-General) William Deane and the Reverend Denis Oakley, the public face of both World Vision Australia and the Child Welfare Foundation of Victoria.

As well as a general philanthropic interest, both men had specific reasons for volunteering their time to undertake the tour. Denis Oakley had been quite alarmed by some of the reports being published on South Vietnamese orphans and orphanages, most originating in the United States. He said he believed there might be up to one million children living in South Vietnamese orphanages and he also wanted to verify other reporting suggesting that among those living in orphanages, up to 90 per cent were either intellectually impaired or dead before they reached their fifth birthday.[1] The Australian Red Cross had sent more than A$10000 to an orphanage at Can Tho in the Mekong Delta, and William Deane wanted to see how that money had been spent. In South Vietnam, their focus was on orphanages and child treatment facilities.[2] The two men spent two weeks in South Vietnam in October 1972, crisscrossing the country and speaking to officials and volunteers at all the institutions they visited. On their return to Australia they prepared a report and submitted recommendations to the Council for Overseas Aid, the coordinating body for thirty Australian relief agencies, and gave several interviews. During one interview, Denis Oakley reported that there were 126 orphanages in South Vietnam catering for around twenty thousand orphans. 'We created the problem,' he added. 'Let's do something to help repair it.'[3]

•

In the 1969 Australian federal election, there was a 7 per cent swing away from the conservative Liberal/National Party government to an invigorated Australian Labor Party under its new leader, Gough Whitlam. For the December 1972 election, Whitlam and Labor campaigned under the slogan 'It's Time'. The 5 per cent swing towards Labor, although smaller than the party had hoped for, was still sufficient to hand it power with a comfortable nine-seat majority. Although it lacked a majority in the senate, the government felt it did have a clear mandate for reform, and so Gough Whitlam and his team of senior ministers set to work to reshape Australia and its relations with the rest of the world.

•

Meanwhile in South Vietnam, two events early in the new year of 1973 would help to define the direction that Rosemary's team would follow in the coming years. The first was the signing of the Paris Peace Accords, agreed to in the French capital on 27 January and designed to end years of conflict in Vietnam. This agreement, signed by both Vietnamese and American representatives, would see US forces withdraw within sixty days and ongoing talks leading to Vietnam's unification. There were commitments, guarantees and international observers to ensure that all aspects of the accords were respected, but there were no readily accessible dispute-resolution mechanisms. The only guarantee of South Vietnam's territorial integrity seemed to be the implicit threat of American re-engagement.

The second event was more direct and existential. Vietnamese authorities issued an expulsion order against Rosemary Taylor, who had by now worked in South Vietnam for almost six years, claiming that she and her nurseries were not affiliated with an internationally recognised agency. Rosemary had intentionally chosen not to be affiliated with any agencies, fearing that this would curtail her freedom to decide what was best for her orphan charges. Her agreement with Terre des Hommes was only considered a subcontract. Rosemary's quest for independence, free of international fetters or constraints, now came back to threaten everything she had worked towards.

An appeal to the Australian Embassy in Saigon received a somewhat tepid offer of support, but a similar appeal to the US Embassy prompted a much more vigorous response. Acting on its advice, Rosemary immediately flew to Denver to meet with Wende Grant. There, FCVN was formally registered with and licensed by the Colorado Department of Social Services as an adoption agency. Rosemary and Wende then flew back to Saigon, where they went through the process of registering FCVN in South Vietnam and applying for an operating licence. They were successful in both processes, assisted considerably by the full support of the US Embassy. By the end of March 1973 they were again able to operate without fear of being shut down.

The registrations and approvals stimulated a new period of activity and growth, in part assisted by a further influx of staff. In late 1972, Christie Leiverman, a 23-year-old nurse from St Paul, Minnesota, arrived as a volunteer. While Christie was the oldest of eleven children, she was the youngest of Rosemary's expatriate staff. In mid-1973 another American volunteer, Julie Chinberg, from McPherson, Kansas, joined the team. A registered nurse, Chinberg was immediately made the administrator at Allambie, overseeing all the senior nursery's operations.

In May 1973, another American volunteer would become a critical part of their nursery operations. Sister Susan McDonald, originally from Colorado, was the oldest of nine children. She announced to her family at the age of four that she was going to become a nun and look after orphans.[4] It was a path she followed with some determination. After graduating from a college run by the Sisters of Loretto, Susan joined the order and completed a nursing degree, specialising in paediatric nursing. After serving for a year at a Loretto Motherhouse, in 1970 she was appointed administrator at the St Joseph Infirmary in Louisville, Kentucky.

Susan had maintained an interest in the children of Vietnam for several years, first becoming aware of them through television coverage. She was especially taken by the images of street children and wide-eyed babies in understaffed orphanages.[5] She wrote to nine different agencies that she knew had representatives in South Vietnam and offered her services to each. One letter was addressed to Rosemary Taylor, whom she knew of after watching a television special. Rosemary was the only one to reply and there was a brief correspondence between the two. Although Rosemary was a little ambivalent about taking on a young nun, Susan's qualifications in paediatric nursing and her obvious enthusiasm won the day and she was offered a position in the nurseries. Susan arrived in May 1973 and almost immediately took over the running of Newhaven and its fifty orphans.[6]

With a growing staff and the full backing of FCVN, which brought with it a certain innate professionalism, Rosemary's nursery and adoption operations again rose to a new level. Americans who wanted to adopt a Vietnamese orphan applied to FCVN, which would then arrange for a 'home study' of the prospective parents. The study was designed to see whether the adoptive family was capable of raising and caring for a child from another country, and also to discover whether or not their neighbourhood would accept an orphan from another country and culture. It was a process that Wende Grant had insisted upon, but it was one that would set up competing priorities within FCVN, creating some stress.

The internal tensions within FCVN that had become apparent in early 1973 came to a head in October of that year. They centred around the allocation of resources between the agency's welfare activities and its support for intercountry adoptions, with those involved in the latter, led by Wende Grant, arguing for a greater share of those resources. When their calls were ignored, those involved in intercountry adoption resigned en masse. Wende, with Rosemary's full knowledge and approval, immediately formed, incorporated and registered in Denver Friends for All Children (FFAC). The agency was also very quickly registered in South Vietnam. There, Rosemary and Margaret commenced discussions with South Vietnamese government departments, discussions that led to the signing of a two-year agreement in February 1974. With that, Wende became Director of Adoptions for FFAC. Mrs Hazel Richards, wife of the British Ambassador to South Vietnam, Brooks Richards, became chairwoman of its South Vietnam branch, and Rosemary continued to administer its South Vietnamese operations.

The split was not without consequences. Even though it was caused by issues over funding intercountry adoptions, FCVN continued to operate in that space and replaced Rosemary in Saigon with Cherie Clark. Clark was keen and compassionate but lacked Rosemary's experience and contacts. Now there were two agencies with similar names and acronyms dealing with adoptions between South Vietnam and North America, something that would later lead to complications.

•

In Australia, too, things seemed to be starting to move in the right direction for those concerned with intercountry adoptions, especially adoptions involving Vietnamese orphans. By January 1973, the Australian Adoptive Families Association (AAFA) had been formed by a nonsectarian group of parents in Melbourne to work solely around intercountry adoptions. Its initial leader, Rosemary Calder, was herself the mother of an adopted Vietnamese child and through her the AAFA soon established links to Rosemary Taylor and her nurseries in Saigon.

While the association's primary role was to provide advice to prospective adoptive parents, based on the experience of its members, it soon moved into two other areas. The first of these was advocacy: several other state branches were established and the organisation became particularly strong and effective in South Australia. The association also moved into activism, an area particularly attractive to Rena Huxley – formerly Briand – who became associated with the group soon after it was formed.

The new federal government was cognisant that a growing number of Australians wanted to do something to alleviate the conditions under which some of the poorest and most vulnerable South Vietnamese lived. Early in its term, the government sent a request to the United States, through diplomatic channels, for information on ways the US government was approaching the problem of orphans and orphanages in South Vietnam. The reply arrived in Canberra in late May.[7]

The Australian Embassy in Washington outlined how US authorities estimated that there were nineteen thousand children in South Vietnamese government-recognised orphanages and between five thousand and six thousand in unregistered orphanages. The United States supported those children through monthly payments of 600 piastres (around US$6) per child, paid to the South Vietnamese Ministry of Social Welfare. That amount was under review by US authorities and was likely to be increased by 50 per cent. As well, food aid was supplied to South Vietnamese authorities at the rate of US$3 a month while several other food and financial aid packages had also been implemented. All up, US officials estimated that their country's support to orphan relief in South Vietnam had totalled around US$125 million over the previous five years.

In June 1973 the Whitlam government announced that it would treat Vietnamese orphans adopted by Australian families as assisted migrants. People who wished to adopt Vietnamese orphans, provided they had approval from both their state government and the South Vietnamese government, could apply to the Immigration Department for assisted passage for the child. This was primarily rhetoric, as nothing had yet been done to establish a coherent and coordinated set of protocols covering intercountry adoptions from South Vietnam. To address this shortfall, in November 1973 a major interdepartmental meeting was held in Canberra where it was revealed that there were forty-five adoptions from South Vietnam between 1968 and 1973. As a result of the meeting, several recommendations were made, including the need for further discussions and standardisation across jurisdictions, as well as the possibility of basing a social worker in Saigon. It was a convenient outcome for the federal government as well as several of the states, as it meant they were not forced to make a decision on whether or not the adoption of non-European orphans was politically risky. Input from bodies such as AAFA was not sought.

•

All of this was of only passing interest to Rosemary, Margaret and their team at work in Saigon. They had far more immediate and pressing problems, including keeping their children alive and healthy enough to actually be considered for adoption. None of the young women ever completely came to grips with this struggle. Those who had been nurses had seen death up close before, while those who had spent time in Vietnamese orphanages knew it was a constant presence – but the loss of one of their little ones was always traumatic. The carers each reacted to this loss in their own way. Rosemary would carry on, burying inside her the grief and the frustration of knowing that so many of these deaths would, in other circumstances, have been avoidable. She would later write about how 'this uncelebrated ending to a life that had never been lived weighed heavily on us all'.[8]

Ilse Ewald was physically and emotionally affected by these deaths, becoming depressed for a time after each one. Margaret Moses, devastated, would on occasion lock herself in her room for days as she tried to understand the mechanisms in the universe that allowed an innocent child who had barely known life to die. As a coping mechanism, Margaret began writing an anecdotal history of their work. She observed that, 'whatever good times we had at To Am, I never got over the horror of children who had never lived, dying. I found myself battering my head against the paradox.'[9]

Over time, a small ritual developed whenever an orphan died. If the child died in hospital they would be brought back to their home nursery, where their body would be washed, usually by Ilse, and then wrapped in a clean sheet or blanket and placed, carefully and gently, into a coffin fashioned from a cardboard box. Margaret would help to tape up the box, carry it to the nursery ambulance and drive it to a cemetery at one of Saigon's orphanages where she would conduct a brief burial service.[10] At the end of 1973, around Christmas, Margaret wrote a poem entitled 'New Light Over Jerusalem'. In it she described 'the still, small voice of nobody's child'.[11] Margaret Moses continued to carry a heavy load.

•

The independence that Rosemary and her team now felt was manifested in the immediate completion of two projects that had been under consideration for some time. The first was Ilse Ewald's pet project, an intensive-care nursery for the seriously ill orphans who comprised a significant proportion of the children they received. It was a need that partly responded to several children suffering from infectious diseases being refused admission to public hospitals in Saigon. It was also partly a response to the mortality rate in their orphans, with a feeling that, had better intensive-care facilities been available, at least some of those deaths could have been prevented.

The new intensive-care nursery was established in a nearby villa and named Hy Vong, Vietnamese for 'hope'. Ilse had identified several specific responsibilities for the facility, including treating dehydration and pneumonia, isolating potentially fatal contagious diseases, the short-term treatment of malnourished children, and emergency care. Hy Vong was also responsible for the preliminary screening of all babies brought in from provincial orphanages. To assist in all this work, Hy Vong would be provided with an ambulance and, best of all, the entire project was underwritten by a series of grants totalling US$100 000, provided by USAID.[12]

Ilse Ewald had a large role in designing and commissioning Hy Vong and took over the nursery as soon as it was officially opened on 1 November 1973. She was assisted there by another German nurse sponsored by Terre des Hommes' German branch,

Birgit Blank. The vivacious Birgit was an excellent nurse, hard-working and looking forward to contributing at Hy Vong for eighteen months before returning to Germany to marry her fiancé.[13] Within a few weeks of opening, Hy Vong was catering for one hundred ill children.

The second major project, Rosemary and Margaret's brainchild, involved another major upgrade to their facilities that increased the scope of their operations. Shortly after Hy Vong was opened, Allambie moved to a new location near Tan Son Nhut, Saigon's main civilian and military airport. The new Allambie was a wonderful facility – a large villa on a huge allotment that included a swimming pool, a big yard covered with lush grass and another open area that was suitable for the construction of open-air classrooms that could be used for arts and crafts. The multi-storey building contained plenty of spare rooms plus several spaces that could be converted to kitchens and a pharmacy.[14] The recently arrived Doreen Beckett, a Sisters of Mercy nun from Adelaide and friend of both Rosemary and Margaret, was placed in charge of the new Allambie, assisted by Julie Chinberg and another new arrival, American physiotherapist Peggy Hammond.

Given free rein at Allambie, Margaret and the nurses created something special. They named each dormitory room after either a country or a continent. When an orphan first arrived, they would be assigned to Canada, Africa or the like, rather than to somewhere cold and impersonal like 'Room 13'. The dormitories were decorated with posters and large photographs of landmarks and animals consistent with each continent or country. Where children had been assigned to adoptive families and were waiting for the process to be completed, their personal spaces were decorated with letters from and photographs of those adoptive families.[15]

Family was central to the running of Allambie because most of the children were old enough to understand both where they were and where they might be going. Each themed dormitory room was, therefore, treated as a family home. There were between five and eight children in each dormitory and a small group of mothercare nurses – who were rarely transferred away from that room and those children – assigned to each one. The night duty 'mother' was responsible for putting the children to bed, helping them to put on their pyjamas and giving them all a cup of warm milk. She would then sleep in the same room as the children.[16]

As a final touch, and to recognise and encourage the individuality and uniqueness of each child, the orphans would be given a cloth bag when they arrived at Allambie. The bags were for any special items and treasures the children might already have or would acquire while they were there. When the child departed to join their new family overseas, the bag and its treasures would travel with them.[17]

•

The old Allambie was retained and, in time, would become a general-purpose complex. Some parts were converted into staff accommodation, others into storage and warehousing, while the main living area became a meeting place. The conversion from nursery to central hub took place over several days, and when the children moved out the rats moved in. While workmen were putting up or knocking down walls and partitions, the carers were seeking out and blocking rat holes. In the end, they permanently sealed thirty-nine rat holes, but the sound of little clawed feet scurrying across bare wooden boards at night told them that there was at least one they had missed. The exercise also provided the inspiration for the name they would give the facility – Rathaven.

•

Heading into 1974, Rosemary and Wende's FFAC operations in South Vietnam included running five separate facilities – To Am, Newhaven, Allambie, Hy Vong and Rathaven. Each of the four nurseries had its own administration and functioned independently in running its own programs. Each had a foreign volunteer as its formal administrator, assisted by a senior local staff member who would serve as both secretary and interpreter when needed. All formal documents, like certificates of registration and contracts, were retained by Rosemary and securely kept at her home office at Phu My. They were now also employing around two hundred Vietnamese staff that included several trained mothercare nurses.

The experience of Susan McDonald, the administrator at Newhaven, mirrored everyone's experience. Susan's first impressions of South Vietnam were very confronting. The poverty she saw all around her was almost overwhelming and, on top of the culture shock, the two French nurses who had been running Newhaven departed two weeks after Susan arrived, leaving her in charge of fifty orphans. From those nurses she had learned that her orphans had been brought in from other orphanages where their main source of nutrition had been rice water – water in which rice had been cooked. While it contained some nutrients, it provided few calories and was a significant factor in the orphanages' high mortality rates.[18]

Susan immediately assumed responsibility for purchasing all the food for her orphans and drew up shopping lists and menus based on her experience and training. Early on, she learned a lesson in Vietnamese economics. Used to chicken being a cheap meat in the United States, she found out the hard way that it was an expensive meat in Saigon. Instead of meat, she turned to vegetables as a staple of the children's diet. Each week she would stock up on vegetables at the local markets, which she would put through a blender to make a basic food for the nursery.[19]

Susan also learned early on the intricacies of the South Vietnamese bureaucracy. Just obtaining a passport for one of her orphans could be a major undertaking. The orphanage – in Susan's case, Newhaven – named the child to be adopted and would then seek that child's birth certificate, a process that could involve court action. Sometimes the requirement for documentation became farcical, and included requests for tax certification for children too young for kindergarten. At times, detailed dossiers on adoptive parents had to be prepared for the authorities and, finally, health certificates and exit visas obtained. Unfortunately, endemic bureaucratic corruption interfered with the process, although Rosemary and Margaret seemed to be able to overcome even that.[20]

Finally, Susan learned the lesson that all the expatriate volunteers would learn in Vietnam – that life as an adoptee overseas was far better than life in a Vietnamese orphanage, even one as well run and caring as Newhaven.

•

The expanded FFAC operation would handle large numbers of orphans from Phu My and the provincial orphanages. These babies and small children were handed in or left at markets, churches and government offices, or sometimes simply on the side of the road. Many of them arrived with no known history, no known families and no known neighbours. As a response to and a result of this, nursery staff established the system of giving these children 'nursery names', which would stay with them while they remained at an FFAC facility.

Considering the large number of children who were now moving through the nurseries, the staff needed to become increasingly inventive when it came to selecting original names for them. Some were given simple Western names like Elizabeth, Roy, Abraham and Brian. Tran, Dinh, Tien, Be and Ngoc-Thanh went by Vietnamese names, perhaps given to them before they arrived at one of Rosemary's nurseries. Other names reflected the religious or political leanings of the Western staff, such as Thomas More, John of the Cross and Cesar Chavez.

In early 1974, one orphanage entered a classical naming phase, coming up with names that would have been quite perplexing to their Vietnamese staff. Jocasta, Plato and Athena were simple enough, but Sophocles, Aristophanes and Euripides posed quite a phonetic challenge. There were strange and sometimes silly names as well. One child was called Nuoc-Mam, which means 'fish sauce' in Vietnamese; another was called 'Stiff Legs' in Vietnamese, while some were simply whimsical, such as Minnehaha, and twins Sun and Flower. All, though, were names bestowed and used with love.

•

By 1974, the FFAC organisation had grown to include fifteen foreign volunteers – nurses and administrators from all around the world. The staff also included up to four hundred Vietnamese nurses, physiotherapists and childhood development specialists, as well as cleaners and gardeners, and support and administrative workers. Their work was still primarily supported by private individuals and groups outside South Vietnam, FFAC and Terre des Hommes and several others in Europe, North America and Australia which had contributed over the previous six years. The one major difference now was that USAID was in the background as a source of advice and support and, more importantly, grant money.

Late in the year, FFAC again looked to expand its operations in the region. In December 1974, following a trip to Phnom Penh, the capital of Cambodia, by Margaret, Wende and two others, FFAC decided to open a nursery there, to be set up later that month. Funded by FFAC's new Canadian branch, the facility would be known as Canada House.

That month also saw the arrival of some additional volunteer staff from Australia. They were now joined by two older women, Margaret Moses senior and her friend May Ewin, both from Adelaide, and another young nurse from the same city, Lee Makk. The older Margaret was soon christened 'Adelaide' Moses to distinguish her from her daughter while recognising her hometown. She and May Ewin had travelled to Saigon primarily to assist as escorts on the small convoys of adoptees who were now flying regularly to Europe and North America to join their new families. Both Margaret Moses senior and May were hard workers, and rather than sitting around waiting for a group to be sent abroad, both women jumped right in to assist with the everyday running of the nurseries.

Lee Makk was another highly skilled and highly motivated young woman who had volunteered to help Rosemary and FFAC in their work. She had been born Gyoparka Maria Makk in Hungary in 1945, the third daughter in a family that would grow to include seven daughters and a son. In 1956, the Makk family fled Hungary in the wake of the invasion by Soviet forces and, after spending time in a refugee camp in Austria, was accepted for resettlement in Australia, arriving in January 1958. After living in Ipswich, Queensland, for four years, the family moved to Adelaide where Gyoparka decided to follow her older sister into nursing. It was while training that she was given the name Lee by her fellow trainees, who struggled with the correct pronunciation of Gyoparka.

While undertaking her initial nursing training Lee decided to specialise in working with the mentally ill. Following graduation, she began working at Hillcrest Hospital (until 1964 known as Northfield Mental Hospital) in Adelaide. While there, Lee asked for leave to work in Saigon with Rosemary and FFAC, which was granted. Once there, she threw herself into work, using her spare time to learn Vietnamese and put together letters and cassettes for her family in Adelaide.

To assist with their enlarged operations, Rosemary employed another remarkable Vietnamese, Dolly Bui Van To. Dolly was a French national married to a Vietnamese engineer who had been granted permanent residency in Germany, which meant that Dolly was able to travel on a German passport. The couple had several children, aged from toddlers through to mid-teens, and the older children sometimes helped Dolly at work. She was a real worker. Fluent in several languages and familiar with the intricacies of the South Vietnamese bureaucracy, Dolly soon assumed the role of general factotum, solving dozens of problems that seemed insoluble to others, and always with a smile on her face.

The increased scale of FFAC's South Vietnamese and Cambodian operations in 1974 drew the organisation closer to USAID and what it was trying to do in the same areas. It also drew Rosemary, Margaret and Wende closer to a remarkable

American family, the Starks. Merrit and Dorothy Stark were also from Denver, he a doctor and she a nurse. They had raised six children, two boys and four girls, in a large and fun-filled home. Their first exposure to Vietnam came in 1966 when their eldest child, Tom, announced that he had enlisted in the Marine Corps. The next two children, daughters Eileen and Laurie, became anti-war activists around the same time. Towards the end of Tom's first tour of duty in Vietnam, Merrit Stark joined a program run by the American Medical Association called Volunteer Physicians for Vietnam. He spent two months working in a coastal town in the south before returning to Denver, where he found he could not forget what he had seen in Vietnam.

After family discussions, Merrit decided to return to Vietnam in 1968. Those discussions widened, and in the end four Starks – Merrit and Dorothy and two of their daughters, Laurie and Ann – decided to go to South Vietnam to undertake volunteer work. While three of them worked on and through programs run or funded by USAID, Laurie Stark worked as a teacher at the Madame Curie School. She, especially, took to Vietnam with a passion and within six months was almost completely fluent in Vietnamese. By 1974, Laurie and a young Vietnamese colleague had started their own preschool, which they called Mother Hubbard. By then, too, all four Starks had become close friends with Rosemary and Margaret, and had become part of the network of friends the two Australian women had created.

As 1974 drew to a close, all those involved in what FFAC was doing in South Vietnam had many reasons to feel proud of what they had achieved to date. The 'salvage operation' they had put in place was running at peak efficiency, and during that year alone several hundred orphans had been successfully placed with adoptive families around the world. It was also running at close to peak capacity. Hy Vong, for example, now cared for 150 ill and recovering babies. Rosemary and Wende were, however, not without concerns. The fighting in both Vietnam and Cambodia, for two years a kind of background rumble to their work, had recently intensified in both countries and, looking ahead to 1975, the best that could be said about the future was that it appeared problematic.

4

ENDGAME

SOUTH VIETNAM, DECEMBER 1974 TO MARCH 1975

Margaret Moses noticed a change in South Vietnam towards the end of 1974. It was harder to purchase supplies and have them either collected or delivered, and increasingly difficult to get orphans out of the country. Their contacts in the various South Vietnamese ministries were either no longer available or were too busy to see them, and Margaret realised that there was a massive churn in the bureaucracy as senior officials tried to whisk themselves and their families out of the country. However, there was no official warning for Margaret or anyone associated with FFAC operations that the military situation had taken a turn for the worse or that their operations – or their nurseries – were in any sort of danger.

To be on the safe side, they decided to limit their work placing orphans overseas until the future became a little more certain. By December 1974 they had more adoptive families on their books than they had orphans available, and the backlog would take almost a year to clear. Rosemary in Saigon and Wende in Denver decided that they would temporarily close adoption applications to all but those willing to take a child with a disability.

•

By December 1974, North Vietnamese leaders and military forces believed they were strong enough to risk a series of attacks in South Vietnam, attacks designed to test the military readiness of South Vietnam and the political will of the United States. The first of these attacks took place in Phuoc Long Province, to the north of Saigon on the Cambodian border. It opened on 12 December 1974 and, after a series of small, local skirmishes, culminated on 2 January 1975 with the provincial capital, Phuoc Binh, being placed under siege. The town surrendered four days later.

North Vietnamese planning and the People's Army of Vietnam (PAVN) easily passed the test. On the battlefield, the South's Army of the Republic of Vietnam (ARVN) showed a lack of equipment, leadership and morale, and was swept aside in almost every clash. To the North, they represented an army and a government that lacked will, while to many leaders in the South the fighting in Phuoc Long was simply a series of small-scale clashes with no significance for the wider struggle. To the North as well, the failure of the United States to intervene in what was clearly a breach of the Paris Peace Accords suggested a clear lack of will to re-engage in combat operations in South Vietnam.

The dust had barely settled on the battlefield, however, before further and more ambitious operations were being planned by North Vietnamese strategists. When, in February, an American congressional delegation visited the South to assess the political and military situation there and to then advise Congress and President Ford on what level of support South Vietnam should continue to receive, those plans were put on temporary hold. The delegation departed after a week with all indications being that they intended to advise a reduction rather than an increase in the provision of civil and military aid. In the North, operational planning now proceeded at a breakneck pace.

•

As early as 11 February, Wende had written formally to Rosemary from FFAC headquarters in Denver to express concerns about the future of their operations in both Cambodia and South Vietnam. Noting the US Congress' seeming reluctance to approve any additional funding to support President Thieu's fight against the NVA (North Vietnamese Army) and the Vietcong, Wende noted that it seemed to be the appropriate time to 'start planning to withdraw along with the others'.[1]

•

On 10 March, the PAVN launched its final major campaign against the South, believing that since the United States seemed to have lost its will to fight any more battles in South-East Asia, it would be fighting the South by itself. Those in the army command and their political masters were confident that if they pushed hard enough for long enough, they would be victorious. In anticipation of what was also to be the largest campaign they had attempted, they moved 100 000 fresh troops without fear of American interference down the Ho Chi Minh Trail, now a sophisticated and modern logistics route flanked by an oil pipeline.

The first battle of the campaign came at the town of Ban Me Thuot, the capital of Daclac Province, in the central highlands, and by 13 March the town had fallen to North Vietnamese forces.

A counterattack to recapture the town the following day barely moved beyond its starting point and soon fizzled out.

Instead of protesting against North Vietnamese naked aggression, the next day President Nguyen Van Thieu made a decision that, above anything else, determined the war's outcome. He ordered the secret redeployment of all ARVN forces from the central highlands to the major coastal cities to regroup and then return to recapture the territory they had lost. It was not to be. The withdrawal and redeployment on 16 March, expected to take three days, descended into a rout.[2]

The secret nature of Thieu's instructions had unexpected and tragic consequences. The unexplained and almost overnight disappearance of substantial ARVN forces from major highland centres like Pleiku and Kontum fuelled rumours that a secret agreement had been reached and that large swathes of the South – the central highlands and the northern provinces – were about to be handed over to the communists.

The mass movement of military forces and civilian refugees from the highlands to the coast would become known as the 'Convoy of Tears', and would contain firstly tens, then hundreds of thousands of panic-stricken men, women and children. Masses of civilians choked the roads and impeded the military's withdrawal to the extent that the rapidly advancing North Vietnamese forces caught many of the ARVN units in the open and cut them to pieces. Any chance of a counterattack in the highlands died with any troops on those roads.

When the extent of the military contribution to the unfolding humanitarian and national disaster became apparent, Thieu sought to redeploy some of his ground forces to the vital northern provinces. This was another disaster, as the units sent north simply disintegrated before they made contact with any

North Vietnamese forces. Once again, masses of people, a mix of military and civilians, fled either south to Nha Trang and Saigon or east to the major ports of Hue and Da Nang, hoping to find some kind of sailing craft to carry them south, always south.

Defeat built upon defeat and surrender followed surrender. Cities and whole provinces were abandoned to the North Vietnamese without a shot being fired. Saigon was perceived as some sort of sanctuary, a key position that could and would never be overrun by communist forces. As such, it became the target for masses of refugees and, as this desperate dash for safety became a flood, all sorts of discipline began to unravel. Among the military there was desertion, with soldiers throwing away both their uniforms and their weapons. Some deserters kept their weapons to turn on their officers until the breakdown involved individuals or groups of armed and uniformed men doing whatever it was they chose to do. Even Saigon itself was not immune to the mania taking over the country.

•

Things had also begun to come unstuck in Saigon from early February, as the first refugees from the fighting in the north as well as the central highlands began to stream into the city. Hidden among them were deserting soldiers. Those soldiers seemed to set some kind of precedent – soon both soldiers and policemen in Saigon began to abandon their posts. Before long, armed gangs appeared on the streets, robbing individuals and businesses seemingly at will. In one incident at Gia Dinh in central Saigon, a drunken soldier walked into a restaurant where he demanded food and alcohol. The owner refused and asked the soldier to leave. Shortly afterwards, a hand grenade was thrown through the door, exploding and killing or wounding many patrons.[3]

To further disconcert the people of Saigon, the Vietcong increased their pressure on the city, undertaking small hit-and-run attacks. Other units outside the city launched rocket and artillery barrages before melting back into the jungles, small hamlets and villages. There were no obvious targets or timings, and this unpredictability kept all Saigonese on edge.

It seemed like the city was dying a slow and painful death. The very atmosphere was thick with apprehension, and when there was silence for more than a few minutes, the renewal of distant explosions and firing was almost like a return to normality. With essential services breaking down, the streets gradually came to be filled with broken-down, damaged and abandoned vehicles. When fires, either accidentally or deliberately lit, broke out, the only ones able to fight them were those who were directly affected, and they rarely had the resources they needed. All knew what was happening to the north, in the central highlands, and that knowledge filled most of them with dread.

•

The privately supported orphanages in Saigon were not exempt from the anxiety that slowly gripped the city. Most had good connections with smaller orphanages in the up-country areas, those provinces where fighting was taking place, causing wholesale dislocation of the social fabric. They received urgent telephone calls pleading for assistance, for help in moving their children somewhere safe, and for food, milk and all those things that were becoming increasingly difficult to procure. The Saigon orphanages had little to offer beyond prayers and best wishes as they, too, were struggling to cope with an increasingly dire situation.

In early 1975, there were an estimated 134 orphanages operating in South Vietnam, collectively caring for just under twenty thousand children. Their situations worsened as the military situation deteriorated. Those dependent on direct government support found that support evaporating at the same rate as the country fell apart. Those supported by religious and humanitarian organisations also suffered, so they too called for government assistance – assistance that simply wasn't available. In the provinces, there was always the possibility of sourcing food from the countryside, an option not always available in larger cities like Saigon.

Typical of many of them was Andre Vung's Sancta Maria Orphanage, smaller and less well-endowed than most and thus more vulnerable when the country began to fall apart. Founded in 1964 by Andre Vung, the son of a family of wealthy Vietnamese businessmen, the orphanage had grown from just a handful of children into a sophisticated operation involving almost five hundred children, most of them of primary-school age and some even a little older. About a third of the children had some form of disability, and their time was divided between a well-built, clean and tidy facility in Saigon and a farm a few hours outside the city where the older boys lived in a dormitory and learned how to be farmers.

Sancta Maria's food supplies – even those from their own farm – suddenly became problematic and the orphanage increasingly relied on what they could source from either the few donor agencies still operating or the black market. The orphans and their carers soon experienced hunger, which became incrementally worse as donations dried up and black-market prices suddenly skyrocketed. All grew weaker and the weakest of them began to die.[4]

•

Wende Grant's concerns about FFAC's South-East Asian operations intensified after her February letter to Rosemary, and on
11 March, at the same time the PAVN was launching its final
major campaign against the South, she flew into Saigon with
two objectives. The first was to supervise the closure of the
Canada House facility in Phnom Penh, now in harm's way as
Khmer Rouge forces closed in on Cambodia's capital city. The
second was to assist Rosemary in placing and evacuating the six
hundred children who were crowded into FFAC's four nurseries
in Saigon. She was prepared to stay for however long it took to
complete both tasks.

The next morning, Wende's short flight from Saigon touched
down at Phnom Penh airport among the daily rocket barrage
unleashed by Khmer Rouge positions outside the city. It would
not be easy to evacuate the Cambodian orphans – approvals
for neither their adoption or for landing in Vietnam had been
completed. The late decision to evacuate the orphanage meant,
too, that the children's transportation had not yet been arranged.
Fortunately, Wende was able to organise a charter flight out. She
was doubly fortunate as all commercial flights to and from Phnom
Penh had just been suspended indefinitely. The only qualification
to the charter was that the airport had to remain open.[5]

Back in Saigon, Margaret Moses set herself to doing what she
did best: working her way through the bureaucracy, seeing the
people she needed to see, in the right order, and saying exactly
what she needed to say to them.

It was not that easy in Cambodia. After two days of going
from the Canadian Embassy to various Cambodian government
departments and agencies, Wende and the two Canada House
administrators finally filed papers to adopt the five children
still at their nursery – two sets of twins and a single baby. To

expedite the process, Wende herself applied to adopt one set of twins. The following day a *laissez-passer*, a group passport and permission to leave were granted. On 17 March Wende, the five orphans and all the expatriate volunteers flew back to Saigon.

Wende's return coincided with continuing broadcasts of military reversals in the central highlands and northern provinces. After a brief discussion, she and Rosemary agreed to proceed with organising the evacuation of their orphans. That decision put in train several actions. The two women were concerned about the possible interdiction of food and medicine, and their timelines for evacuation would be determined by both their available stockpiles and the supply of essential items. They estimated that they still had a minimum of three to four weeks to organise the evacuation. That timeline could be impacted, though, if Saigon were swamped by refugees or if the airport at Tan Son Nhut were shut down either by enemy action or by being overrun with Vietnamese trying to leave. Wende knew what could happen if commercial airlines shut down services, so she began a search for possible charter flights.

There were additional complications for the two women to consider. The six hundred children for whom they were responsible were being cared for by an expatriate staff of fifteen and a local staff of four hundred. However, should the situation in Saigon suddenly deteriorate, many of those local staff members would be unable to report for work and then the nurseries could not function. Without them it would also be physically impossible to transport the children to the airport or to any of the helicopter pick-up points in the event of an emergency evacuation.

While Wende and Margaret Moses set to work to organise the logistics for evacuating their six hundred orphans, Rosemary concentrated on the paperwork that would identify each child.

For the best part of five years, Rosemary had been preparing similar paperwork for the dozens of orphans who would be sent overseas to new homes each month. Now she had, at best, six weeks to complete what would normally take place over six months. Her small one-roomed home at Phu My soon had stacks of files climbing towards the ceiling in every available space.

This time, too, the task was a bit more complicated. Many of the children who had arrived in recent months had come in without the usual identification documentation. Some arrived without names, others with very limited family background details. Given that all would be with new adoptive families within a few weeks, Rosemary was determined to provide as much documentation as she could for every one of them, hence the mountains of paper in her room.

She began by drawing up a series of lists of orphans' names – either their birth names or those they had been given when they arrived at the FFAC nurseries. Each list was organised by country of destination with, if known, the children's names and birthdates, together with their adoptive parents' names and addresses. All the known information for each child was also transcribed onto an index card and, again if available, a photograph and copy of their birth certificate were attached to the index card.[6]

Rosemary also wanted to make identification bracelets, like those worn by patients in hospitals, for each orphan. At the very least, these bracelets should contain the child's real and/or nursery name and the nursery where they resided. These could then be cross-referenced with the index cards she was compiling. Additional bracelets could be made, Rosemary decided, containing details of the child's adoptive family, their destination and even health and useful medical information, such as allergies or what kind of formula they drank. It might mean that some children would be wearing several bracelets when they left, but it would certainly make things easier for officials and volunteers along the way.

Suddenly, a lot of other considerations came into play. While most children were some way through the adoption process, there were quite a few nearer the start than the finish. Some children were considered unadoptable, while others were too ill to be considered anywhere near ready for adoption. Some were so ill that they were being treated in hospital and were assessed as being too sick to travel. Some were in orphanages in other parts of the country waiting to be collected by Rosemary's team. There were also a few, a very few, who had arrived so recently that they had been neither assessed nor registered.

Another consideration was the nurseries themselves. Rosemary and Wende knew that refugees were streaming down from the north and they knew, too, that the South Vietnamese government was talking about establishing new refugee camps just to the north of Saigon to house them, although nothing seemed to have progressed beyond talk. They knew that there would be orphans among those refugees and that, after FFAC had made an orderly evacuation, the state could use their facilities to house those orphans. They might even be able to continue their operations there for some time after their own children had left. That role was something they had discussed since early March, when calls started coming in from orphanages in places like Da Nang asking them to send someone up to collect their orphans. But then, towards the end of the month, the phone calls stopped coming.

•

Rosemary Taylor and Margaret Moses were not the only two Australians in Saigon that March worrying about what the future might hold for vulnerable people for whom they had assumed responsibility. At the Australian Embassy on the fifth floor of the Caravelle Hotel, Australia's Ambassador to South Vietnam, Geoffrey Price, was facing a raft of similar problems. Canberra had been asking more and more of Price since the beginning of the year as the unfolding situation in Vietnam carried a clear set of Australian political priorities above any Vietnamese and international relations ramifications.[7]

On 19 March, Price dispatched a cable to the Department of Foreign Affairs (DFA) in Canberra, a regular update which opened with the words:

> The pace of the deterioration of the military situation which has been gathering momentum over the past ten days appears about to quicken rapidly. The expected and predicted escalation of the war by the NVA has been launched on a more massive scale than anticipated . . .[8]

In response to a request from Canberra, Price would send a daily Situation Report (Sitrep) to Canberra from 21 March. These gave the prime minister and his senior ministers the latest updates on the military situation in South Vietnam plus all the local political responses to that situation. Anything else considered relevant to Australian policymakers was also to be included. The second Sitrep on 22 March, for example, included information about the flight of up to one million refugees ahead of the advancing communist forces.[9] Within a week, the Sitreps were touching on the plight of Saigon's orphans and orphanages, and offering observations on Australia's possible obligations to both.

•

Rosemary, Margaret and Wende were growing increasingly concerned. As villages, towns and cities in the north fell with little or no resistance, the unthinkable was suddenly becoming possible. In recent weeks, and boosted by daily communiqués from the presidential palace, there was a belief, which was perhaps more a hope, that the ARVN was being withdrawn to defensible positions to the north of Saigon and that the capital city and the Mekong Delta would be defended to the death. There was, too, the ultimate belief/hope that the United States would re-enter the war and the B-52 bombers would again pound the north and the Ho Chi Minh Trail, and North Vietnam would be forced to sue for peace. But President Nixon, the man who promised such action, was no longer in office and President Thieu, upon whom so much now rested, was proving incapable of any meaningful action.

All hope from just a few weeks earlier was gone and had been replaced by fear and trepidation. The trepidation was about what might happen to them all should the previously remote prospect of a communist victory eventuate, and the fear was over how that victory might be achieved. Most believed that a final battle for a Saigon crowded with millions of refugees would include a rain of rockets and shells, and that the city would be cut off from its hinterland. When it was, that supplies of food and medicines would dwindle and disappear from everywhere but the black market, where prices would make them simply unobtainable. They would be trapped, too, because Phnom Penh had shown that the commercial airlines would cease operations and that the airport would be shut down by enemy action.

For Rosemary and the other administrators there was an additional layer of concern: should the situation in Saigon suddenly deteriorate into the kind of street fighting that some were predicting, the majority of their staff would be unable to get to work, and their supply lines for food and other consumable items – and even their lines of communication to provincial orphanages – would be disrupted at least and destroyed at worst. When the news came in of how the approach of North Vietnamese forces was leading to an almost complete collapse of civil order in Hue and Da Nang, it acted to strengthen their resolve. What had been a priority – evacuating the orphans before a communist takeover prevented them from leaving – now became a matter of life and death.

•

The full horror of the breakdown of law and order in Da Nang could not be told until Ken Healy's World Airways 727 arrived back in Saigon, and for most of the flight there was no certainty that they would even make it. The scheduled 45-minute flight on 28 March took two hours to complete. The rear stairs remained lowered throughout the flight, which meant the rear door couldn't be closed and this, in turn, prevented the cabin from being pressurised. To ensure that everyone aboard could breathe, Healy kept the aircraft below three thousand metres. He had thought about making an emergency landing at Phan Rang because of the difficulty he was having controlling the 727, but abandoned the idea when he was informed that Phan Rang airport had no firefighting equipment. He then directed Don McDaniel, the pilot of the third 727, to rendezvous with him above Phan Rang, and sent Dave Wanis back to Tan Son Nhut to help them prepare for the emergency landing he knew he would now have to make there.

McDaniel had been flying at almost ten thousand metres but descended in time to meet Healy's 727 over Phan Rang and then fly a slow circuit around the other aircraft, observing it from above and below. One of his first observations was that there appeared to be a body hanging out of the nose wheel well. There was – one panicked ARVN soldier had climbed into the wheel well and as the front wheel retracted he had somehow become trapped and was crushed. The soldier's body prevented the wheel from fully retracting, which probably saved the lives of the eight other people who had squeezed into the well before him.

The aircraft's left wing appeared to be quite badly damaged, and shrapnel from the exploding grenade had cut through control surfaces and severed control lines. McDaniel reported that while the nose wheel had only partially retracted the other wheels appeared to have retracted correctly. Healy had hoped this was the case but was unable to confirm it since the hydraulic sequencing system for retracting all the wheels had stopped working. McDaniel added that Healy's cargo door was open and that the cargo hold appeared to be full of people. This information plus the knowledge that his aircraft was steadily losing fuel convinced Healy to fly directly to Saigon where, if he couldn't lower and lock all the wheels for landing at Tan Son Nhut, he would attempt to put the plane down on the Saigon River.

McDaniel flew his 727 ahead of Healy's down to Saigon and as Healy prepared to land, McDaniel reported to him that all the 727's wheels were down and appeared to be locked in position. That was a relief to Healy, but he remained uncertain whether those wheels and the struts that supported them would withstand the impact of landing. They did, first the side wheels and then the front wheel, although other mechanical issues meant that he was forced to use a fair amount of the almost five-kilometre-long runway to slow down to taxiing speed. When he did, though, he turned the 727 around and moved slowly along the taxiway to the World Airways terminal, where he parked the aircraft and turned the engines off.

For a moment, the silence was almost palpable and gave those on board the aircraft a few seconds to gather their thoughts. Many, perhaps most, were on reflection ashamed about their actions back in Da Nang. They had pushed and kicked and sometimes even killed to gain the sanctuary of the aircraft, and while a quick headcount in the main cabin suggested a figure of more than 250, the true number aboard would never be known. On that evacuation flight, though, and in that aircraft, there were just ten women and one baby. The rest were men, almost all military age and many still wearing their uniforms.[10]

Others aboard, the flight and cabin crew, could hold their heads up and be proud of what they had all achieved under exceptionally difficult and trying conditions. Ed Daly's courage could not be questioned but his judgement would be, not for the first time and certainly not for the last. The journalists, reporters and camera crews were given the opportunity to ply their various crafts and by the day's end the story of the last flight from Da Nang was spreading across Saigon and across the world. As it spread it raised one question above all others: if one evacuation flight into a provincial city could descend into such chaos, what would happen if there was an attempt to evacuate people from Saigon under the same circumstances?

•

After the soldiers and civilians had been escorted from Ken Healy's 727 and after Healy, Ed Daly and Joe Hrezo had departed for drinks in Daly's suite at the Caravelle Hotel, and long after Bruce Dunning, Mike Marriott and all the other journalists and cameramen had rushed back to their studios and offices to spread the news of the dramatic flight, the last two people aboard the 727 walked down those rickety stairs and across to the World Airways terminal. They had tidied themselves up a bit – as befitted their role – and now Jan Wollett and Val Witherspoon were going to do a bit of winding down of their own. It was Good Friday, after all, and with a little bit of luck they had a holiday weekend ahead of them.

5

LOOKING FOR AN EXIT

Saigon, Easter 1975

Easter, usually a time of peace and reflection, almost passed without notice in Saigon that year. The nuns, ex-nuns and civilian volunteers running FFAC's nurseries were simply too busy to do anything but recognise the special days with private prayers and reflections. If anyone had harboured doubts about the decision to evacuate all the children (and no one seemed to), those doubts were brushed aside on Easter Sunday. The official and unofficial news from Da Nang revealed more detail about the human and humanitarian disaster that continued to unfold there, and Wende and Rosemary directed that all efforts were now to be put into preparing the children and the documentation necessary for them all to successfully complete an overseas evacuation. They were to do so while trying to remain calm themselves, doing everything in their power to avoid frightening or distressing the children.

Plans for that evacuation were extremely fluid, in part because their main hope for an aerial evacuation was partly dependent on one of the most controversial figures then in South Vietnam, Ed

Daly. Late on Saturday night, 29 March, Wende and Rosemary agreed that, given his heroics at Da Nang, Ed Daly might be both willing and able to assist them with their evacuation plans. With Rosemary ensconced at Phu My, Wende telephoned Daly in his rooms at the Caravelle Hotel to ask if she could talk to him about possible evacuation flights from Saigon. Daly, just finishing a late-night drinking and talking session with several expatriate journalists, invited Wende to come over immediately.

Elaine Moir had arrived from Australia the previous week to assist with the evacuation and Wende asked her to accompany her to the meeting. The two women contacted the mission warden and arranged for a car and driver to take them to Daly's suite at the Caravelle, arriving there shortly after midnight. Things were a bit tense at the start of the meeting. The two women were completely focused on the wellbeing and safety of their six hundred orphans while Daly wanted to talk, to sound them out while expounding his own theories on the fate of South Vietnam and how World Airways could help almost everyone with almost everything. Then, after listening to several recountings of the events surrounding his evacuation flights to Da Nang, Wende raised the specifics of their request for assistance with a charter flight. Their organisation FFAC, she said, was caring for several hundred orphans in their nurseries, and they wanted to evacuate those children from South Vietnam. Was Mr Daly in a position to assist? Daly said he could, would and, moreover, was able to offer them the charter of a Boeing 747 jumbo jet, then the largest passenger aircraft in the world. A verbal agreement was reached and at 2.30 a.m. Wende and Elaine departed the Caravelle Hotel feeling extremely hopeful about the possibility of an early evacuation.

By mid-morning the next day, Easter Sunday, 30 March, Ed Daly's overnight offer had changed. He told Wende that there was a change of plans because the Boeing 747 was no longer available. They should not be concerned, though, because he had been able to source two substitute aircraft, both passenger jets. He now planned to use one to fly a group of orphans directly to the United States while the other aircraft would fly to Australia, carrying those orphans who were not scheduled to go to North America. He would contact them again when he had more details on the aircraft's movements. It was not a major impediment; Wende and Rosemary agreed to proceed and decided that all Europe-bound orphans would travel with the small group bound for Australia, and further arrangements would be made there.

However, Daly's change of aircraft and arrangements was not what they wanted to hear at that time. Further details of the military debacle and human disaster that had occurred at Da Nang were emerging, and if any of them harboured doubts about what the future held, those doubts were removed when they received formal notification of the US evacuation plan for their citizens in Saigon, a number that included several FFAC volunteers. Part of the plan stated:

> Should it be felt necessary for US personnel to report to their designated assembly areas, a coded message will be broadcast over American Radio Service. This message will be broadcast every fifteen minutes for approximately two hours. If you hear the above message, report with travel documentation to your nearest assembly point. Stay tuned to American Radio Station FM 99.9 (primary) or FM 90.1 (secondary) for further announcements.[1]

Sunday was a day of furious activity despite all these distractions. During the morning prepared memos were sent from Rathaven to the four nurseries requesting details on all the children each nursery was then holding. As the information on each child came back it was collated and transferred to an index card to which a photograph of the child was stapled. Even as the requests went out and they continued collating the material they already had, Rosemary and Wende knew they would be unlikely to complete all other paperwork necessary for the evacuation of six hundred children, but they kept going anyway. Their last task that Sunday night was to write a letter to South Vietnam's deputy prime minister, Dr Phan Quang Dan, who was also the Minister for Social Welfare, requesting a *laissez-passer* for all 600 FFAC children, allowing them to legally leave the country.

•

By now, Rosemary and Wende had almost given up hope of gaining any assistance from the Australian government, which they believed was struggling to cope with the way the Vietnam conflict had changed so rapidly in the last few months. There seemed to be a policy vacuum in Canberra, and until there was a clear indication of commitment to the government and people of South Vietnam, the fate of Rosemary's nurseries and their orphans – and thousands of other South Vietnamese who had Australian connections – would be in the hands of a government with little or no apparent commitment to or interest in those people. It was easy to see why they would feel that way and it was an assessment that wasn't all that far wide of the mark.

The seeming indifference to the fate of South Vietnam and its orphans was partly the result of the realpolitik that had brought the Whitlam government into office in the first place. Australian foreign and immigration policy was more the product of Whitlam himself rather than his foreign minister, Don Willesee, or his Immigration Minister, Clyde Cameron. And when it came to South Vietnam, Whitlam was prepared to let the decision about the country's fate be determined by the Vietnamese people themselves, and if the North prevailed in that contest of arms, then so be it. His government would recognise the reality of a Vietnam reunited by battlefield success and would follow accepted international protocols when dealing with the new Vietnam, including those protocols governing the acceptance of refugees.

The problem was that in Australia many people believed that Whitlam was less than even-handed when it came to the two Vietnams. Since the opening of the North Vietnamese offensive in the early months of 1975, a number of Whitlam's senior ministers, including Jim Cairns and Tom Uren, had made public comments suggesting that they, and perhaps the government as a whole, considered that the fall of South Vietnam's government and a communist takeover there were not necessarily a bad thing.[2] The suspicions went back a lot farther than that, however, and in a New Year's Day editorial that year, one of Australia's leading newspapers observed, 'The government has so far been less than even-handed in its condemnation of the Saigon government for breaches of the Paris Peace Agreement and its failure to voice any criticism of the war effort controlled by Hanoi . . .'[3]

Whitlam himself would urge DFA officials not to dismiss statements from communist authorities in Hanoi and their front organisation in the south, the Provisional Revolutionary Government, that the people of South Vietnam had nothing to fear when the communists took over.[4] He was also in the process of setting up a formal diplomatic relationship with

North Vietnam and wanted nothing to disrupt this developing rapport.[5] Finally, Whitlam was almost paranoid about what significant numbers of South Vietnamese refugees could mean for Australian politics. He had seen how anti-communist refugees from Eastern Europe – he referred to them as 'fucking Balts'[6] – had pushed conservative politics further to the right during the 1950s and 1960s, and was determined that the process would not be repeated during his prime ministership.

In some ways, Rosemary Taylor's orphans were hostages to this political posturing. Their plight, and the plight of hundreds of thousands of their compatriots in South Vietnam, did not go unnoticed in Australia. Amid the alarmist predictions of a possible bloodbath following a communist victory in the south, more reasoned voices – especially those who already had adoptive families waiting for them in other countries, including Australia – were highlighting the orphan issue. Here, the lead was taken by the AAFA, which claimed that there were at least one hundred orphans in South Vietnam who were simply waiting for the adoption procedures to be completed before they could join their new families. The problem was that it was taking between six and twelve months for those procedures to be completed in Australia on top of however long it took in South Vietnam. There was a real chance that many orphans would be dead before they could be adopted. And for every orphan bound for Australia, there were dozens more bound for other countries.[7]

•

Facing criticism from the public and the mainstream media over a number of policy failures, Whitlam and his senior ministers realised that public opinion was clearly in favour of Australia doing something beyond uttering platitudes to ease the unfolding humanitarian disaster in South Vietnam. In a series of carefully worded press releases commencing on 30 March, Whitlam announced that the Australian government continued to monitor the military and civilian crises in South Vietnam and was committed to doing all it could to ease the suffering of those who had been impacted by the fighting. The government would, Whitlam trumpeted, be instructing the RAAF to undertake an ongoing relief operation while the crisis continued, an operation that would be purely humanitarian in its planning and execution, one that would deliver relief supplies to those who needed them most.

The relief operation would comprise RAAF elements already in the area and based at RAAF Butterworth in Malaysia, and RAAF assets based in Australia. As well as the flying and ground support crews, headquarters would be placed in the Australian Embassy in Saigon where a direct and secure radio link between all operation components would be established.[8] To involve the wider Australian community in the relief effort, the prime minister also announced that the government would launch an appeal to raise funds to support the refugees displaced by the fighting currently underway in Indochina.

When the various elements of the RAAF relief operation were brought together into a single unit, that unit would be known as Detachment S and would be under the command of Wing Commander John Mitchell of 36 Squadron. Its role would be to assist in the distribution of Red Cross supplies to refugee camps and/or areas cut off by the fighting,[9] plus other non-specified but certainly non-military tasks. Because there was a distinct possibility that some of their missions might take them to disputed areas, a small team of airfield defence guards were assigned to the detachment to secure their aircraft when they were on the ground at Tan Son Nhut and elsewhere in South Vietnam.

Detachment S's mission did not get off to an auspicious start. Its first operational flight the very next day, Easter Sunday, departed Butterworth for Saigon. As the C-130 was on its final descent into Tan Son Nhut, the pilot was asked by air traffic control whether any of those aboard were armed, as bringing weapons into South Vietnam aboard a humanitarian relief mission was clearly a breach of several Geneva conventions. The C-130 was carrying the airfield defence guards and their personal weapons, and when this news was reported to air traffic control, the C-130 was ordered to return to Butterworth, where the guards were to store their weapons. This was done, and the aircraft returned to Saigon later that day, ready to begin relief operations as soon as those operations were identified.

•

Gough Whitlam's was not the only government caught off balance by the double blow of a crumbling South Vietnam and public outcry for something to be done about the innocent victims of that collapse and the thousands of orphans whose long-term survival was now being called into question. In the United States, President Gerald Ford was caught in a dilemma of his predecessor's making. He was unable to win congressional approval for the kind of support that former President Richard Nixon had promised South Vietnam if just such a contingency arose. Until the end of his presidency, Nixon had maintained that any form of North Vietnamese aggression would be met by an overwhelming US military response. Gerald Ford, diminished by both the words and actions of his predecessor, struggled to gain support for any form of increased American support for the beleaguered South Vietnamese government. He was also hamstrung in his ability to respond to those who demanded some kind – any kind – of action to ease the suffering of the innocent victims of a nasty war. He did, however, send one of the Pentagon's senior officials, General Frederick Weyand, the US Army's Chief of Staff and former commander of US forces in South Vietnam, to Saigon to see if there was anything the United States could do that might make a difference.

When Weyand met with US Ambassador Graham Martin a possible course of action became apparent. Martin was regaling Weyand with stories about Ed Daly and his antics at Da Nang. He recounted Daly calling him a 'jumped-up used-car salesman', something that didn't bother him as much as the fact that he believed Daly did everything with one eye permanently on ways to generate free publicity for himself and his airline. It was this oversized showmanship, this egotistical theatricality, that most annoyed Martin. The ambassador was also aware that Daly was currently working behind the scenes organising an airlift of Vietnamese orphans to the United States. Martin knew Daly's history, knew that he was himself an orphan, and didn't doubt his sincerity, but he also knew that such an operation would simply become a huge publicity campaign for Ed Daly and World Airways.[10]

It was this dynamic that gave Graham Martin an idea. If the United States were to organise its own airlift of orphans, on a much larger scale than Ed Daly envisioned, the images of hundreds of Vietnamese babies and small children arriving to sanctuary in the United States might just be the spectacle that aroused enough public sympathy and public pressure to force Congress to release some of the South Vietnamese civilian and military aid packages that it had blocked. Weyand agreed that the proposal might just work.

Weyand was in Martin's office that Easter weekend not just for a meeting with the ambassador but also because he was about to take part in a conference call with Gerald Ford and Secretary of State Henry Kissinger, who were both in Palm Springs, California. When Martin outlined the proposal both Ford and Kissinger were in favour of it, Ford commenting that he did not want to see Daly and World Airways 'grandstanding' on the back of what would be a humanitarian mission.[11] Kissinger also pointed out that such a proposal fell under agreements already reached by the United States and both President Thieu and South Vietnam's Minister for Refugee Affairs.[12]

The meeting ended with Martin agreeing to write a letter to that minister outlining what the United States hoped to achieve through the orphans' airlift and Kissinger saying that, from their end, it would be presented as a State Department initiative, to be delivered by USAID. All agreed to put the necessary wheels in motion as soon as possible.[13]

•

For the workers and volunteers at the FFAC nurseries, there was no indication that Easter Monday, 31 March, would be any less hectic than the previous day or that the pressure that continued to build in Saigon would in any way be released. The first task of the day was to deliver the request for a *laissez-passer* to the deputy prime minister's office and one of the senior Vietnamese staff, probably Dolly Bui, was sent off with it. That morning, too, all available volunteers came to Rathaven to begin collating material and preparing documentation for each child. Further instructions were also sent out to each nursery. They were asked to have any children in foster care returned to their home nursery, while any children who were in temporary FFAC care were to be returned to their families.

Several additional requests were also sent out. On the lists of children, each nursery was asked to add notations on each child's health and their ability to travel. They were also asked to pack travel clothing and food for all of them. Foreign staff, too, were included in the requests sent from Rathaven. They were instructed to make up a travel pack of their own belongings and to have that at Rathaven by 9 a.m. on Tuesday morning. Rosemary added a note saying they should only take the bare minimum of personal effects.

That instruction brought home the seriousness of the situation to the expatriate volunteers. Out at Allambie, Lee Makk quickly finished and then posted an audio cassette to her family in Adelaide. On the tape, Lee spoke of her admiration for the local girls they worked with, praising their diligence and their obvious love for the orphans in their care. She described how, although she liked walking, she usually caught a cyclo when travelling around Saigon as doing so helped the driver support his family. She spoke of local village customs, her daily routines and the weather and spoke, too, of the staff with whom she worked and how much she enjoyed caring for her little orphans. Finally, she let her family know that she had begun the process of adopting a little girl herself. Lee knew that her family would not receive the cassette until early April, but she also knew that they would all be thrilled when they did.[14]

Christie Leivermann returned to Rathaven later that morning after completing another shift as night manager at Newhaven, where she had seen all the instructions that Rosemary and Wende had issued. Spotting Wende, she called out, 'Well, Grant, do we evacuate today, or should I go to bed?'

Wende replied, 'We're not sure yet, Christie. Sleep, but put your evacuation outfit at the end of the bed just in case.'[15]

Christie didn't go to bed, though, staying up for an extra couple of hours making identity bracelets. She repeated this harmless banter each morning in the coming days, continuing to make bracelets when her shift was over.

•

Also working hard was Geoffrey Price, Australia's Ambassador to South Vietnam. His daily reports were becoming essential reading for politicians and public service mandarins in Canberra, providing, as they did, a clear exposition of the death throes of a small nation. On 27 March, his Daily Sitrep had warned that the situation in Da Nang was deteriorating rapidly and that civilian violence was highly likely. The next day he commented on fears among the civilian population and included a paragraph mentioning that 'one senior VNAF (Vietnamese Air Force) officer stated this week that at least 500 000 service officers and government officials can expect to be executed if the North Vietnamese achieve a complete military victory'.[16] It was certainly food for thought.

On that Monday, 31 March, Geoffrey Price was also thinking about emergency evacuations, and put those thoughts into an Immediate cable to his department in Canberra. Price stated his belief that several small orphanages in Saigon would most probably approach the Australian Embassy requesting assistance with transporting their orphans to safety. When they did so, Price believed priority should be given to those orphans already assigned to Australian adoptive parents. He added that he had received a list of forty-five orphans from one agency and believed that an RAAF aircraft could be used to fly them to Australia. Price added a word of caution about Rosemary Taylor and her six hundred FFAC orphans, suggesting that committing to assist with their evacuation could lead to unnecessary complications. He also suggested that Canberra might raise the issue with the Americans because, while many of Taylor's volunteers were Australian, the nursery operations were funded primarily by Americans. By then, Canberra was already aware of Rosemary's concerns.

When Rosemary and Wende decided that the only safe alternative for their orphans was overseas evacuation, they contacted FFAC headquarters in Denver and their friends and supporters in Australia and asked them to lobby for government support for a complete evacuation program. By 31 March, that effort had already started and was not being particularly well-received by the heads of the Departments of Foreign Affairs and Prime Minister and Cabinet, or by the prime minister himself. The bureaucracy thought that Rosemary and her supporters were trying to play departments off against each other, while Prime Minister Whitlam, facing a raft of issues threatening his government, had little sympathy for the plight of Vietnamese refugees, irrespective of their ages or backgrounds. Price was told that his initial response was, 'the Vietnamese sob stories did not wring his withers'.[17]

On Easter Monday, Rosemary raised the pressure several notches when she made direct contact with both the deputy leader of the Labor Party, Lance Barnard, and Immigration Minister Clyde Cameron. She described to both men the rapid deterioration of South Vietnam and her fears for both the security of Saigon and the safety of the six hundred children in the nurseries. She said she believed the South Vietnamese government had or was about to issue exit visas for at least two hundred children and urged the Australian government to come to their assistance. While she wished for the complete evacuation of all six hundred orphans, there were 165 she would like evacuated immediately, among whom were seven who already had adoptive families waiting for them in Australia. Both men said they would see what they could do.[18]

•

Ed Daly's withdrawal of his offer of a 747 jumbo was a setback but the counteroffer of two other passenger jets offered some hope. The change of plans also encouraged Rosemary and Wende to continue exploring every possible avenue of escape, and soon staff in both Saigon and Denver were scrambling to try to find an airline able to carry their children out of harm's way. Wende learned of a Pan American Airlines (Pan Am) 747 that was sitting on the tarmac at Hong Kong airport, but their hopes were dashed after learning that the aircraft had already been promised to another adoption agency, probably Holt International.[19] They quickly discovered, too, that there would be no chance of flying out small groups of children on the regularly scheduled commercial flights. The three main carriers – Pan Am, Air France and China Airlines – were booked out for the first three weeks of April and were loath to take bookings beyond that.[20]

Requests about charters elicited a similar response. Both Pan Am and Air France were vague when approached directly about the possibility of chartering flights for the orphans. Air France stated that it would need more time to both consider and organise a charter flight. Pan Am, although admitting it had several planes available in the Far East, appeared incapable of making a decision on a charter. The fact that there were now seven adoption agencies in Saigon, all presumably looking to evacuate their charges, may have influenced those responses. China Airlines was simply not interested so World Airways remained their best bet for evacuation.

The day's only really good news came in the early evening. At 7.30 p.m. a telephone call to Rathaven from the deputy prime minister's office in Saigon informed Wende that all their orphans would be granted exit visas.

•

Two middle-aged Australian women, Margaret Moses senior and May Ewin, worked away quietly in the background while all the swirls and eddies of politics and personalities threatened to engulf the activities of the FFAC nurseries and those who ran them. They had earlier volunteered to assume primary responsibility for making name tags for the children, allowing the other volunteers to devote their time and energy to preparing all the travel documentation and travel packs that their children would need. Margaret had been hoping to escort a forthcoming convoy of orphans to Europe but that was put on hold the previous week when the security situation deteriorated rapidly. Now, she was hearing talk about a possible evacuation flight to the United States and thought she might put her name forward for that if there was a call for volunteers. She had never been to America and her daughter had spoken quite glowingly of her time there.

6

THE NOOSE TIGHTENS

April Fools' Day

The communist noose tightened perceptibly on April Fools' Day, Tuesday 1 April 1975. That day, after a brief burst of resistance by the ARVN's 22nd Division, the key coastal cities of Qui Nanh, Tuy Hoa – the town where Rosemary was first posted – and Nha Trang were all abandoned by South Vietnamese forces. In doing so they surrendered the northern half of South Vietnam to the NVA, reducing the area controlled by the south by more than 50 per cent. As the communist forces rolled down the coastal plains, hundreds of thousands of refugees and families displaced by the fighting fled ahead of them.

As this was happening in the north, NVA and Vietcong forces opened a second front in the south. Operating out of sanctuaries in Cambodia, they pushed into Long An Province, just to the south of Saigon, where they threatened to cut Highway 4, the capital's main link to the Mekong Delta. Small units attacked government forces and set up small fire bases in the country-side outside Saigon, and every night those crowded in the city could hear gunfire and explosions from somewhere in the darkness. That darkness came earlier now, too, as the government continued to extend the curfew.

It appeared as well that all eyes were increasingly being drawn towards Tan Son Nhut airport. The airport buildings and surrounds were now crowded with refugees, many of whom were in small family groups camped in odd corners, desperately trying to buy seats on departing aircraft. They didn't care where those aircraft were going; they just wanted to get out. Anticipating that the airport and its flight paths might come under direct enemy fire, South Vietnamese civil aviation authorities now instructed all aircraft to take defensive measures when both landing and taking off.

•

For Geoffrey Price, 1 April was simply a continuation of what had started the previous week with the collapse of ARVN forces in the country's north. Canberra was now ravenous for news of the political, military and civilian developments in South Vietnam, and Price and his staff were struggling to answer all the questions and service all the requests that were being made of them. One item included in that day's Sitrep was an assessment that South Vietnam may not be able to hold out much longer. The continuing setbacks in the north and the numbers now flooding into Saigon to escape the fighting suggested a possible refugee crisis arising there. If Australia were to become involved in addressing such a crisis, Price wrote, they would need to categorise those refugees and decide which categories they would accept.[1]

Rosemary's telephone calls to Lance Barnard and Clyde Cameron the previous day had prompted an immediate response, and Price promptly received a cable from Canberra asking him to comment on Rosemary's request for an RAAF evacuation operation to take all orphans back to Australia. Price was cautious in his response, knowing that any action he advocated might create a precedent. While he agreed that the evacuation of orphans destined to be adopted by Australian families should be a priority, he again pointed out that most of FFAC's orphans were bound for other countries. Price noted, again, that Rosemary Taylor's organisation was based mostly in the United States, so it was not really an Australian responsibility. His final concern was the possibility that if such an operation became public knowledge it had the potential to cause some kind of panic in Saigon.[2]

•

A number of volunteers stayed up late into the night on Monday 31 March, working on travel and identification documents for the orphans, while others were up early on Tuesday to continue that work. They all knew it was going to be another busy day but no one knew how it would end. Wende Grant made a decision early that day. She had been scheduled to leave South Vietnam on 1 April, flying out of Saigon aboard a Pan Am flight as part of the escort for a convoy of FFAC orphans that included the Cambodian twins that she and her husband were planning to adopt. Those little girls and the other Cambodian orphans had previously been brought in from a temporary facility at Tu Duc to Rathaven and they had been camping on the pharmacy floor.

In the rapidly changing circumstances, Wende discussed these plans with Rosemary and chose to stay in Saigon until 1 April to assist with evacuation preparations for all the FFAC nurseries. She had authority and experience, two attributes they both knew would be invaluable in the days to come. Her replacement proved surprisingly easy to find. A phone call to Merrit Stark revealed that their daughter Anne would be willing to accompany the convoy on its journey to Seattle.[3] That agreed, the travel packs, which included the children's special possessions, were prepared for the convoy. Two hours later, the children and their escorts were gone.

It would become a day of sadness in addition to those farewells. The Vietnamese staff at the nurseries and Rathaven were all aware of the planned evacuations and, although clearly worried about the deteriorating security situation in Saigon, continued to report for work and care for the children. Now, though, some of the women approached expatriate volunteers – some quietly and others in tears – to express fears about the safety of their own children and to ask if there was any possibility that their children could be included in the evacuation. Many broke down when they said they understood they may never see their children again, but still begged for the opportunity to send those children away. All requests were politely and compassionately refused but each such refusal exacted a toll on all concerned.

•

Ed Daly just couldn't help himself. His various schemes and plans were constantly being thwarted by the unavailability of aircraft. The aircraft were either already engaged on other contracted missions, out of action being serviced, or somewhere on the other side of the world when he needed them here, in Saigon. Late on April Fools' Day, still trying to work out what he needed to do, Daly was drinking with a group of journalists at the Caravelle Hotel. There were at least two Australians in the group, and Daly revealed to them that he planned to fly fifteen hundred orphans to Australia and the United States, and would fly them with or without the approval of either government.

The Australian journalists lapped it up. They would later characterise Daly as 'a flamboyant, larger-than-life character whose company, World Airways, had been flying into Phnom Penh to support government forces fighting the Khmer Rouge'.[4] They would also report that he was famous, or infamous, for organising the chaotic last evacuation flight out of Da Nang. Warming to the task, Daly told the journalists that he was aware that the Australian government would refuse him landing rights for his orphan flights but also said that, if he was aboard, 'no further clearance is needed'.[5] He then retired to his suite where he made two telephone calls, one to Rathaven and one to Australia.

The call to Australia was to Sir John Knott, the former senior public servant who was now World Airways' Australian representative, to inform him that he planned to fly a planeload of FFAC orphans to Australia the next day, departing Saigon around 2 p.m. He had not sought permission from Australian authorities for the flight, and he and Knott discussed how it could be done. He then telephoned Rathaven and invited Wende to send someone to the Caravelle Hotel to discuss evacuation flights.

Wende asked Elaine Moir if she would represent them at the meeting and, when Elaine agreed, the mission warden was contacted and a car and driver soon came. Elaine arrived at Daly's Caravelle suite after midnight and listened as Daly outlined his plans – to say she found them unusual would be an understatement. Daly said he would carry four hundred orphans and forty attendants in an aircraft that would depart Saigon late in the morning that day. The aircraft would fly via Brunei and Darwin to Sydney and he gave Elaine a list of the times and distances for the various legs of the flight. He had all the options covered, he told Elaine. Should the authorities in Australia attempt to interfere with the flight, he would fly to Adelaide Airport where he knew there were no immigration authorities.[6]

That was it. Daly said he would confirm the arrangements early in the morning and Elaine left, uncertain about exactly what had happened during their meeting and what was likely to happen later that day.

•

The pressure was also building on the other side of the world. In the United States, Americans were watching the tragedy in South Vietnam unfold on their television screens every night and wondering about what would happen next. Several 'special reports' detailed the plight of thousands of children living in foreign-run orphanages, waiting for their adoptions to be organised and approved. Particular attention was paid to those children believed to have been fathered by American servicemen – their future under a communist government was thought to be especially problematic.[7]

Many, many Americans were concerned about the fate of a country that fifty thousand of their young men had died to defend, and most concerned of all were those with a direct interest in those vulnerable orphans – prospective parents, supporters of the various adoption programs and those in church and welfare groups that had been involved in Vietnam for many years. These people had been writing letters and making phone calls to the media, radio, television and newspapers, and putting pressure on their elected congressional representatives to do something, anything, to assist the plight of the Vietnamese orphans. As the pressures on him continued to build, President Gerald Ford scheduled a press conference at the San Diego Convention Center for 2 April 1975.

•

In Canberra, Whitlam and his senior ministers continued to grapple with two pressing issues. The first was how to target Australian aid to a South Vietnam that was now seemingly doomed to fall to the communist forces that were on the offensive, and winning, across vast swathes of the country. Most there believed it was a matter of weeks, and some just a matter of days, before South Vietnam fell. Senior figures in Canberra knew that the government could not afford to be seen to be doing nothing. Equally, they knew they could not afford to put the country's defence personnel in harm's way, or appear to do anything that might destroy the developing relationship with Hanoi, whose forces were now very, very close to claiming victory in the south. The second issue was how to release some of the public and opposition pressure building around accepting Vietnamese refugees and, in particular, Vietnamese orphans. Some in cabinet believed the two issues were inextricably linked.

Whitlam's preference was for Australia to play an extremely limited role in accepting Vietnamese refugees and probably would have preferred not to accept any at all. In this he was opposed by both his deputy leader, Lance Barnard, and – sometimes – by his Immigration Minister, Clyde Cameron. When these two approached Whitlam about accepting Vietnamese refugees, he snapped back at them, leaving them both in no doubt that it would be he who would be making all the decisions about what offers would be made to assist South Vietnam.[8] Barnard's subsequent support of a fellow Labor parliamentarian's plans to bring Vietnamese orphans back from Guam was the beginning of his fall from the prime minister's grace. From that point onwards, Barnard would play no meaningful role in the debate about Vietnamese refugees.

Whitlam received strong support from the head of the Department of Foreign Affairs, Alan Renouf, who was especially concerned about Australia agreeing to act as a transit point for refugees, only to then find that those refugees couldn't – or wouldn't – be relocated to another country. Even Renouf, though, agreed that something needed to be done, and late on 1 April a series of announcements, some deliberate and others leaked, began to emerge from Canberra. A report came out suggesting that the government had agreed that people on tourist visas from any part of Vietnam would be allowed to remain in Australia until the current conflict in South Vietnam had concluded. As well, it was suggested that the government planned to announce that a significant amount of money in new aid would be offered to the United Nations Commissioner for Refugees. This was in addition to the A$200 000 announced in March and given to the Red Cross. There was even a rumour that the government was looking at the possibility of an airlift of orphans. The only official comment on this was a statement by a government spokesman that, yes, the government was looking at the question of Vietnamese orphans in those areas of the south that the South Vietnamese government still held.[9]

•

In Saigon, Detachment S was given its first assignment. At the personal request of South Vietnam's deputy prime minister, Dr Phan Quang Dan, one of the detachment's C-130s was to fly refugees from Phan Rang, then directly in the line of advance of NVA forces, to Can Tho in the Mekong Delta. While one C-130 was undertaking that mission, another would be ferrying Red

Cross supplies from Saigon to Can Tho. There was an immediate issue with the request as the detachment was only allowed to undertake operations that had personally been approved by Whitlam, but the prime minister was temporarily out of touch somewhere on the Gold Coast in Queensland.

When apprised of this, Dr Dan suggested that he was expecting to receive a request from the Australian government about a possible airlift to Australia of Vietnamese war orphans whose adoption by Australian families had been approved in both countries. He then proceeded to make it perfectly clear that no orphan airlift would be approved if the Australian Government was not prepared to authorise in-country humanitarian missions in South Vietnam. After a flurry of telephone calls and cables, the necessary approvals came through from Australia and a single RAAF C-130 departed Tan Son Nhut. When it arrived over Phan Rang, the captain considered the conditions at the airport too unsafe to attempt a landing and the C-130 returned to Saigon. John Mitchell promised Dr Dan they would double their efforts the next day.

•

In New York City on 1 April, the South Vietnamese Ambassador to the United Nations made a public appeal for American help with the evacuation and resettlement of refugees from his homeland. He stressed that there was an immediate and urgent need to move around two thousand orphans from Saigon to the safety of a friendly country.[10]

At the time the ambassador issued his appeal, USAID officials in the United States and South Vietnam, and Australian government officials in Canberra and Saigon, were working towards that end, with American efforts well ahead of the Australian. In the

United States, there was an ongoing problem caused by President Ford issuing verbal directions rather than written instructions about what he wanted done; however, USAID and the State Department were professional enough to be able to turn those verbal instructions into concrete operational plans. Those initial plans were for up to two thousand orphans to be uplifted at Tan Son Nhut airport in Saigon and flown to Clark Air Base in the Philippines where all would be given comprehensive medical checks before flying on to the United States via either Yokota Air Base in Japan or the US Navy facilities at Guam.

•

Rosemary, Wende, Margaret and all the other volunteers at Rathaven were only dimly aware of the government proposals for orphan airlifts, if they had any knowledge of plans at all. Most were now into their second day of working with the children on their normal shifts and on documentation and travel packs during any spare time. Sleep was something they grabbed an hour at a time if they could. If they had heard whispers of a large orphan airlift, they may well have thought it was just another rumour in the hundreds of rumours now sweeping through Saigon. There were persistent stories of nightly gunfire in the villages surrounding the capital and well-placed sources predicted the city would soon be completely cut off from its hinterland. There were even better-placed sources who said that the six hundred Eastern Bloc members of the International Commission of Control and Supervision, there to oversee the implementation of the Paris Peace Accords, had all booked flights and would depart Saigon that week. If that wasn't enough, there were rumours that Ed Daly had a fleet of aircraft on their way to rescue them all.

7

A PARTIAL IMPLOSION

Wednesday 2 April

Wednesday would be another very busy day for Geoffrey Price, who was becoming quite used to the number and tenor of the cables arriving from Canberra, predicting what would be coming in the next cable by the level of concern that had been expressed in the last one. One of the early messages handed to him that day was for Price personally and came from the department's secretary, Alan Renouf. It read:

> Australians here connected with Rosemary Taylor are contending that GVN [Government of Vietnam] has already given approval for 200 orphans to leave for Australia. These circles are embarrassing us with demands for explanation of why the Australian government is not getting on with the movement. Please confirm or deny at the earliest possible moment whether the GVN has given approval or not.[1]

He suspected that today was going to be all about Rosemary Taylor and her Vietnamese orphans.

•

If it was to be a busy day in Saigon, it would be a frantic day in Canberra, one that certainly did not get off to a good start for the prime minister. During the morning, the official spokesman for the Immigration Department announced that Lance Barnard, the Minister for Defence, and Immigration Minister Clyde Cameron had granted conditional approval for two hundred Vietnamese orphans to be flown to Australia aboard a special RAAF flight. However, because of concerns previously raised by Geoffrey Price, when Alan Renouf heard the announcement he came out swinging, insisting that the Immigration Department immediately quash the story. Whitlam responded even more vigorously, stating publicly that the proposal had been suspended because it did not align with Australia's stated intercountry adoption policy. He added that there was no disagreement between himself and two of his senior ministers. However, from that moment, Whitlam assumed full control of all Vietnamese relief and orphan operations and insisted that all government statements on both would only be issued by him.[2]

Whitlam then went on the front foot. Later that day the government released Press Statement 478, which formally detailed the Australian government's response to what it described as the unfolding crisis in South Vietnam. The statement said a further $1 million would be made available for relief work among Indochinese refugees, noting that this was in addition to the $200 000 announced on 28 March. The prime minister pointed out that he had earlier decided to make available seven C-130 Hercules aircraft as well as others based at Butterworth for use in a humanitarian role in Vietnam. He offered reassurance that the aircraft were to be used 'to ferry supplies and materials to meet immediate and critical human needs'.[3]

Whitlam also disclosed that he had given permission for the RAAF to fly Vietnamese orphans to Australia provided that all formalities had been completed in both countries and that there was an appropriate adoptive family waiting in Australia. Finally, he announced that a public appeal would be launched on behalf of the Council for Overseas Aid's disaster emergency committee, to raise $5 million to further assist refugees in Indochina. Critics of the government's tardy response, a group that included almost everyone involved in welfare and relief work in South Vietnam, suggested that the package was too little, too late and smacked of cheap political opportunism. Most, though, remained transfixed by images of what was happening in that poor country.[4]

•

At around the same time as things were starting to heat up in Canberra, they were developing rapidly in Saigon as well. There, the US Embassy decided that Ed Daly had gone beyond being a loose cannon and was rapidly becoming a positive nuisance. With an imminent announcement of a major presidential and State Department initiative addressing the issue of South Vietnam's orphans, Daly's attempts to put together a planeload of them for a publicity flight was in danger of becoming more of an impediment than an embarrassment and had the potential to interfere with the USAID planning then underway. A decision was made, possibly by Graham Martin, to cut off Daly's access to both orphans and orphanages. Early that morning, someone at the US Embassy telephoned Rosemary at Rathaven and made a counteroffer to what Daly was proposing.

If Taylor and FFAC broke off their negotiations with Ed Daly, the US government would facilitate the evacuation of her orphans from Saigon. There were now regular US Air Force missions bringing in supplies and materials to replace those that had been lost in the recent fighting. Those flights were staged out of Clark Air Base near Manila and returned to that base, empty, after each resupply mission. Rosemary was asked whether the FFAC would be interested in utilising that empty space. Yes, Rosemary replied, they certainly would.

•

As promised by Wing Commander Mitchell, the other Australians then involved in relief efforts, Detachment S, were in the air early that Wednesday. Two C-130s flew out of Tan Son Nhut at mid-morning, landing at Phan Rang airport thirty minutes later. During what would become a very long day, the C-130s would each complete either five or six missions carrying between fifteen and eighteen hundred refugees from Phan Rang to Can Tho, a direct flight of 150 kilometres. They would also come very close to getting caught up in the kind of panic-driven chaos that Ed Daly had experienced in Da Nang the previous week.

The aborted flight the previous day had shown that the airport security at Phan Rang was questionable, and with the NVA closing in on the city, everyone on the ground was understandably jumpy. A group of ARVN soldiers was present when the RAAF aircraft landed and set up a cordon around the aircraft, acting as both a guard force and a police force directing refugee movements on the tarmac. It all went well until four NVA rockets landed around four hundred metres from the aircraft and the crowd panicked. As they surged towards the C-130s, one ARVN soldier fired into the air to try to restore order. Unfortunately, he was near the rear of one aircraft at the time and several of his bullets struck the tailplane. A number of soldiers forced their way onto one aircraft, knocking a pregnant woman out of the way to do so. Disciplined soldiers and airmen eventually sorted the situation out.

The last flight of the day was also problematic. As the pilot eased the C-130 along the taxiway, he found his way was blocked by two fuel tankers parked intentionally to do just that. As he sat there helpless, the air traffic controller informed the Australian that the tankers would be moved if the Phan Rang authorities received assurances that the RAAF aircraft would resume evacuation flights the following day. Those assurances were given and the tankers were moved, allowing the C-130 to depart safely. The assurances that had been given would never be met. When Gough Whitlam learned of the two incidents that had occurred at Phan Rang that day, he ordered that no more such flights would be authorised. Detachment S would now involve itself only in the delivery of humanitarian aid.[5]

•

As he had promised Elaine Moir during their late-night meeting, Ed Daly contacted Rosemary at Rathaven on Wednesday morning to talk about the proposed evacuation of her orphans scheduled for some time that afternoon. Daly said he now had good news and that he would be able to fly all six hundred orphans out later in the day aboard a DC-8 cargo jet that was due to arrive quite soon. However, he was going to have to put some conditions on the operation. Loading the orphans aboard would have to be completed within a thirty-minute window as he had contracted a television crew to film the operation and they would only be able to film at Tan Son Nhut for that period of time. Rosemary thanked Daly and said that she needed to talk to some other people before she could agree to the charter conditions.

Rosemary discussed Daly's latest proposal and its conditions with the other senior administrators at Rathaven, all of whom had considerable experience with orphans travelling on international flights. To begin with, none could visualise the conditions under which six hundred children could be accommodated aboard a cargo jet; the numbers were simply too great, and their safety had to be considered first and foremost. There had been no mention of seats and/or cots, so presumably Daly thought they could be laid out in rows. The women's experience suggested that one carer to five or more children was possible for older children with no medical needs, but there would be many babies and children with ailments among the six hundred. The absolute minimum would be one carer to every eight to ten children, meaning at least sixty carers would be needed. Where they could be found and how they would fit on the aircraft was anybody's guess.

The other condition, loading six hundred fearful and distressed children and their carers aboard an aircraft in hot and steamy conditions within a thirty-minute timeframe, was physically impossible. The women only discussed it briefly as it was so outrageous and then, on reflection, decided that Ed Daly's overall demeanour and behaviour were also outrageous. It was a short step from there to deciding that he was so unreliable that they would no longer deal with him. This gave Rosemary the ammunition she had been looking for and she phoned Daly back to inform him that their dealings were over. All their eggs were now in the USAID basket.

•

Press Statement 478 was just one of Whitlam's moves that day, and he sent personal appeals to every state premier, relevant department heads and Opposition Leader Malcolm Fraser. In them he asked for their full cooperation, particularly with the placement of Vietnamese orphans into Australian adoptive families. In particular, he asked the premiers to try to have their welfare departments expedite processing adoption applications that were either expected or were already in the system. He set about getting the orphans together and bringing them back to Australia. The figure of two hundred that Lance Barnard and Clyde Cameron had bandied about that morning seemed a good starting point. He then proceeded to set up a Vietnam Crisis Task Force to coordinate what he wanted done.

Somehow, by the time the directive had travelled from the prime minister's office in Canberra to the ambassador's office in Saigon, the general notion of two hundred orphans had become a specific request for exactly 212 orphans. The number didn't really matter. Geoffrey Price was given until 4 April – two days – to identify and collect that number, and make all the necessary arrangements at his end for the airlift to Australia. It was a big task, but he had a good staff and promptly commenced scoping the problem and the best way to implement what his prime minister had decreed was to happen. He almost immediately ran into problems.

After just a few enquiries to his staff, Price learned that only a few of the children nominated for adoption had any of the necessary formal checks completed, while some had just their health and immigration clearances finalised. Double-checking enabled him to establish that the embassy had ninety-eight children with adoptive parents waiting in Australia on its books, twenty-three of whom he believed would be at an acceptable state of clearance for entry into Australia. He also learned that the total number of potential evacuees could be pushed up close to 150 if the expected nominations from the various adoption agencies were added in.[6] It was an improvement on ninety-eight but still well short of the prime minister's figure of 212.

Price also had an interesting conversation with Group Captain Lyall Klaffer from Detachment S. The RAAF Liaison Officer told Price that a C-130 could carry up to seventy-five orphans and between five and ten carers. If necessary, the aircraft could be configured for a medevac mission, fitted out with stretchers and other medical equipment and fly directly to either Adelaide or Melbourne. The only reservation Klaffer had was about the spartan conditions aboard a military transport aircraft. He said a flight that could take up to fourteen hours aboard an aircraft that had limited heating in its main cabin would prove trying for small children in good health and hazardous for those with an ailment.

Later in the day, Price spoke with Rosemary Taylor, who asked about the possibility of sending several of her orphans to Australia, saying that seven of them had been assigned to and accepted by adoptive families in Australia, while admitting that only one or two of them actually had all the necessary adoption formalities completed. She also had another ten orphans who were not Australian adoptees but who had been scheduled to travel to Australia for important medical treatments. Finally, in the last couple of days, Rosemary and FFAC had assumed responsibility for an additional eighteen orphans, all from orphanages in areas that had since been overrun by North Vietnamese forces. She hoped the Australian government would see its way clear to evacuating any or all of those children.

Price explained that, irrespective of what he personally thought, in this instance his hands were tied. The government's criteria were clear – only those orphans who had adoptive families waiting for them in Australia, and who had completed all the required procedures in both countries, would be considered for evacuation to Australia. Rosemary, by her own admission, had only one or two children who might fit into those criteria. Besides, FFAC was an American-based organisation, and Price was sure the Americans wouldn't let Rosemary down. In response, Rosemary expressed extreme disappointment on behalf of FFAC at the approach adopted by the Australian government. On a personal level, too, Rosemary left the ambassador in no doubt as to what she personally thought of the Australian government and of its prime minister in particular.[7]

•

Ed Daly was not the kind of man to give up easily. He had an aircraft and he had a plan; he had never needed much more than that in the past. Rosemary and the FFAC declining his offer was a setback, and it was soon followed by another when Holt International also declined to accept his offer to fly its orphans out, telling him it had now chartered a Pan Am jumbo for its children. Daly's daughter Charlotte had previously been involved with both Save the Children and the FCVN, and she suggested to her father that he contact the FCVN orphanage at Tu Duc, a small village on the outskirts of Saigon. He did, and to his delight FCVN – probably through its Saigon director, Cherie Clark – accepted the offer of an evacuation flight to the United States. Preparations for that flight began immediately.

In the end just fifty-seven orphans aged between eight months and eleven years would be evacuated on that flight, but the World Airways DC-8 would also be carrying twenty-seven escorts for them, six of whom would turn out to be South Vietnamese citizens who did not possess the requisite exit visa. By the time the orphans and their escorts were transported to Tan Son Nhut, it was late afternoon. By the time they had been organised aboard the cargo jet, it was dark and there was another hold-up. A Vietnamese official was making noises about the aircraft not being equipped to carry babies and sick children. When he left to seek further direction, Daly told Ken Healy, again flying a critical mission, to take off, quipping, 'How are they going to stop the plane, shoot it down?'[8]

As Healy steered the DC-8 out onto the taxiway and towards the main runway, air traffic controllers ordered him to stop the aircraft and return to the World Airways terminal. He ignored the calls and concentrated on getting his aircraft into the air. As it turned onto the runway, as a last resort air traffic control turned off all the runway's landing lights. It was too late, and it wouldn't have mattered anyway. As he turned onto the darkened runway, Healy powered up the engines, gathered speed and lifted off into the night sky.[9]

•

Around the same time as Ken Healy's DC-8 disappeared into the sky above Saigon, Geoffrey Price was putting the final touches to a long cable to send later that night, intended to be on the desks of Alan Renouf and other senior DFA officials when they arrived for work on Thursday morning. After providing a summary of what had been achieved to that time, Price turned to the subject of Rosemary Taylor, something he knew would raise a red flag in Canberra. He outlined his discussions with her and her 'bitter disappointment' over what she perceived to be the indifference of the Australian government, adding, 'I believe that they [Taylor's supporters] will attempt to attack the government on the issue and play heavily on all the emotional factors that can be considered.'

Knowing what Renouf and others thought about Rosemary, Price sought to balance his criticism of her:

> As for Miss Taylor, we do not wish to defend her intemperate tactics to move her orphans. In mitigation, however, it should be explained that pressures on her and her small volunteer staff have been immense in trying to, as she sees it, do the best for the 600 or so children under her care. It should also be explained that a number of the orphans will remain in Vietnam, come what may, and now some of the Australian workers have volunteered to stay with them. Unfortunately, she has a tendency to lash out but it has to be admitted that what she has done here in the past eight years is highly praiseworthy.[10]

Price concluded with some observations and recommendations of his own based on what he had seen and heard that day. To begin with, he believed that airlifting babies and small children from Saigon to Australia aboard RAAF transport aircraft would be an undertaking fraught with difficulties and dangers, and raised the possibility of using chartered Qantas passenger aircraft instead. He also suggested an increase in the number of attendants travelling with the orphans, believing experience had shown that it was better to have too many than too few. Given the situation in South Vietnam, he believed consideration should be given to allowing orphans to travel to Australia before all checks were completed and noted that South Vietnamese authorities had indicated that they would issue exit visas to all children nominated by the Australian Embassy. Price concluded by suggesting the 4 April deadline he had been given was unrealistic, especially in the conditions under which it was expected to be met. Satisfied with what he had written, he sent the draft to the communications room for transmission to Canberra. Then Geoffrey Price went home.

•

Ed Daly, Ken Healy and their passengers flew over the South China Sea en route to Japan. Daly had already informed Healy that they would be flying direct to Yokota Air Base to the west of Tokyo and one of the Military Airlift Command's (MAC) major Asian bases. There was likely to be an issue with this because unless a civilian aircraft was under charter to the US armed forces, it would be denied permission to land at Yokota. It was a problem Daly said they would deal with when it arose. As the World Airways DC-8 approached Yokota from the south, Healy contacted the base and asked for landing directions. Both he and Daly were taken aback by the air traffic controller's response. In a calm, clear voice, he informed Healy that because his aircraft had never officially left South Vietnam, it could not officially land in Japan. Then, after a pause for effect, he said, 'Welcome to Yokota!'[11]

The welcome at Yokota only went so far, however. The aircraft was refuelled but none of the Vietnamese citizens aboard were allowed to disembark. A medical team was sent in to examine the children and was quite disturbed by what it found. Twenty-eight of the fifty-seven children required some form of medical attention, and two of those were dangerously ill from severe dehydration and malnutrition. Judged too ill to continue with the flight, they were taken off the aircraft and admitted to a hospital nearby. Assurances of full medical treatment in the United States were given and the DC-8 was allowed to continue on to its destination, the World Airways terminal at Oakland International Airport. There, the aircraft was met by a cheering crowd and reporters and cameramen documenting the first airlift of orphans from Vietnam.

It was all very glitzy, very Hollywood, very Ed Daly – cameras filming the head of World Airways smiling and waving before panning to a fleet of taxis waiting to take the children to a US Army facility in nearby San Francisco. Daly had his moment in the sun but it was brief and it had already been overtaken by a formal announcement from USAID in Washington, DC, earlier in the day, and would soon be eclipsed by a speech by President Gerald Ford, sitting in front of a phalanx of cameras and microphones some distance to the south of Oakland in California, on the main stage of the San Diego Convention Center.

•

Earlier in the day and on the other side of the country, USAID headquarters in Washington, DC, released a statement saying that up to two thousand Vietnamese orphans would be airlifted from Saigon to the United States. Funding for the rescue operation would be sourced from a special foreign aid children's fund and was expected to be released in tranches beginning around noon the following day when President Ford made a formal announcement about the operation in San Diego. All relevant US departments and agencies had been apprised of the operation and had been instructed to remove any bureaucratic obstacles to its success. It was also believed the South Vietnamese government was about to announce a blanket approval of exit visas for all those orphans.

At noon, as the formal press release detailing the operation was released across the United States, Gerald Ford spoke to a press conference he had called at the San Diego Convention Center where he had been attending a conference. Speaking from notes he had prepared over the past two days, Ford opened with a statement:

> We are seeing a great human tragedy as untold numbers of Vietnamese flee the North Vietnamese onslaught. The United States has been doing and will continue to do its utmost to assist these people. I have directed all available naval ships to stand off Indochina to do whatever is necessary to assist. We have appealed to the United Nations to use its moral influence to permit these innocent people to leave and we call on North Vietnam to permit the movement of refugees to areas of their choice.
>
> While I have been in California, I have been spending many hours on the refugee problem and our humanitarian efforts. I have directed that money from a two million dollar special foreign aid children's fund be made available to fly 2000 orphans to the United States as soon as possible. I have also directed American officials in Saigon to act immediately to cut red tape and bureaucratic obstacles preventing these children from coming to the United States.[12]

In the question-and-answer session that followed Ford's announcement, he confirmed that all Vietnamese children currently identified for adoption by American families would be part of the airlift and that several international child welfare organisations had asked to be part of it. That airlift would, in the first instance, be undertaken by elements of the US armed forces, specifically the MAC. The entire airlift, from planning to evacuation to the delivery, had been given a name – it would now be referred to as 'Operation Babylift'.

PART II
OPERATION BABYLIFT

8

LAST-MINUTE NERVES

Thursday 3 April

From a distance that day, Thursday 3 April, parts of the Canberra bureaucracy would have resembled an ants' nest that had been poked with a stick. Furious activity was occurring – a lot of which seemed to be activity for activity's sake, but did on closer examination have a clear purpose. This time, those doing the scurrying were trying to put together the hundreds of individual components that would be brought together into an operational plan that, when implemented, should see 212 Vietnamese orphans flown thousands of kilometres to new homes in a new homeland. The man with the metaphorical stick was Gough Whitlam and he – like all those now scurrying – knew that time had become their greatest enemy.

•

The prompt replies to Whitlam's call for cooperation from the federal Opposition, the bureaucracy and the state premiers is a good indicator of how significant they thought the issue might be to the general public. The tenor of their replies also suggested that those state premiers believed there might be some political capital in the issue. The tone was set by Opposition Leader Malcolm Fraser, one of the first to respond, who asked precisely what the government intended to do while also offering full support to the government's humanitarian moves.[1]

Overnight, the premier of New South Wales, Tom Lewis, leading a conservative Coalition government in that state, cabled a reply to the prime minister which read:

> The New South Wales government has been shocked at reported statements by ministers of your government regarding the situation in Vietnam. We urge you to take immediate action to assist in relieving the suffering of the South Vietnamese people caused by the brutality of communist domination. New South Wales stands ready to assist with personnel, medical supplies and food.[2]

Victoria's Coalition premier, Rupert 'Dick' Hamer, also sent a similarly worded cable to Whitlam that night. His closed with, 'I look forward to your views on the best method by which this form of assistance can be coordinated and put in hand.'[3] From the north the most conservative of them all, Joh Bjelke-Petersen, the National Party premier of Queensland, also got in on the act. After describing Jim Cairns's comments on the possible fall of Saigon to communist forces as 'callous and cynical', Bjelke-Petersen softened his tone and went on to offer Queensland's support to any relief actions the Commonwealth government might care to take.[4]

At 1.40 p.m. on Thursday afternoon, Whitlam replied to all the premiers with a telex that was forwarded to each personally. Noting that his government was concerned 'that Australia should play its part in helping to alleviate the hardship and suffering now being endured by the people of South Vietnam', he asked them all to work quickly to remove any impediments to the adoption of Vietnamese orphans by Australian families.[5] Copies of the telex were also sent to the secretaries of all relevant government departments.

If that wasn't enough to cause ructions in government departments at both state and federal levels, news from the United States added an additional fillip. The USAID announcement of orphan airlifts, made in Washington on 2 April, arrived overnight in Australia and added to the work to be done that Thursday, especially as Australia did not want to be seen as being more restrictive than the United States over who it granted entry to. The DFA almost immediately announced that Australia would simplify its regulations for admitting orphans, specifically those around procedural checks, and Gough Whitlam sought assurances from the state premiers that they agreed and, moreover, that they would accept children for approved families 'whatever their condition'. For good measure, he asked the premiers if they would accept the orphans brought from South Vietnam, even if their adoptive families didn't.[6]

Several media commentators noted this almost complete backflip on the admission of South Vietnamese orphans. Senior public servants and members of Whitlam's government explained then and later that it wasn't a reversal, but rather an 'extension', of past policy. It was neither. It was a circumvention of past policy and it was one of the reasons that public servants were scurrying all over Canberra, and Saigon.

•

One of the first cables from Canberra to land on Geoffrey Price's desk that morning was a special telex addressed to and to be read only by Price. Although his name did not appear on the document, its author was in all likelihood Alan Renouf, and it included the revelatory, 'For your own private information Prime Minister shares our qualms about Taylor, whose organisation has flouted Australian immigration procedures in the past, and it will be necessary to ensure that other organisations are adequately represented in the uplift.'[7] That was all well and good from a desk in Canberra, but the facts on the ground in Saigon were that over 80 per cent of intercountry adoptions in the past five years had been from Rosemary Taylor's nurseries and hers remained the largest operation of its kind in South Vietnam. When a later cable from Canberra upped the number of orphans required for the Australian Babylift to 246, Price knew that the much-maligned Rosemary Taylor would have a key role to play in his quest for an Australia-bound planeload of orphans.

That quest occupied a lot of the embassy's time that day, and its chances of reaching the new target were bolstered by the circulation of a letter in both government and non-government circles in Saigon. Written by the deputy prime minister, Dr Phan Quang Dan, the letter urged the South Vietnamese govern-ment to expedite the evacuation of all orphans in Saigon. Such a mass exodus of children, Dr Dan predicted, would be given wide coverage in the American media, which would create a groundswell of sympathy for the South Vietnamese, which would ultimately help the Thieu regime. It wasn't an official document, but it would give Price's staff some additional leverage as they searched for orphans to fill designated spots on their aircraft.

Given the apparent restrictions on offering places to Rosemary Taylor's orphans, the embassy net was cast far and wide. Holt Children's Services, World Vision and International Social Service were all approached and were able to nominate some of their orphans, but their intercountry adoption operations were tiny compared to FFAC's and the total number of orphans they provided was fewer than twenty. They had more success with Cherie Clark at FCVN. While Ed Daly's unauthorised evacuation flight had carried fifty-seven of its orphans, all had come from the main orphanage at Tu Duc. It had a second, smaller orphanage in Saigon, and Clark agreed to release twenty-one of its orphans to the Australian Babylift operation.

Embassy staff had even more success at the Sancta Maria Orphanage. Sancta Maria was one of the better-run and better-appointed orphanages in South Vietnam.

An unidentified senior official from the Australian Embassy visited Sancta Maria on Thursday morning. After discussions with Andre Vung, it became clear that there were several Sancta Maria orphans suitable for evacuation to Australia. Andre's sister Caroline, one of several friends and relatives who worked at the orphanage, mentioned an affiliated institution that might also be able to contribute. Known as Halfway House, its administrator was Béla Venczel, Caroline's husband, who had formerly worked with FCVN. Between them, it was agreed that the two institutions would provide fifty orphans for evacuation. The official asked that those orphans be brought to Tan Son Nhut airport some time during the morning the next day, Friday 4 April.

Other officials found other orphans at other institutions like Phu My, but it was obvious that they would not get near the figure to which Australia had committed without Rosemary Taylor's FFAC nurseries contributing a significant number. Fortunately for Price and Renouf, they would not be in the majority, which was something at least. An official phoned Rosemary at Rathaven that afternoon and asked her whether she would be interested in taking up an offer to fly some of her orphans out on an evacuation flight to Australia from Tan Son Nhut around midday the next day. He told Rosemary that there were fifty places available and she replied that they would take them all and would certainly be there. They would be part of a much larger group FFAC was sending off, which would help with their logistics, Rosemary added before thanking the official.

•

Earlier in the day, USAID summoned the foreign-run relief and orphan support agencies to a meeting at its headquarters in downtown Saigon. There, a senior official told the assembled representatives that the US president had authorised Operation Babylift and that in the coming days USAID would organise the airlift evacuation of approximately two thousand South Vietnamese orphans. Those present were left in absolutely no doubt that USAID would be the organising, coordinating and final authority in the operation, and that their role was a subsidiary one. All they had to do was find and prepare the children for evacuation. The USAID spokesman was happy to answer questions, though, and Rosemary and Wende, FFAC's representatives, were certain they heard the spokesman say that among the evacuation aircraft there would be a Nightingale, a specially equipped DC-9 used for medical evacuations.

While there was no specific timetable given for the evacuation flights, both women were under the impression that Operation Babylift was going to commence in the near future. And while specific numbers or quotas were not mentioned either, they also thought that all the children in their nurseries who were fit to travel, even if their ultimate destination was not an American family, would be eligible for evacuation. Back at Rathaven, they briefed the others on the USAID meeting and then reviewed where they were with their own planning. Through FFAC headquarters, they had contacted Terre des Hommes' French and German branches to ask them whether it would be possible for them to organise transport for adoptees heading to families in their respective countries. They were yet to hear back from either branch. FFAC in Denver was also continuing its attempts to obtain private chartered aircraft to evacuate its orphans, again without success.

When the Australian Embassy phoned with its offer of fifty places on an evacuation flight to Australia, it helped with several problems. The carers had all been concerned about the risks of international, long-distance travel for some of their babies, especially those with pre-existing ailments. Several of their orphans were simply too ill to travel, and they would remain either in hospital or at Hy Vong until they recovered. There were numbers of others who were ill, but who were thought to be well enough to travel if aboard adequately equipped aircraft on flights short enough to not be adversely affected by the stresses air travel placed on vulnerable infants. Dehydration was a particular threat, and they had all seen its effects when they escorted convoys of adoptees on long-haul flights to Europe and North America.

The flight to Australia would probably occupy around twelve hours in the air; those to the United States could be up to double that. Because of the comparative travel times, Rosemary and Wende decided that the children whose health was poor would be allocated to the Australian Babylift operation and the healthier children to the American. Hy Vong, home to most of the children with health issues, would obviously provide most of those to be sent to Australia. Mary Cusack, the administrator at To Am, was also asked to nominate any of her children that she thought might struggle on the longer journey. At Hy Vong, Julie

Chinberg was given responsibility for choosing which children should be evacuated to which country. It wasn't an easy task and the destinations for the last eight children were determined by the draw of a card. There were two blind boys at Hy Vong and Julie decided both would go to Australia with personal escorts. She would accompany one, and Elaine Moir the other.[8]

•

The day would become a bit of a blur to Geoffrey Price, who at times must have felt more like a juggler than his government's senior representative in South Vietnam. He had already experienced two little victories, one when his recommendations about the suitability of the RAAF C-130s were accepted. Now those aircraft would only be used to ferry the orphans on the short flight from Saigon to Bangkok, where they would be transferred to a chartered Qantas flight to Australia.[9] Easing restrictions on who they could send was also a victory of sorts, as it meant that children with incomplete documentation, or who might otherwise be rejected on health grounds, were now allowed to travel, enabling the embassy to almost reach the number of orphan evacuees they were supposed to find and forward.

The day hadn't been without its interruptions. In a somewhat transparent attempt to prod Price and his team, someone at DFA headquarters in Canberra (and Alan Renouf is the prime suspect) had sent a cable that spoke of 'the advanced state of preparations here, strong public interest and compelling sense of urgency'.[10] They again reminded Price that one condition the government had imposed was that either both a child's parents had to be dead or both had to have signed a consent document for them to be eligible for evacuation to Australia. But that was in Canberra and he was in Saigon. Under South Vietnamese law, a child with only one living parent was legally an orphan. All the children on Geoffrey Price's list would be orphans.

•

The decision to airlift over two hundred orphans to Australia from Saigon via Bangkok caused a lot of late-night work at the RAAF base at Butterworth. The air force already had a flight of C-130s operating relief missions in South Vietnam, but those aircraft were configured for carrying emergency supplies and unsuitable for transporting babies and children. Two additional C-130s were fitted out as medevac aircraft, with cots and additional medical equipment found and fitted, tasks that occupied ground staff well into the evening.

Flight crews also had to be found and briefed. Each aircraft would carry two two-person aeromedical teams, each comprising a nurse and a medical orderly trained to cope with a range of common medical ailments and emergencies. The four teams were sourced from the RAAF's No 4 Hospital, also based at Butterworth, while other staff from the hospital volunteered their time that night lining cut-down packing cases with foam rubber to make little cots for the evacuating babies. All would be ready by morning, when aircraft and crews would depart on their first mission as part of Detachment S.

•

Canberra was also achieving results from frantic action, and a comprehensive plan for the Australian Babylift operation was compiled within twenty-four hours of being mooted by the prime minister. The two C-130s would carry the orphans from Saigon to Bangkok; there should be 246 of them but few believed the target would be met. At Bangkok International Airport the orphans would be transferred to a specially chartered Qantas Boeing 747 jumbo jet, on flight QF 180 to Sydney. The charter would cost $71500 and the DFA would meet that expense plus any other costs associated with the operation. Possible avenues for cost recovery would be explored later.[11]

QF 179 would depart Sydney for Bangkok carrying personnel and supplies. In its cargo hold would be twenty-five tonnes of food and medical supplies, the former including milk powder, rice and corned beef. At Bangkok these supplies would be transferred to the C-130s that had brought the orphans from Saigon and would be sent there for distribution to refugee camps. The flight would also carry a medical team comprising three doctors and twenty nurses, managed by Dr William 'Spike' Langsford, First Assistant Director General of the Public Health Division in the Commonwealth Department of Health. Also travelling and representing the government would be Bill Morrison, Minister for Science and Minister Assisting the Foreign Minister.

Very little was left to chance. QF 179 would depart Sydney's Kingsford Smith Airport at 9 p.m. on 4 April and arrive in Bangkok some seven and three-quarter hours later at approximately 1.45 a.m. local time. There, the aircraft would remain in the international departures area until all the orphans brought across from Saigon had been checked, cleared and boarded, a process expected to take two hours, during which time the aircraft would be refuelled and reprovisioned. Also boarding at Bangkok would be several dependants and non-essential staff from the Australian Embassy in Saigon. When boarding was complete, the aircraft would fly direct to Sydney, where it was expected to touch down during the middle of the afternoon of Saturday 5 April.

There was also an element of control at work. Operation Babylift had generated considerable and genuine interest in the fate of South Vietnamese orphans. However, given that the operation was partly a political gesture to blunt criticism of the government's policies towards South Vietnam and its orphans and refugees, it was important to the government that media coverage represented the exact measure it wished to convey. No private media representatives would be allowed on either the outward or homeward legs of the flight, despite considerable pressure from that media. There would be one Qantas staff photographer aboard who would make photographs from the flight available to the press on their return to Sydney. Spokespeople would be there as well to answer any questions, which would be directed to the appropriate area.

•

Rosemary continued working late into the night at Rathaven, drawing up and refining lists, putting together travel documents and health records, and checking to see how other volunteers were coping. Midnight came and went, and in the early hours of Friday morning she called the mission warden and was driven back to Phu My, arriving there at 2 a.m. She had meant to go straight to bed but began sorting files and dossiers. She might have slept at her desk for an hour or two because, suddenly, it was light again. Rosemary was back at Rathaven by 8 a.m.

Wende Grant also had an interrupted night. In the early hours of Friday morning she received a telephone call from her husband at home in Colorado. Duane told her that a Pan Am pilot in Hong Kong had contacted FFAC headquarters in Denver. He was calling, he said, because there was a Boeing 747 in Hong Kong that he would later fly back to the United States, and it was empty. If FFAC contacted Pan Am and the airline agreed to a charter, he could fly to Saigon, collect a substantial number of orphans and their carers, and fly them all back to the United States. Duane said that FFAC would continue to pursue that possibility from Denver but thought that some additional pressure applied in Saigon might assist the cause. Wende promised that someone from Rathaven would be there when Pan Am's Saigon office opened later that morning.

Somewhere in Canberra, an anonymous desk officer was putting the final touches to a cable that would be on Geoffrey Price's desk when he arrived on Friday morning. It was considered very important, according to the cable, that the embassy attempt to collect all available documentation for every child it would be sending to Australia. It was, they repeated, very important . . .

9

TAN SON NHUT

Friday 4 April

Rosemary barely had time to say hello to Wende and Margaret when she arrived back at Rathaven; they were soon out the door and on their way to the Pan Am office. They weren't the first there. As the two women sat in the reception area, they heard a conversation in an adjoining office. As that conversation continued, they realised that they were listening to a representative from another adoption agency successfully negotiating the charter of the jumbo jet currently sitting idle at Hong Kong. As that realisation began to sink in, the receptionist told Wende that there was a telephone call for her.

The caller was a senior USAID official named Bob King, and he told Wende that the Operation Babylift evacuation plan that had been outlined at the previous day's meeting would be implemented later that day. Some time in the next few hours, an Air Force C-5A Galaxy cargo jet would be arriving at Tan Son Nhut bringing in a load of replacement equipment for the South Vietnamese armed forces. Once it had been unloaded, the aircraft would be available to evacuate orphans to the United

States via Clark Air Base in the Philippines. If they had orphans ready to leave, the C-5A would evacuate 230 of them. FFAC was his first choice, King continued, but if it was not interested, he would offer those spaces to other agencies.

In case Wende was concerned about the aircraft that was being offered, King said that the C-5A was in no way comparable to the DC-8 that Ed Daly had used two days earlier on his unauthorised evacuation flight. To begin with, Daly's aircraft lacked what most people would consider essential safety equipment. The C-5A – the largest cargo aircraft in the world – was a multipurpose aircraft that had a dedicated passenger compartment with appropriate seating and safety features. It would have seatbelts, oxygen masks and a full complement of emergency and safety equipment.

Wende asked King for just a minute or two to discuss the offer with one of her senior administrators, Margaret Moses, who was with her. Wende and Margaret discussed the offer, weighing up the pros and cons, and decided that it was an offer that they simply couldn't pass up. After Wende informed King that FFAC accepted the USAID offer, the two women returned to Rathaven by 9.30 a.m. and quickly informed the staff there that 230 of their children needed to be prepared for departure to the United States that afternoon.

•

The senior American military officer based in South Vietnam, General Homer Smith, was also happy to learn that a C-5A was to depart Saigon with a complement of orphans. Smith, whose Defence Attaché Office (DAO) was based in a large cantonment adjacent to Tan Son Nhut, was very conscious of the dangers his staff would face if the South Vietnamese military and government structures simply collapsed under the weight of the continuing communist offensives. Smith was responsible for the several hundred DAO staff whose roles revolved around supporting South Vietnam's armed forces while avoiding any direct involvement in the prosecution of the war. More than three-quarters of his staff were civilians and a large proportion of those civilians were women, and therein was the nub of the problem the C-5A might help him solve.

Smith wanted to start evacuating his staff, beginning with most of the civilian women, but did not want the South Vietnamese authorities knowing, because of the clear message it would send to them. Operation Babylift would give him the opportunity to evacuate some staff in a way that would not attract unwanted attention. When the C-5A flight was scheduled, Smith and his staff went to work. Combing through lists of DAO employees by function and experience, they began to do what Rosemary and her staff had been doing for some time: preparing lists of evacuees.

When the DAO's staff began their normal working day that Friday morning, forty of them, all female civilians, were called to a meeting in their conference room. There, a senior officer informed them that General Smith had formally designated them as non-essential staff, which meant they could officially be evacuated home to the United States. That evacuation would happen later in the day. Each was to be nominated as an escort for the first Operation Babylift evacuation flight, a C-5A mission expected to depart in the early afternoon. They were allowed to return to their accommodation within the DAO compound to pack up their belongings before returning to the conference room to await departure. Each was allowed to take two small bags; any other belongings they left behind would be packaged up and forwarded to them later.[1]

As it turned out, not all of the forty non-essential personnel were in a hurry to get home. One or two did not want to leave while others had commitments to, or with, Vietnamese families that they could not easily get up and walk away from. They simply remained in their quarters for the rest of the day and returned to work on Saturday. Thirty-six of them eventually reported for evacuation and were joined by twelve others who had managed to talk their way into the non-essential cohort. In this latter group were five nominated dependants of the evacuees; the wife and two small children of an army sergeant posted to the DAO; and a young woman, a dependant of an Esso employee, who somehow found her way onto the DAO evacuation list.

The CIA, which had a substantial station based at the US Embassy, also viewed Operation Babylift as an ideal opportunity to extract a few of its female staff from the country. Best of all, as far as their station chief Tom Polgar saw it, by designating those staff as escorts for the orphans, someone else would pay for it.[2]

•

Because this was the first of the long-haul flights to the United States, Rosemary, Wende and Margaret came to the sensible decision that they would send their healthiest children on it and quickly identified 228 evacuees, several being some of their older children. All orphans at Allambie were included, along with fifty-two from Phu My, twenty-two from Newhaven and fifty from To Am. Their ages ranged from just a few months up to six years. It was decided, too, that they would choose some of their more experienced and more widely travelled staff to accompany the children.

While USAID said that some civilian evacuees would act as escorts and carers for the orphans, and that there would be medical specialists aboard the flights, Wende and Rosemary knew that it was important that at least some escorts had previous experience in the role or that they were familiar with some of the children travelling. They were fortunate that Dolly Bui was willing and available. The entire Bui family was in the process of leaving South Vietnam: Dolly's husband, To, had secured employment as an engineer in France and the family would be moving there. In fact, To Bui was leaving later that day on a German evacuation flight and Marina Bui, one of their daughters, was leaving the following day as an escort on a Canadian evacuation flight. So Dolly volunteered too, providing other escorts as well. Her daughter, Tina, and her sons, David and Michou, would travel with her and help with the orphans.

Other escorts self-selected. Lee Makk had always intended to remain with her children at Allambie, but they were all being evacuated. Even though there would always be something to do in Saigon, Lee volunteered. She let Rosemary know that she was available and, late in the morning, received a request to accompany the children just as they were being assembled. Lee quickly threw together a travel bag, but in the rush forgot to pack her passport. Ilse Ewald also volunteered immediately, but she was too important to the nursery operations for Wende to let her go while there were still children to care for. Ilse nominated for evacuation a delightful little girl named Monique who she was in the process of adopting, and who would stay with friends in the United States until Ilse could leave with the children who remained. Her fellow German, Birgit Blank, could go in her stead.

Several Australian, American and European volunteers were also asked to accompany the orphans, some to return later and others to remain in their home countries and aid there. An additional escort was selected late in the process. Christie Leiverman and the bulk of her Newhaven orphans were not scheduled to be evacuated until a bit later in the process, but Wende and Rosemary decided that she could be spared for a few days. She could fly to San Francisco with the C-5A children, hand them over to authorities and fly straight back to Saigon.

When Christie arrived back at Rathaven from her night shift on Friday morning, she went through the usual exchange with Wende: 'Well, Grant, am I leaving, or can I go to bed?' The answer was unexpected: 'Stay up, Christie. You're flying home today.'[3]

•

There would be at least one more familiar face aboard the aircraft. Dr Merrit Stark, the USAID public health doctor who was a friend to Rosemary and her nurseries, had agreed to act as the medical director aboard the USAID evacuation flights. He was not surprised that morning when, arriving at work, he was asked to prepare what he needed for an evacuation flight that afternoon. After putting a medical kit together, Stark was driven to the school where his wife worked and told her about flying out on an evacuation flight to the United States that afternoon. He headed home to put together a change of clothes and the personal items he thought he might need. While there, his daughter Laurie arrived at the family apartment. That day was the last day of term at the school she had helped to found, the Mother Hubbard School, and she too was scheduled to fly home as an escort the following day. Merrit suggested that she travel with him and Laurie agreed to the change of plans.

She quickly put together her travel pack, then father and daughter loaded their things into the USAID car still waiting for them outside. They returned briefly to USAID headquarters before being driven out to the FFAC facility at Allambie to pick up the travel orders authorising all the flights they would be making in the next few days.

•

At Rathaven later that morning, a circular letter arrived from the Australian Embassy, addressed to Rosemary Taylor. The circular advised all Australian citizens and residents to leave South Vietnam while commercial travel facilities were still available. It further warned that the Australian Embassy could not later either guarantee their safety or arrange their departure. Rosemary could have been forgiven for thinking that this was all a bit rich given the distinct lack of support the embassy had given her during her eight years in South Vietnam. She appreciated, though, the consul's handwritten note across the bottom of the circular offering to send her personal belongings back to Australia with his.

•

A short time earlier, a convoy of trucks, guarded by a contingent of American troops, had arrived at the Sancta Maria Orphanage. The evacuating children were escorted to the courtyard, many apprehensive about what was happening.[4] That apprehension was heightened by the large crowd drawn to what appeared to be some kind of armed convoy. As the children were helped onto the trucks, many of those in the crowd realised that they were being evacuated, and several broke through the cordon of guards, trying to climb onto the trucks as well. The soldiers responded vigorously, trying to dislodge those who had made it onto the trucks and who were now clinging to bonnets, mudguards and canopies.

While one group of soldiers formed a line and, with fixed bayonets, tried to keep the crowd at bay, others dragged the interlopers off and from within the trucks. Where threats failed, fists and rifle butts were used. Some civilians were so desperate they had to be knocked unconscious before relinquishing their grip on the trucks. Watching all this from close range, many of the children began to cry and scream, which they were still doing when the drivers started their engines. At that, the crowd moved in to block the exit from the courtyard. In response, the line of soldiers cocked and raised their rifles.

The stand-off lasted just a few seconds. A Vietnamese interpreter accompanying the troops stepped forward and in a loud voice called out that the soldiers would certainly open fire if the crowd did not move. That was enough to make them give way, allowing the trucks to depart. The mob had to be satisfied with hurling abuse, rubbish and rocks at the trucks as they drove past.

It was a scene that would be repeated along most of the evacuation route. Whenever the convoy slowed down or stopped, a crowd quickly gathered and some of that crowd would try to force their way on board, prompting a repeat of the scenes from the orphanage. Those who managed to get aboard were smashed with fists and weapons until they jumped or fell off. The trucks were continually pelted with rocks and rubbish and, on several occasions, it sounded like shots were fired at the vehicles.[5]

For the children, the noise and violence were complemented by what they saw of their city from the back of the truck. They made their way through scenes of devastation – shops looted and their windows smashed. There were bodies lying in the streets – mostly civilians but occasionally one in a police or army uniform, killed by the mobs they were trying to control. There seemed to be fires everywhere, some caused by communist rockets and shells, but most seemingly lit by the city's own residents. Eventually the trucks stopped in an area of relative calm. They were outside the Caravelle Hotel, where they waited for some Australian officials to join them.[6]

•

Through USAID, Wende and Rosemary arranged for their children to be taken to Tan Son Nhut. Their departure had originally been scheduled for 11 a.m., but was delayed by one, then two hours and finally scheduled for 4 p.m. Wende was supposed to leave with the children and around midday went to her room to pack her bags. As she carried them to the front door she walked past Rosemary, who was still working on documentation. Wende paused to say goodbye to her friend but then, on impulse, asked if Rosemary preferred she stay until all the children had been evacuated. Rosemary replied that she would very much appreciate that and, decision made, Wende went to find young Margaret Moses to see whether she would fly to the United States rather than Australia as had originally been planned.[7]

Margaret was not happy about this last-minute change but agreed with the reasoning behind it. At that, she asked her mother to prepare a small travel bag for her, while Wende and Rosemary unearthed an old and battered suitcase to pack with the travel and identification documents for the United States–bound children. There was no attempt to sort them into any order – the others would be able to do that when they arrived at their destination. Grabbing both the travel bag her mother had prepared and the old suitcase full of documents, Margaret called out 'See you!' before catching a ride out to Allambie, where all the orphans and their escorts would gather before the short trip from there to Tan Son Nhut.

Shortly after Margaret departed, Rosemary found that the telephones were out of order at To Am and Newhaven. She sent a messenger to To Am with news of the latest developments and decided to walk to Newhaven to see how they were going there and to tell them that they needed to have twenty-two of their strongest children ready to depart in an hour. Along the way a passing car stopped and she was called over. It was Sister Ursula Lee from the Good Shepherd Convent and orphanage at Vinh Long. She had actually been on her way to see Rosemary to tell her that the Good Shepherd had received a number of children from orphanages in Da Nang and other northern centres and wanted to find out if FFAC would be able to accommodate any of them.

In exchange, Rosemary explained Operation Babylift to her and how, that afternoon, 230 of their orphans would be flown to the United States. The only problem they had was a shortage of nurses and carers to escort the children. Sister Lee, who had considerable experience in both areas, said that she would be happy to assist. She herself was due to return to her native Malaysia but could do so after she returned from America. She then had her driver drop Rosemary off at Newhaven while she continued to Vinh Long to tell the other sisters what was happening and to prepare for her own departure.

Rosemary decided to stay at Newhaven. She could help to prepare the children for their journey and assist them aboard the USAID bus. She thought she might even travel with them out to Tan Son Nhut.

•

Susan McDonald had been working hard at Newhaven since receiving news from a messenger that the first evacuation flight was that afternoon and that she should prepare twenty-two of her healthiest children to travel to the United States. The telephone system's failure and the relative silence of the streets – all cyclos had now been banned – had left Susan feeling very alone, so she was more than happy when Rosemary arrived. Together, and with the help of the local staff, they had their evacuees ready to go shortly after 2 p.m., half an hour ahead of the time when USAID had said they would be collected. The twenty-two children were placed in shade in the front yard with their travel packs, each one containing bottles, nappies, pyjamas and blankets.

There was no pick-up bus at 2.30 p.m. but that was no cause for panic. Susan had arranged for several cars to be available in case of just such an emergency and the children and their travel packs were soon bundled into those and driven out to Allambie. A bus organised by the Australian Embassy was due there at 3 p.m. to collect children for the Australian Babylift operation and Susan guessed, correctly, that there would be no objection to her children also travelling on that bus. Shortly after they arrived at Allambie, Margaret Moses phoned Susan. Margaret wanted to let Susan know of the change in travel arrangements and when she learned that Rosemary was also at Allambie, she asked Susan to pass on the news that everything was so far, so good. Again, she ended with a cheery, 'See you!'

•

Elaine Moir had been given responsibility for organising the Australian Babylift component of the FFAC evacuations. When she learned of the swap of escorts involving Wende and Margaret Moses, she realised that the Australian evacuees would need a replacement escort. Around noon, she telephoned Mary Cusack at To Am and asked her if she would be able to travel to Bangkok with the evacuees. There, she would hand over responsibility to the Australian government representatives for their onward journey to Sydney. Because of the logistics associated with the RAAF involvement, Mary would have to fly from Bangkok to Butterworth aboard the C-130, returning to Saigon aboard an RAAF aircraft the next day.

Mary told Elaine she was happy to fit in with that proposal. When the USAID bus arrived at To Am at 2 p.m. to take the fifty orphans headed for the United States to their assembly point at Allambie, Mary stood at the front of the nursery and farewelled them all. As that bus was pulling away, a second bus pulled up. It was the bus organised by the Australian Embassy for the Australian Babylift flight. There were just a few To Am babies for that flight. Mary helped them onto the bus with their Vietnamese carers before picking up her travel bag and climbing onto the bus after them.

•

The trucks from Sancta Maria sat in the hot sun for five and then ten and twenty minutes outside the Australian Embassy, the children and carers aboard growing uncomfortable and restive. They had been joined by several vans in that time and eventually the enlarged convoy formed and headed off to Tan Son Nhut, where they joined a line of traffic held up at the main entrance gates to the airport.

Earlier, the four carloads of children from To Am had joined the two hundred other children who had been brought together at Allambie. Lee Makk's last-minute decision to volunteer to be part of the US evacuation team quickly proved fruitful. Smiling and encouraging her young charges, she somehow seemed to make them all think they were going on a special journey to a special place. The babies going to Australia had been separated from the babies going to the United States, and organised by placing two of the smallest into each of the prepared baskets. There were a few last-minute issues – twins had been separated at To Am and Elaine was waiting behind at the Australian Embassy for another orphan – but taxis and an element of luck finally brought the complement together.

At Allambie, all children and escorts boarded buses for the short drive to Tan Son Nhut. All went well until they were refused entry by the guards at the main gate. It appeared the guards had not been told about the imminent arrival of hundreds of orphans destined for evacuation and were not prepared to admit them, despite the arguments and entreaties of Dolly Bui and Merrit Stark. A senior officer was summoned.

Conditions aboard the buses were by now uncomfortable and would soon be unhealthy. April is a hot and humid month in Saigon and the children, especially the babies, were disturbed by the conditions and were now bawling and squawking incessantly. More concerning for the carers was that, on every bus, the supplies of boiled water were running out and more and more of the children began to show signs of dehydration. Fortunately, an officer appeared and, convinced by Merrit Stark and the copy of Dr Dan's letter he had with him, ordered the guards to open the gates and create a passage through the crowds that had gathered at the gates with the liberal use of boots and rifle butts, directing the buses across the tarmac to where three aircraft stood in a little cluster. Two of those aircraft were large; one was gigantic.

•

That gigantic aircraft was a Lockheed C-5A Galaxy, which was at the end of a journey that had begun at Travis Air Base in California. When the C-5A had left Travis, it had been loaded with seventeen 105-millimetre howitzers for the South Vietnamese armed forces. There had been few concrete results from General Frederick Weyand's study trip to South Vietnam, but one of them was an agreement to replace materials and equipment the ARVN had lost in the recent fighting against the NVA. The original flight plan saw the C-5A unload the artillery at Clark Air Base for transhipment on to Saigon and then return to Travis. At some time during the trans-Pacific flight, that plan changed. The aircraft was now the flag bearer for Operation Babylift. It would still touch down at Clark, but only to refuel and take on board some supernumeraries; it would then proceed to Tan Son Nhut, offload the artillery pieces, and take on board 230 orphans and their carers before returning with them to Travis, again via Clark Air Base.[8]

The C-5A's pilot was Dennis Traynor III, an air force captain with eight years' experience in MAC, who was always called 'Bud' Traynor.[9] He would take on board a medical team from the 13th Air Force's 9th Aeromedical Evacuation Squadron during the stopover at Clark. The team would be under the command of Lieutenant Regina Aune, a qualified nurse from a military family with two years' experience in the area; this would be the first time Regina had acted as Medical Flight Crew Director. When the C-5A landed at Clark Air Base, the new mission was explained to Traynor, who in turn briefed his flight crew. He was also told that because of the changed nature of his cargo, he should take whatever he thought necessary for the flight from the base's stores. His crew then collected all the nappies they could find as well as five hundred bottles of juice and five hundred bottles of milk, plus blankets, pillows and empty baby bottles.[10] After Aune and her team of eight were taken aboard she was able to assure Traynor that additional medical staff would join them as soon as they could be organised.

Traynor's C-5A departed Clark Air Base at 10 a.m. on Friday morning. After an uneventful flight it touched down at Tan Son Nhut at 12.50 p.m. before taxiing to the secure freight area. The aircraft had front and rear cargo doors, enabling its payload to be driven on and off. They had to wait a few minutes for American and Vietnamese television crews to arrive – both governments wanted the delivery of the large artillery pieces in the enormous aircraft to be filmed and released to the wider media as a demonstration to the Vietnamese people that the United States was still solid in its support of the Thieu government.

Traynor left one engine running to provide power for the aircraft's air conditioning while it was quickly surrounded by a perimeter of armed guards, both American and South Vietnamese, who were still in place at 2.30 p.m. when another American aircraft, a C-141, also landed and taxied across to the freight area. It carried the additional medical staff promised at Clark. When that staff were told that their C-141 would only be evacuating adults back to the Philippines and that all children would be aboard the C-5A, they all volunteered to travel on the larger aircraft. As they walked across the tarmac, another larger group was also walking towards the cargo jet. It was the DAO staff who were escorting the children.

As those two groups mingled in whatever shade they could find, a convoy of buses and trucks passed through the airport gates and drove slowly towards what was becoming a hive of activity.

•

Back at Clark Air Base, everyone now knew about the C-5A's mission. Later that evening it would be returning with over two hundred orphaned children, babies and toddlers en route to a new life in the United States. Here at Clark, they would all be given comprehensive medical checks and only those fit enough for a trans-Pacific flight would be on the aircraft when it departed for Travis the next day. The orphans, when they arrived, would probably be frightened and upset at their sudden change of circumstances, so a welcoming party was organised for the children. There would be kids' movies in the gymnasium, kids' meals in the canteen and toys – lots and lots of toys.[11]

10

AMERICAN BABYLIFT

Merrit Stark was in one of the first FFAC vehicles onto the tarmac and was one of the first off that vehicle. After exiting, he stopped to take in the scene in front of him. There were three aircraft parked quite close to each other. He knew the two RAAF C-130s were there to carry orphans part of the way back to Australia. Towering over them was the C-5A which would carry him and many FFAC orphans to the United States. As he watched, the last artillery piece was towed out of its cargo area and away from the aircraft, with several of the plane's load-masters walking in its wake. The doctor noted that he wasn't the only spectator: a small group of Australian and American airmen gathered together under a wing nearby, talking quietly. He noted, too, that the entire scene was being filmed by several Western television camera crews. It would make a good news segment, he thought – weapons, ammunition and bombs off and babies and children on. None of the many armed guards nearby seemed at all concerned that the entire area was posted with signs strictly forbidding the taking of photographs.

•

Of all those on the tarmac, Rosemary Taylor may well have been the most nervous. Her adult life had revolved around selflessness – suppressing any temptation to live a life for herself, instead choosing one that was about the larger community of humanity. The last eight years of that life had been lived here in Saigon in South Vietnam, and they were years during which she saved hundreds of lives while organising new and better futures for many who previously had nothing to look forward to. Friday 4 April 1975 was the beginning of the end of that endeavour. Two hundred and thirty of her children were departing and in the coming weeks, perhaps even just days, most of the children in the nurseries she had founded would be leaving for new lives somewhere else in the world. A few of her children would stay and Rosemary would stay with them for as long as she could. But today she was nervous and worried and agitated. She held it together because she was helped and supported all the way by people she loved and who shared her vision and, with her, they were at the front of what was now happening at Tan Son Nhut.

Rosemary caught up with Margaret as they both made their way towards the C-5A, Margaret struggling a bit with the old suitcase and wearing a pretty dress that Rosemary had not seen before. As they walked together, Margaret explained how she'd borrowed the dress from one of their American volunteers, Lydia Brackney, because she wanted something a bit brighter than the work clothes she usually wore. They also spoke about the evacuation flight, both women expressing some concern over the small number of nursing staff they were able to send with their children. Apart from Margaret, FFAC would only have Christie

Leiverman, Birgit Blank, Lee Makk, and Dolly and Tina Bui on the flight, although they could add Sister Ursula Lee to their group because she had worked closely with them for several years now.[1] All the other escorts and nurses were strangers to the children and, worse, with little or no experience caring for such numbers on long-haul flights.

They couldn't do anything about that now, and the women continued walking to where they could watch people boarding the aircraft. As they drew closer, Rosemary took a baby from one of their Vietnamese helpers and Margaret lifted the suitcase into her arms. Men and women in US Air Force flight suits or uniforms were directing people just ahead and, reassuringly, it looked like they knew what they were doing.

•

USAID's Bob King had been a little bit disingenuous when describing the C-5A's qualities to Wende Grant earlier in the day. He was certainly accurate when he described it as large – the top of its tailplane stood six storeys off the ground and its cargo compartment, running the length of the fuselage, reminded those who had seen it of a high school gymnasium. But it was not and could never be considered a passenger aircraft, as the passengers who normally travelled on it were young, fit men who had been ordered aboard and who, if they thought the amenities weren't up to scratch, could always join the navy.[2]

The C-5A was made up of several discrete fuselage components. At the front and on the top level was the cockpit, with a small crew rest area attached to it. Immediately behind that was the troop compartment, the area where passengers were normally carried. When the aircraft's front and rear clamshell cargo doors were open, passengers would enter the cargo compartment and

climb up stairs to the troop compartment. That troop compartment had seats for seventy-three passengers arranged in rows of
six, with three either side of a central aisle. All seats faced the
aircraft's rear, several of them normally occupied by the loadmasters. There were toilets at both the front and the rear of the
troop compartment and a galley near the rear stairwell. That
stairwell, and another behind the crew rest area, were the only
access points to and from the enormous cargo compartment that
had just housed seventeen large pieces of field artillery.

Before their first passengers arrived, Bud Traynor and Regina
Aune agreed that the babies they carried would be accommodated in the troop compartment's seats and the toddlers, older
children and adults could travel in the cargo compartment, and
those were the instructions they gave the aircraft's loadmasters.
Carers carrying babies would be directed into the cargo compartment and then up one of the staircases to the troop compartment
where the babies would be placed on a seat. The carers would
then return downstairs to collect another baby to take up to the
troop area. The inefficiency of this system soon became apparent
and a human chain was formed, with the babies being passed
along that chain. The nurseries' Vietnamese helpers carried them
from the buses to the start of the chain, most of them with tears
streaming down their faces.

The Phu My orphans were the first children to be boarded
and Rosemary carried one of them onto the aircraft, where the
sheer size of it all stunned her. She carried the baby upstairs
and handed it to a carer there before returning to the tarmac
to offer further assistance. As the babies were brought up to
the troop compartment, aeromedical staff placed them on the
seats. Armrests were removed, allowing two babies to be placed
on each seat. Pillows were placed between those children while

blankets and cushions were used to pad the seatbelts that held each pair of babies in place. Each baby was given a bottle of juice, while any old enough to open the seatbelt were taken down to the cargo compartment and replaced by another child.

Regina Aune remained at the ramp, directing babies upstairs and older children back into the cargo compartment. That enormous space had partially been prepared for them. As the first babies were taken upstairs, the medical team and loadmasters had placed a double layer of blankets on the bare metal floor of the cargo compartment between the two stairwells, and laid out several cargo nets and cargo straps to be used instead of seatbelts. Because of the noise and vibrations when the aircraft was in flight, the cargo compartment's rear section would not be used for passengers. Instead, as the compartment filled up, that space was used as a storage area, and nappies and baby food joined the babies' records, adults' luggage and medical equipment. Because the cases containing that equipment were very heavy, several items likely to be needed by the babies were removed and taken upstairs. All medicines and narcotics were also sent to the secure crew area upstairs.

Bud Traynor's flight orders authorised him to utilise 'the floor-loading of passengers in the cargo compartment, if necessary', which it was.[3] With the troop compartment near to full with babies, Regina had been directing older children and adults into the cargo compartment and it, too, soon filled up. Almost all the Allambie children were either carried or walked into that vast cavern, as were several Newhaven children plus most of those from To Am. Regina and the loadmasters tried to sit them in small groups, keeping children from the same nurseries together with an adult from that nursery. Almost all the civilian DAO employees joined them, and when the cargo compartment was almost full the loadmasters began to show them how to prepare for take-off and landing, and how to use the cargo nets and tie-down straps for safety and stability. There were catwalks and a couple of bench seats, and these would be available to adults and older children after take-off.

Despite the air conditioning still running, the atmosphere inside the aircraft soon became oppressively hot and humid. The fuselage had no windows and the only natural light came from the open cargo doors, adding to the underworldly quality of the scenes in the two compartments. The children and the babies were hot and dehydrated, and many of them cried. Then, without any fanfare, the line of adults and children had disappeared. All were aboard, and the aircraft would soon depart.

•

Christie Leiverman had been one of the last evacuees to board the aircraft as she had been helping more babies, children and escorts from the buses and trucks, and generally directing traffic on the tarmac. By the time she climbed into the C-5A, almost everyone else was aboard preparing for take-off. Once inside, Christie asked one of the aircrew where the small children had been taken and was directed upstairs to the troop compartment. There, she helped to strap and restrap the babies while checking that those already strapped in were comfortable. It was what she was doing when she heard Rosemary call out her name.

Rosemary had been dreading the moment when so many of her friends and so many of her children would be leaving, and so she and Pat Zirk, the American administrator at Allambie, busied themselves helping to load milk, blankets, spare clothing, extra food and small boxes of documents. As the time to leave grew closer, Rosemary wanted to say goodbye to all her staff and volunteers, and take one last look at her 230 babies. To start the process, she climbed upstairs to the troop compartment – and almost immediately wished she hadn't. To Rosemary, it was a scene from hell: 'The babies, sweltering and screaming, were strapped tightly, two to a seat by the well-meaning air force personnel who were helping to board the children. The babies were not supported adequately as there were not enough cushions available.'4

Rosemary followed a crew member down the aisle between the rows of seats, 'numb with horror', as she tried to calm the more distressed babies while making others as secure as she could. She found a canteen filled with fresh water and, using the tips of her fingers, gave as many babies as she could drops of water as she waited for someone, anyone, to bring bottles of water to the children to replace those that were so clearly empty. Rosemary could see only one nurse/escort working with some babies further along. It was Christie Leiverman.

The two women embraced, and Christie said to Rosemary that she had a bad feeling about this trip. She was upset at them having to make the trip anyway, but she was now more concerned about how the babies had been squeezed into the seatbelts and then just left alone. Rosemary confessed that she, too, was worried about that. Still visibly upset, as some other carers arrived they embraced again and Rosemary went back downstairs. At the bottom she met Pat Zirk, who was also quite emotional about the imminent departure and the conditions aboard the aircraft. Rosemary was vaguely aware of children and adults spread across the cargo compartment's floor, but she was now operating on autopilot.

As Pat led her towards the exit ramp, they were stopped by Birgit Blank. Birgit wanted to say goodbye to them both and for them to say goodbye to the little boy she was carrying. His name was Sven and she was hoping to adopt him either before or after her forthcoming marriage.[5] As Birgit and Sven moved back into the aircraft's interior, Rosemary was approached and embraced by Dolly Bui carrying her young son, David. Pat and Rosemary supported each other off the aircraft and were joined on the tarmac by Ilse Ewald, who had just farewelled Monique, her daughter-to-be. A photographer wanted to take a photo of the three women, but they ignored him and kept walking towards the buses that had brought them here. Rosemary couldn't speak, but the others knew precisely what she wanted to do – get back to Rathaven and bury herself in work.

•

Up on the flight deck, Bud Traynor was becoming impatient. After eight years in the military, he was used to orders in triplicate and movements on and off his aircraft being made with military precision. He had seen none of that today and the process of loading orphans and escorts had seemed at times chaotic to the military professionals aboard. There had been no pallets with supplies, no crates with personal items, and everyone seemed happy to carry their belongings aboard and just stack them in the cargo compartment's rear. Worst of all, he had no idea of how many people were aboard his aircraft. Neither Traynor nor any of his loadmasters had been given a passenger manifest for the orphans and their carers and nurses. All he had was a list of forty-three DAO staff.

Traynor sent his chief loadmaster, Ray Snedegar, to have his crew conduct a headcount and continued his own pre-flight checks. Soon after the last passengers had been helped aboard, USAID contacted him to ask if a small group of photographers could come aboard for five minutes to take some photos that the agency would use to document the operation. Traynor knew that there were already two combat photographers aboard – they had arrived with the second medical team aboard the C-141 – but he also knew that USAID was funding the operation and agreed to the request. He said that after those five minutes, all doors would be shut and locked. If the photographers were still on his aircraft, their next photo opportunity would be in the Philippines.

Just before 4 p.m., and just over an hour after the loading process had commenced, Traynor was told that the reporters had finished and exited the aircraft, as had all others who were not scheduled to fly. At that, all the cargo and pressure doors, front and rear, were hydraulically shut and locked in position. As the aircraft's three idle engines were started, Ray Snedegar reported back to the flight deck with a headcount, made in lieu of a passenger manifest. The total crew plus medical teams came to thirty. In the aircraft's troop compartment there were 143 babies and seven attendants, most of them civilian DAO staff. The cargo compartment held 102 children and forty-seven other evacuees; again, most of the adults were DAO evacuees.

As Traynor added these figures to his calculations, several other activities were underway aboard the aircraft. Merrit Stark, believing that the most probable calls for his medical expertise would come from the babies and a few handicapped children in the troop compartment, indicated that he would remain there for the flight. Laurie Stark volunteered to go downstairs to the cargo compartment, where her language skills and experience working with young children would be most appropriate. Christie Leiverman said that she, too, would stay in the troop compartment; she was a qualified nurse and had travelled with convoys of orphaned children of all ages several times in the past. Before settling in for take-off, though, she went downstairs to collect some more bottles of boiled water. She carried them upstairs, showed some of the crew how best to use them with the babies, then took up a position near the front stairwell for departure.

In the troop compartment, crew members moved along the aisle explaining to the civilians how best to position themselves for take-off. As the aircraft began to move slowly along the taxiway they pointed out that, with all the seats occupied by babies or small children, their best position would be to wedge themselves between two rows of seats, their backs against the back of one row and their knees braced against the front of the next. They should aim to fit as tightly as they could, so they wouldn't be bounced around as the aircraft sped down the runway and lifted into the air. If they couldn't do that comfortably between the rows of seats, they should try it across the aisle, holding onto outside arm rests if necessary. Christie chose the former, wedging herself between the first and second row of seats next to the forward stairwell, while Merrit Stark did the same further back in the compartment. Downstairs, the adults made the children as secure as they could and then braced themselves against anything close at hand and unlikely to move.

•

After completing all the pre-flight checks, Bud Traynor ran the engines up and began to steer the C-5A along the taxiway. As he did so, he contacted air traffic control for final clearance and was given authorisation to take off. He also received the latest weather forecast: it was fine and clear for departure and those conditions were expected to continue all the way to the Philippines. Turning onto the main runway, Traynor gradually increased engine power and the aircraft increased speed, slowly at first but then faster and faster until Traynor was able to pull back on the control column and the giant aircraft lifted into the air. It was precisely 4.03 p.m.

Traynor kept the power up after the wheels left the ground, going for a rapid climb at maximum power and maximum angle of ascent to avoid possible ground fire. Climbing through five thousand feet, he started to ease off on both and at sixteen thousand feet he put the aircraft into a shallower and steadier climb to a cruising altitude of thirty thousand feet. He also manoeuvred the aircraft into a gentle right-hand climbing turn that would take them above the coastal resort town of Vung Tau and out over the South China Sea.

As the angle of ascent flattened out, crew members and some of the passengers began to move around the two main cabins. In the cargo compartment one DAO escort, 42-year-old Twila Donelson, had been thinking about what she had overheard shortly before they took off. There were over seventy babies upstairs in the troop compartment, but there were only half a dozen or so nurses and carers with them. Twila was officially an escort and she knew she would be able to assist them. She turned to her friends, told them she was going upstairs to help and made her way to the stairwell.

Elsewhere in the cargo compartment, one DAO escort became airsick during the take-off. Regina Aune went to the woman, trying to reassure and comfort her. Regina said that there were airsickness tablets upstairs in a medicine chest in the crew area, and that she would get some for the sick woman. Regina then followed Twila Donelson up the stairs.

Up those stairs in the troop compartment, Merrit Stark stood up from his crouching braced take-off position and began checking on the health of the children closest to him. He thought that when they levelled off at their cruising altitude, he would talk to the other medical staff and escorts about organising a system for feeding, changing and checking the children.

Christie Leiverman found the take-off very interesting, but also disconcerting. The troop compartment had no windows, so it was impossible to either estimate their height or catch a last glimpse of Saigon receding beneath them. Christie, though, felt the aircraft begin levelling off a few minutes into the flight and stood up to begin checking on the children in her section. Moving from row to row, she collected the empty bottles and replaced them with the full bottles of boiled water she had placed nearby before they departed Tan Son Nhut. As she was doing this, and nine minutes after take-off, the C-5A passed through twenty thousand feet as it crossed the coastline above Vung Tau.

When she had distributed all the full baby bottles, Christie collected as many of the empty ones as she could carry and took them back to the galley at the rear of the cabin to fill with sugar water to take back to the babies. There were several others at the galley's entrance and she had to squeeze around them to drop the bottles off. As she was doing this, one of the crew offered her a small bottle of cold milk, which she accepted with thanks. She drank it down quickly in just a couple of gulps and, as she went to pass the bottle back, was thrown violently to the floor as a large explosion rocked the aircraft.

11

CATASTROPHIC DECOMPRESSION

SOUTH CHINA SEA, 4.20 P.M.

The take-off and rapid climb for initial height had been successful and if anyone had fired anything at the C-5A, they certainly hadn't hit it. At sixteen thousand feet, Bud Traynor had reset the controls for a gentler climb to their normal cruising altitude of thirty thousand feet. He turned the aircraft onto a bearing of 136 degrees as Tilford Harp, the co-pilot, prepared to turn their radio onto the next flight centre's frequency. Below and ahead, a large bank of cumulus cloud was building up, prompting a discussion between Traynor, Harp and Keith Malone, a third pilot who was on the flight deck to familiarise himself with the aircraft. Twelve minutes after take-off, the C-5A passed over Vung Tau and the conversation turned to what the most appropriate response would be to a rapid and catastrophic decompression. It was a conversation the men would never finish.

Shortly after entering airspace above the South China Sea, one of the rear cargo doors, which also acted as a ground ramp, blew apart. A locking bolt snapped, and the remaining door bolts then also broke under the suddenly increased pressure placed on them. As that cargo door blasted outwards from the pressurised cabin, it smashed into the outer pressure doors, shattering them and sending steel and aluminium debris in all directions. Sharp metal edges sliced into the fuselage and tailplane, severing control and trim cables to the elevators and rudder, leaving only one aileron and the wing spoilers operational. At the same time, two of the aircraft's four hydraulic systems were also knocked out.

Almost simultaneously, the flight deck suddenly bucked up and down. The three pilots heard and felt an explosion and at the same time the cockpit filled with condensation, alerting them to what had happened. The sudden fog also suggested to them what they should be doing to address what was obviously an emergency. All three calmly put on their oxygen masks and checked that they were uninjured. The C-5A had gone into an immediate dive and as Traynor struggled with the control column, Tilford Harp called 'Mayday!' into the radio microphone three times and switched on the aircraft's emergency radio beacon, sending out a mayday signal on international distress frequencies. Then he turned to assist Traynor.

The dive had pushed the C-5A's airspeed up towards dangerous levels. It passed 300 knots and reached 370 knots as Traynor pulled back hard and strained through gritted teeth to bring the aircraft's nose up. Eventually he succeeded – the nose started to rise, and the aircraft pulled out of the dive. However, the nose kept climbing and the aircraft's speed dropped away, and it now threatened to stall. To counteract this, Traynor banked to the right and reduced power, and eventually the C-5A returned to a semblance of normal flight. Through trial and error, they regained some control by changing power settings and manipulating the only aileron that seemed to work, occasionally raising or lowering the wing spoilers as well.

With that limited control, Traynor attempted the manoeuvre they had been discussing when the explosion occurred to bring the aircraft down to a level where the air was breathable again: a descending 180-degree turn to the left. When he did so, the C-5A again threatened to go into a dive, but Traynor found that if he levelled the wings and increased power the aircraft would fly straight and level. A quick examination of the control panel showed that the quantity and pressure of fluid in numbers one and two hydraulic systems read zero, and he noted a complete lack of pitch control. Despite his ability to fly to where he wanted to, albeit erratically, the aircraft was almost certainly doomed.

After a brief discussion, the pilots agreed that they would try to fly back to Saigon. Tilford Harp contacted air traffic control at Tan Son Nhut, declaring an emergency and told them that they were attempting to return to the airport. He requested the airport management prepare for an emergency landing. While Harp was doing that, Traynor called the senior loadmaster, Ray Snedegar, to the flight deck and told him that it appeared that their intercom had been damaged in the explosion as he was not receiving any reports from either the troop or cargo compartments. He asked Snedegar to go back and make a full assessment of the damage the aircraft had suffered. He was to do so as quickly as he could and then report straight back to the flight deck. Traynor did not know what the loadmaster would find, but he did know that it wouldn't be good.

•

Christie Leiverman heard two sounds in the aftermath of the explosion that had thrown her to the galley floor. The first was a voice, so loud and shrill that it was hard to tell whether it was a male or female voice. 'OH MY GOD!' it called out. 'OH, MY JESUS GOD, NO!' As a background to the sheer terror in that voice was a sound that reminded Christie of a train entering a tunnel at speed – the sound of powerful engines and rushing wind. Still on the floor, she watched as the air above was filled with pieces of other people's lives – glasses, pens, paper – and what seemed to be part of the material that had been used as insulation in the aircraft's fuselage. The air pressure had changed, and she was finding it difficult to breathe. Christie knew she had to move and move she did.

As she stood up, one of the crewmen near her slid down in obvious pain, grabbing at his legs. He was not her responsibility, the children were, so she moved past him, stepped over a pile of debris at the entry to the galley and began walking along the aisle to her station. She paused at the rear stairwell and looked down. It was hard to make out anything in the gloom but looking back, towards the aircraft's rear, she could see that a large part of the fuselage was missing and glimpsed the ocean a long distance below. As she crouched there, Christie felt a tap on the shoulder and looked up to see another crew member. Shouting to make himself heard above the roar of the wind, he asked the young nurse if she was alright and if she was scared. Christie answered both questions with a single emphatic, 'Yes!' The crewman then provided a modicum of reassurance, telling Christie that the type of accident they had just experienced had occurred before and that the aircraft 'usually landed okay'.[1]

As she made her way down the aisle, Christie became increasingly aware of what was going on around her. She passed two crewmen who appeared to be trying to repair a radio and noted, too, that there were oxygen masks hanging from the ceiling and that they were whipping around in the wind whistling and swirling through the troop compartment. The interior was now quite cold, and she still had some difficulty breathing. Most of all, though, she was affected by that glimpse of the ocean so far below. Despite what the crewman told her, Christie was not convinced that they would 'land okay' and believed that they would most probably come down in the sea. She knew none of the babies could swim and, unfortunately, neither could she.

•

Lieutenant Regina Aune had made her way to the crew area and there collected some motion sickness tablets for the woman in the cargo compartment. On her way back, she thought she may be able to save herself some trips later by checking to see if there were more people airsick below, and so stopped at one of the several grates set into the floor, intending to call out to one of her colleagues in the cargo compartment. Before she could, one loadmaster asked Regina if she needed anything else from the crew area. And then there was a loud explosion and she was enveloped in mist. It soon cleared, though, and Regina stood up and looked around, momentarily uncertain about what to do next.[2]

•

Merrit Stark was just a few metres away from both Christie Leiverman and Regina Aune. He had been systematically checking on the wellbeing of the babies in the troop compart-ment, starting at the front and slowly working his way aft. When the plane shook with a loud explosion and he was temporarily engulfed in mist, Merrit was convinced that an anti-aircraft missile had struck somewhere towards the cargo jet's rear. He suspected that there was considerable damage and that there would be casualties. It was an aeronautical emergency, which he could do nothing about. But it was also likely to be a medical emergency and that was his area of expertise. When the aircraft stopped its violent manoeuvring, Merrit Stark looked for Regina Aune, understanding that they would have work to do.

•

The epicentre of that medical emergency was the cargo compartment. There, it was chaos. When the cargo door blew out, the instantaneous decompression sucked out one loadmaster who had been working among the supplies and personal belongings secured by cargo nets at the rear. A lot of the material he had been restowing had also flown out through the gaping hole. Children who had been watching him were gone along with at least one of the carers. Added to that, the sudden decompression, lack of oxygen and massive drop in temperature had sent several adults and children into physical and emotional shock.

Flying debris caused many more injuries. The sudden decompression and the large hole at the rear had created a vortex and in that vortex anything that wasn't secured was picked up and thrown around by the cyclonic winds. Small, everyday items caused numerous puncture wounds, but far more serious injuries were sustained by humans being picked up and thrown around like toys, crashing into the walls, floor, ceiling and into each other, causing multiple fractures and fatal injuries. Worse, this continued until the aircraft was under control and flying at a height where everyone could breathe easily, both figuratively and literally.

•

With some control over the aircraft – however partial and uncertain – Bud Traynor took the C-5A down to sixteen thousand feet, a height at which there would be sufficient oxygen in the air to breathe without masks. At that height, he and Tilford Harp were able to put the aircraft into a controlled descent towards Tan Son Nhut. When they had descended to 7500 feet, Saigon was visible in the distance. Harp was talking to air traffic control, which directed them to then descend to four thousand feet and fly on a heading of 310 degrees preparatory to a landing on Tan Son Nhut's runway 28 L. By then, those on the flight deck had a fair idea about what was going on behind them in the aircraft.

Ray Snedegar, the loadmaster sent by Traynor to check on damage to the aircraft, made his way back through the troop compartment, careful not to disturb any nurses or carers who were working to keep the babies alive. At the forward stairwell, he went down a few steps and looked into the cargo compartment, shocked by what he saw, 'a massive tornado of fog, spinning aircraft debris, personal belongings and human beings in the wind. At the end of the aircraft, where the twister generated its force, a huge, gaping hole had appeared.'[3] As the C-5A flattened out from its left descending turn, Snedegar was able to continue into the cargo compartment, where adults and children huddled under cargo nets and held onto whatever they could. Several called out, 'The kids have gone', and he looked towards the empty nets and straps further back in the compartment.

After reassuring those near him and looking around very carefully, Snedegar returned to the troop compartment. He arrived just as a pair of crewmen finished repairing part of the aircraft's intercom system. When informed it was now working, Snedegar used it to contact the flight deck. He described what he had seen, detailing the large hole where one of the cargo doors had been and how control lines and cables now hung down and were being blown around like spaghetti. Traynor asked him to stay where he was for further instructions, adding that they were about to line the aircraft up for its final approach.

•

Christie quickly made her way back to the four rows of seats and forty-eight babies that were her responsibility, navigating her way to the first row through the oxygen masks that had dropped from the ceiling when the cabin decompressed. If she was struggling for breath, the babies would be struggling more and she knew she had to get some oxygen to them as soon as possible and keep up the supply until they were back into a breathable atmosphere. She immediately discovered there were several problems with this plan. Each seat had one oxygen mask, but each seat was also carrying two babies. To compound that difficulty, several masks proved faulty, with only two working in the first row Christie addressed.

When Christie pulled down on the first of the masks to start the oxygen flow the entire unit fell out of the ceiling. When she managed to untangle and rearrange the unit and straighten the tube, she found there was no oxygen flow. She also quickly discovered that the masks and tubes were designed for adults and were simply too short to reach the babies in the seats. Rather than panicking, she thought the problem through. She found a mask that worked, put it on and began picking up the babies closest to her, placing her mask briefly over their faces. In doing this, she realised that some babies were in greater need than others and began to be more selective in which babies she picked up. The first three or so to whom she now gave oxygen had become cyanotic, their skin turning blue from a lack of oxygen. When they appeared to be recovering, she moved on to others who also appeared to be struggling.

It was cumbersome, but effective, and when Christie looked around she saw that other carers were doing the same thing. Several moved among the children, looking for those who appeared to be in trouble, while the medical team dealt with emergencies in the troop compartment. The crewman who had collapsed in agony alongside Christie in the galley appeared to have suffered a broken leg; in a cleared space in front of the galley, a flight surgeon and nurse worked on setting and splinting the leg by the light of the combat photographer's lamps. Not far away, a group of loadmasters was attempting to extricate a colleague who had slipped to the bottom of the rear stairwell and who appeared to be in danger of being sucked out through the hole at the rear. With considerable effort, the men succeeded in pulling their crewmate back upstairs.

When Merrit Stark recovered from the initial shock of the explosion, he asked two carers to assist him as he moved from seat to seat, examining each of the babies for a few seconds before moving on to the next. Any who needed oxygen immediately would be handed to one of his new assistants. As Merrit was doing this, a crew member appeared and shouted out to them that the rear cargo door had blown out. While looking for distressed children, Merrit now became very alert to what was happening with the aircraft. He noted that the C-5A had banked into a long, gentle turn and, as his ears started to ache, knew it was also losing altitude. He realised as well that the pilot was having problems controlling that descent; every minute or so he would run the engines up and down again.

At around the same time, crewmen moved through the troop compartment signalling to all the crew and carers that the oxygen masks were no longer needed and that they were now low enough to breathe normally. At the same time, the air grew perceptibly warmer and, somewhat incongruously, scraps of paper began to float through the cabin. Those who were able to looked down the stairwells to the hole at the aircraft's rear and called out that they were now no longer over the ocean and that they could see rivers, rice paddies and villages. At the same time, the engine noise increased significantly, and crew members informed all in the compartment that they should prepare for landing.

Christie and the other helpers immediately dropped whatever they had been doing and moved to secure the babies for landing. This involved checking them all individually, padding the space around them and tightening their seatbelts. If necessary, some were lifted out and their whole seat remade for them. As Christie was checking her babies, the crewman who had spoken to her after the explosion again asked her if she was alright; she answered that she was. As she made her way to her own landing position, Christie noticed that several children had small identification pouches around their necks. She moved quickly to pull the pouches off, calculating that it was better to lose their documentation than to risk them choking to death during the landing. She just made it back to her own landing position when a crewman called out for everyone to brace themselves.

Everyone down below in the cargo compartment was also well aware of what was happening without having to be told. While hanging on for their lives, those who had survived the initial explosion observed the various changes in altitude and direction, and the attempts to fly the aircraft straight and level. From what they could see through the rear's gaping hole, they were over land again and were steadily dropping down towards it. In the minutes still available to them, adults did the best they could to secure children before trying to do the same for themselves. In the compartment above, Ray Snedegar continued to monitor what was happening in those parts of the cabin he could see while making mental calculations about what he would need to do when they landed. As all the carers crouched down between seats, one of Snedegar's loadmasters tapped his shoulder and shook his head. Snedegar sat down on a crew seat, adjusted and snapped on the seatbelt and braced himself as well as he could.

•

On the flight deck, Bud Traynor eased the C-5A into a gentle left turn around fifteen kilometres out from Tan Son Nhut to line up the main runway for the final approach. Air traffic control had confirmed that the airport was prepared for an emergency landing, and Traynor and Harp had agreed on the process they would follow – they would land using maximum brakes and spoilers and then full flaps after they had slowed down. As the aircraft started to straighten out of the turn, Traynor opened the throttles to burn off as much fuel as possible before landing, and then lowered the landing gear. Just as the control panel lights indicated that the gear was locked in position, the C-5A went into a dive, its instruments showing it was dropping at the alarming rate of four thousand feet a minute.

The extra drag caused by the landing gear had reduced their airspeed to 230 knots, too slow for them to maintain level flight and meaning that they would not be able to make it back to Tan Son Nhut. Now, instead of an emergency landing, they were looking at a crashlanding. The two pilots, Traynor and Harp, now worked together, firstly levelling the wings and opening the throttles to again bring the nose up. At just twenty metres above the ground, Traynor retarded the throttles to idle speed and a few seconds later, the wheels touched the surface of a flooded rice paddy. They were just three kilometres short of Tan Son Nhut.

•

The C-5A touched down at around three times its normal landing speed. The landing gear absorbed the initial impact but almost immediately broke off while the fuselage continued to roll and slide across the paddy field at high speed. In the cargo compartment, anyone not secured by a cargo net or tie-down strap was thrown around like a rag doll, smashing into the walls, ceiling and each other. Well above them on the flight deck, Keith Malone said aloud, 'We're going to make it',[4] while Tilford Harp thought that he had actually made worse landings on a runway.

Their sense of relief was short-lived, however. Barely slowing as it aquaplaned across the rice paddy's surface, the C-5A skidded for three hundred metres before crashing into the raised dyke that bordered the field. The solid earthen dyke – which rose to ten metres – acted like a ramp, forcing the plane back into the air while ripping off the number one engine in the process. The aircraft's speed was such that it flew up and over the Saigon River, 150 metres wide at that point, before clipping a dyke on the other side of the river and wiping out a small ARVN outpost as it did so. It then smashed down into another flooded paddy field on the far side of the dyke.

Without any landing gear to absorb the shock, the second impact was much more violent than the first and anyone or anything that wasn't tightly secured continued to be thrown around inside the aircraft. The C-5A bounced once and came down hard again, skidding another three hundred metres across the paddy field. As it bounced and slid across the muddy surface, those inside were assailed by a wall of sound – groans and scrapes and grinding, snapping and breaking noises coming from all around them. It was the sound of a giant aircraft breaking into pieces.

•

The main body of the fuselage remained intact, the troop compartment more or less undamaged while the cargo compartment, which had absorbed most of the impact of the second touchdown, had been largely crushed and shattered. As the fuselage continued to skid across the paddy field for what seemed ages to those inside, the tail, wings and flight deck all broke away. The wings, with their fuel cells ruptured, also burst into flames. As the parts continued to slide, they separated, each now throwing up huge plumes of water, mud and vegetation as they scythed their way through rice plants. When all eventually slowed down and came to rest, they were spread over hundreds of metres. The wings continued to burn furiously, and the aircraft's last resting place was marked by two columns of black smoke climbing into the sky.

•

Crouched and braced between her two rows of seats, Christie Leiverman was painfully aware that the C-5A was being torn apart. Amid the bumping and screams of tortured metal, ceiling panels in the troop compartment broke loose and dangled before falling onto the children below, exposing insulation, wires and cables, and adding to the debris flying around the compartment. At one point, an emergency escape slide suddenly inflated and deployed, tipping over a nearby row of seats and burying the babies beneath. An almost continuous geyser of water, mud and vegetation sprayed up through the stairwell just metres from where she crouched, replaced just once by flames and a blast of hot air when the wings broke away and fuel from them ignited.

As the aircraft continued its mad skid, Christie believed that she might survive. The flames and heat had been intense but momentary and she sensed they were gradually slowing down. All the lights in the compartment had gone out when they crash-landed but, glancing to her left, she saw that a hole had been either worn or torn in the fuselage, and looking through it understood that the aircraft had come down in a rice paddy. As the compartment slowed to a halt, Christie turned her thoughts to the children aboard.

Regina Aune had braced for impact in front of the galley, but it proved to be an unwise choice. As the fuselage bounced and skidded across the muddy field, she was thrown free and cannoned and ricocheted down the central aisle between the rows of seats. Unable to stop, she crashed into several seats before she was brought up short by a bulkhead. Hurting all over, she thought she might be in some trouble as she had clearly felt several bones in her feet fracture.[5] Regina knew it could have been worse, far worse. Nearby was Twila Donelson, the DAO evacuee who had come upstairs to help with the babies. She, too, had been thrown around the cabin and had also crashed into the bulkhead. She had struck it awkwardly, though. Her neck broke and she died instantly.

Further back in the aircraft, Merrit Stark was relieved to find that the plane had stopped and that he seemed to have survived without serious injury. His first thought was how to evacuate the aircraft; he would find an emergency exit, open it and activate the inflatable slide. As he searched in the darkened compartment he was joined by several other crewmen, and they soon had emergency exits opened on both sides of the fuselage. It was only when the doors were opened that they realised they were sitting in the mud and water of a paddy field and the doors were not even two metres above the surface. Stark looked around carefully outside and spotted another part of the aircraft burning furiously. He didn't know which part it was, and he couldn't do anything about it anyway. Gathering with the other crew and carers, he began methodically to do what he could to save the lives of as many passengers as possible.

●

One hundred metres away, those on the flight deck were oblivious to anything but their own situation and, when their cabin finally slowed to a halt, they weren't even certain what that situation might be. They, too, had lost all power after the initial impact and after the second touchdown in the rice paddy they lost sight of everything, as the windscreen was soon covered with a thick encrustation of mud. They were aware that their compartment had slid and spun for a considerable distance and when it, too, came to a halt, Traynor, Harp and Malone all exhaled loudly and thanked the providence that saved them. Bud Traynor and Tilford Harp undid their seatbelts almost simultaneously – and both fell down to the roof. None of the three had realised that the flight deck had finished upside down.

After working out where everything was in their upside-down environment, Traynor opened the large emergency exit window in the windscreen. Normally ten metres above the ground, it was now almost level with the rice paddy's surface and the three men simply climbed through the window and stood up. The first thing Traynor saw when he looked around was a large section of his aircraft burning furiously. His heart skipped a beat when he thought that the flames were coming from the remains of the fuselage and so was relieved to clearly see in another direction the fuselage appearing almost intact. As he watched, an emergency exit opened halfway along it and people started climbing and jumping out.

•

Christie experienced a moment of panic when the aircraft finally slid to a halt. She believed that, somewhere nearby, children were dying and she wouldn't be able to save them all. But she could save some and when she was sure she was uninjured, she stood up and carefully checked all the children in the rows that were her responsibility. Fortunately, none seemed to be seriously injured. The next step would be getting them out of the aircraft and that, too, had been partially done for her. The emergency exit closest to where Christie had braced herself for landing was now behind a wall of debris, but two further back on either side had been opened and people were clustered around the one on the right-hand side.

The airman who had broken his leg when the cargo door blew out was seated at the emergency exit, handing babies passed to him to other crewmen outside who were in turn placing them alongside the fuselage. Merrit Stark seemed to be supervising the process, but as Christie arrived he indicated that he was going to set up a casualty treatment area, also alongside the aircraft. He was accompanied by a nurse who appeared to have a broken arm. Following them to see if she could be of assistance, Christie saw that two of the babies passed out from the aircraft had partly turned over and their faces were now almost in the water. She splashed over to them and propped them up before returning to the aircraft when Stark indicated she would be more useful there. She re-entered the C-5A using a knotted rope to climb back up into the emergency exit.

Christie went immediately to a first aid kit that had been near her station and which had burst open in the crash. Collecting bandages and other items she thought Merrit Stark might need, she carried them back to the emergency exit and passed them out to him. She then joined the human chain that was passing babies along the aisle and out through the emergency exit. The outside helpers had learned their lesson about placing babies down on the paddy field, even if they were propped against the fuselage's side. The risk of them drowning was just too high, so they were now taken to any flat surface that was above the water, either part of the fuselage or the raised earthen walkways that crisscrossed the paddy field.

When the last children had been removed from the seats and passed outside, Christie started at the front of the troop compartment and worked her way towards the rear to make certain that no babies had been overlooked. With the assistance of one of the aircrew, she uncovered and turned over the row of seats that had been upended when the escape slide had inflated. She was thrilled to find the seats' six occupants a bit ruffled but otherwise unharmed. She had a real fright when she spotted a tiny arm protruding from underneath a tumble of debris – roof panels, insulation and the like. Fortunately, all the material was light. Christie easily moved it and was again thrilled to find several uninjured babies underneath.[6]

While Merrit Stark and an injured Regina Aune took charge of the injured and babies outside, air crew began examining the fuselage's remains. In what was now the triage area, Ray Snedegar assisted Regina in her efforts to assist the injured. Early on, she heard one loadmaster call out to her. He was on the ground, his back against the fuselage, and half-covered by mud and water. A quick examination confirmed that the airman's injuries would prove fatal, and that he didn't have much longer to live. Regina did what she could – a smile, a hand clasp – and made the man as comfortable as possible in his last moments. She wanted to remain with him until he died but understood that there were probably others who needed her expertise more than this man needed her compassion.

As they worked, Regina and the other survivors became aware of the sound of many helicopters coming near. Both Air America and the South Vietnamese Air Force had helicopters in the air and on standby for the emergency landing, and several of them witnessed the crash, albeit from a distance. They flew directly to the crash site, the first touching down on a dyke wall nearby no more than five minutes after the C-5A went down. From that point onwards, for an hour and a half, there was a constant shuttle of helicopters between Tan Son Nhut and the crash site. In the beginning, those helicopters carried babies and injured adults back to a fleet of ambulances that had assembled at Tan Son Nhut. The ambulances waited to take the injured to one of Saigon's hospitals, with most going to the Seventh Day Adventist Hospital next to the airport.

Later, helicopters brought rescue workers to help in the search for survivors. They also brought body bags. Most of the survivors, though, had been flown back to Tan Son Nhut long before the recovery operation switched from the living to the dead. Among the last of the living to leave was Christie Leiverman. Christie had been working with Regina Aune, nursing the many who were injured in the crash and who were waiting to be flown out, when she suddenly realised just how badly injured Regina was.[7] The air force nurse eventually collapsed, so Christie and one of the flight crew half-carried and half-dragged Regina across to an evacuation helicopter and helped her aboard. After the helicopter departed, Christie asked the crewman the question she had been too afraid to ask earlier. How were the adults and children in the cargo compartment, she asked. The answer was a sad and simple, 'No.'

•

Even as babies were being passed out and down from the troop compartment, surviving air and medical crew were trying to find survivors in the cargo compartment. It was a grim task. Early on, two survivors were pulled from the debris: a medical technician and the daughter of one of the DAO escorts. Both were badly injured but Bud Traynor, who was assisting with the recovery effort, believed that both would survive their injuries. Two more survivors, a crewman and an escort, were also recovered but both had suffered what were clearly life-ending injuries. They were made as comfortable as possible while the search continued, but it was not a search that held out any real prospects of success.

When they thought the troop compartment had been cleared, Merrit Stark made one more inspection of what remained. He walked back to the compartment's rear, where a number of seats had become entangled with other debris. Fearing the worst, he looked carefully into the pile but could see no bodies within it. Finished there, he climbed slowly down into the muddy field and walked back towards the burning wreckage some distance away in the paddy field, wondering whether his daughter was somewhere on the other side of the flames. As he walked, he was approached by an Air America helicopter pilot he knew. That pilot told Merrit that there was nothing more that he could do and led him across to a South Vietnamese military helicopter that was about to return to Tan Son Nhut. Stark was its only passenger; he also believed he was the last survivor to leave the scene.[8]

•

When the wider search was called off after an hour, an additional six children and two adults with a range of injuries had been found alive. The initial estimate of the number killed in the cargo compartment was 141. It was not a surprise that so many had died; it was a surprise that anyone had survived.

The first casualties in the cargo compartment were those killed or injured when the cargo door failed and there was a massive explosion followed by a catastrophic decompression. Some of those towards the rear were dragged out the back of the C-5A in the sudden vacuum that was accompanied by cyclonic winds. Some died from shock, hypothermia or a lack of oxygen. Others were killed outright or fatally wounded by the debris swirling through the compartment, and in the minutes that followed some succumbed to those injuries. Others survived a few minutes longer only to be killed during either the first or the second impact with the ground. Most, though, died in that second impact when the cargo compartment was completely crushed as it absorbed all the forces of the crash landing. Several among those who survived that impact were either drowned or suffocated when the remains of the compartment were immersed in water, mud and vegetation.

It was a tragedy that more than 150 men, women and children fleeing danger were killed during that flight, dying in just a few minutes and in terrible circumstances. It was a double tragedy when it was learned that it was an accident that should never have occurred.

12

AUSTRALIAN UPLIFT

Tan Son Nhut, 4 April

Meanwhile, shortly after midday Eastern Standard Time on Friday 4 April, the Australian Department of Foreign Affairs in Canberra sent a restricted and urgent cable to its chargé d'áffaires in Hanoi. The chargé was asked to inform the relevant North Vietnamese authorities about the forthcoming RAAF operation out of Tan Son Nhut airport in Saigon that would involve airlifting over two hundred South Vietnamese orphans to Bangkok for transfer to a chartered commercial aircraft that would then fly them to Australia. If necessary, the chargé was to stress that this operation was nothing out of the ordinary and was simply a continuation of past practices. The cable, which was copied to the Australian Embassy in Saigon, concluded with the words, 'The adoption of Vietnamese orphans is a long-standing private expression of concern at the suffering caused by war and the government, with the full support of all segments of the Australian people, is accelerating the movement of orphans.'[1]

•

If the process at Tan Son Nhut was frustrating for the adults that day, it must have been frightening for the children, especially those old enough to be aware of their surroundings. The FFAC staff appeared to be the best prepared of the carers accompanying the children but most of their children were being evacuated aboard the big American C-5A and the lines of communication (and control) were becoming a little fluid around the Australian Babylift operation. Not for the first and certainly not for the last time, the volunteers who had been involved in orphan care for months or years were being eased aside by bureaucrats and well-meaning amateurs, several of whom seemed more concerned about being seen to be involved rather than the actual value or contribution of that involvement. Gradually, though, some order crept into an otherwise chaotic picture.

There would be four flights scheduled for the RAAF C-130s that day, with each aircraft making two runs between Saigon and Bangkok. The planned procedures for each flight were identical, an example of wishful thinking at its best. The first flight saw lines of orphans and carers mingling with other lines of orphans and carers, some of them destined for the C-5A and others for the RAAF flights. Escorting those allocated to the first of those flights was Don Whitelum, a pharmacist from Adelaide who had travelled to Saigon in early 1975 to help Rosemary organise the FFAC's dispensary. Assisting to load that first C-130 was an experience Whitelum would never forget. 'It was hell. We carried them onboard . . . strapped them in or put them in cardboard boxes . . . and off we went . . .'[2]

The older children walked up the ramp into the fuselage and, like many of the adult escorts, were quite dismayed by what confronted them. The C-130 was a military transport aircraft, so passengers and passenger comfort were very much a secondary consideration in its design and outfitting. The fuselage was primarily a large, spartan, open space with an array of fixing points for cargo and tie-down straps. The bespoke baby carry-cases were arrayed towards the front of that space and the very smallest orphans, those just days and weeks old, were carefully placed in them. Older babies, those up to two years of age, were then placed crosswise on the medevac litters the medical team had brought with them. Depending on their size, each litter could hold up to five children. All the babies were given bottles of water to drink to help them avoid dehydration and to help them adjust to the changing air pressure.

The oldest children, a group that included several teenagers, were told to sit on the floor and were shown how to secure themselves for take-off and landing using the aircraft's tie-down straps. Toddlers and the remaining children were either strapped into the metal seats along each side of the fuselage or placed on the laps of adults in those seats, or with others sitting on the floor, again secured in place with tie-down straps. Many of the younger children were by then ill and all were distressed to a greater or lesser degree. Their fears and their cries increased substantially when the cargo ramp retracted and the rear doors closed. For them, the semi-darkness of the cargo hold was frightening and their fear only increased as the engine noise reached a crescendo and the aircraft began to move, slowly at first, and then picked up speed, lifting off at 4.15 p.m. Adding to their fears, the windows were set too high for any of the children to at least see where they were going.

Things improved only marginally, if at all, during the flight to Bangkok. It was a relatively short flight of around ninety minutes, but it was a flight that none of the older passengers would ever forget. The oppressive heat that had gathered in the aircraft when it had been sitting on the tarmac at Tan Son Nhut gradually dissipated, but that discomfort was replaced by two others – noise and vibration. The engine noise in the cargo compartment was so loud that any form of normal conversation was impossible. The older children said it was difficult to think and most developed headaches.[3] The vibration was just as bad. Although normal, it made it feel like the aircraft was trying to shake itself apart. Those who spent the flight sitting on the fuselage floor arrived in Bangkok feeling that every bone in their body was broken.[4]

Don Whitelum felt that he was fighting a losing battle during most of those ninety minutes in the air.

> I think I was the only one or two who actually looked after the children on the flight. All of them (the children) were just screaming . . . and I spent the whole time feeding and changing nappies and running around generally . . . and it was hell . . . All these babies – they were screaming, crying and frightened out of their wits, so it was quite traumatic.[5]

As well as the crying, there were illnesses that the children had brought aboard with them, plus airsickness. An already bad situation was made worse by the lack of RAAF air and medical crews; there were simply too few people to meet the needs of many sick, scared and disoriented children. The older children did what they could to help the younger ones, but that first C-130 to land in Bangkok carried a cargo of traumatised orphans, now suffering from headaches, earaches and dehydration on top of whatever else was ailing them.

•

The first RAAF aircraft had carried fifty-nine orphans plus carers, medical and aircrews from Tan Son Nhut, where it had taken off at 4.15 p.m. Approximately eight minutes later, the US Air Force C-5A piloted by Bud Traynor crash-landed in a paddy field just three kilometres from the airport. Even before the pillars of smoke became visible from the tarmac, many of those at Tan Son Nhut knew that there was something wrong with one evacuation aircraft. From radio traffic, the crew on the flight deck of the second RAAF C-130 were aware that it was the American plane that was in trouble and had crash-landed, but that knowledge was yet to filter back to the medical teams and volunteers working to load more orphans onto their aircraft. Many of those at the rear automatically assumed that it was the first RAAF aircraft that had crashed.

Waiting in the shade of one of the buses was Mary Cusack, To Am's administrator, trying to keep her children calm as their final security clearances were completed. As she waited, Mary heard several fire trucks and ambulances speeding somewhere with their sirens wailing. In the distance she could see smoke rising into the sky and when someone said that it was from an aircraft that had crashed, she just assumed that it was a South Vietnamese military aircraft and that it had probably been sabotaged by the communists.[6] Just fifty metres away, Margaret Moses senior was helping board the group of small children she was escorting back to Australia. She, too, saw the smoke and was told that it was the C-5A and that most of the passengers were dead. Margaret thought that there was nothing she could do about that and, besides, there were some very small and quite ill children who needed her help. She continued working.

It was quickly confirmed that it was the C-5A that had crashed and that, moreover, it had crashed after an explosion had blown one of the rear cargo doors off. What was uncertain was the cause, with speculation fixing on three main possibilities.

Mechanical failure could not be disregarded but then neither could sabotage or a small bomb deliberately placed aboard the aircraft. A surface-to-air missile was considered the least likely cause but was not entirely discounted. To guard against the possibility that the crash was the result of a bomb placed aboard, all future evacuation flights – American, Australian and all other nations' – the evacuation aircraft and all they carried would be subjected to a thorough search before they would be permitted to depart. This would continue for the duration of Operation Babylift.

Because of this, the departure of the second C-130 was delayed by around thirty minutes. Mary Cusack oversaw the loading of her children directly from the buses onto the RAAF aircraft and supervised, too, the examination and loading of green plastic garbage bags filled with nappies, clothes formula and bread. She would farewell that plane and help load the next and would not depart herself until all the To Am babies were on their way to Australia.

•

As the shuttle flights of orphans arrived at Bangkok from Saigon, their occupants joined a growing band of refugees heading for Australia who were gathering there. The Australian Embassy in Bangkok had been given responsibility for coordinating the movement of the South Vietnamese orphans and had organised a transit lounge and associated facilities to accommodate them between their arrival in Bangkok and their departure for Sydney. The arrival of the first two C-130 flights shortly before 6 p.m. showed just how inadequate those arrangements were. The flight and medical crews and several carers had struggled to cope with the fifty-eight children on the ninety-minute flight, and now RAAF personnel were preparing to return to Saigon as the second flight was on its final approach to Bangkok.

When it became obvious that the small number of the embassy's diplomatic and locally engaged staff and the children's carers would struggle to cope with the orphans' needs, an urgent call for assistance went out to the Australian diplomatic community resulting in five wives of embassy officials volunteering their services. Unfortunately, that was still nowhere near enough and the official in charge authorised the hiring of additional staff. Sixteen ground hostesses and one safety officer were hired from the British Overseas Airways Corporation (BOAC, the forerunner of British Airways) and the Borneo Company.[7] They made a significant difference, but the situation was still far from ideal.

Some of the tensions that emerged on the tarmac at Tan Son Nhut – the responsibilities of the carers versus the prerogatives of those charged with implementing Operation Babylift – were exacerbated by the conditions at Bangkok. As well as trying to organise the orphans' welfare and wellbeing, officials from the Australian government and military and the Red Cross attempted to remove the volunteer carers from any decision-making. When those carers, who knew the orphans and had experience in caring for them, offered suggestions or advice, they were either ignored or asked to not interfere. At best, they found they were patronised by people whose sense of moment was matched by their self-importance. Unfortunately, it was an attitude that would continue and that would also have consequences.

The final shuttle flight from Saigon arrived at Bangkok at 10.18 p.m. that night and a rough headcount in the orphans' transit lounge came up with a total of between 185 and 200 children plus seventeen adults being evacuated. Orphan numbers could not be narrowed down because there were now civilian evacuee children in the lounge. When the chartered Qantas 747 touched down in Bangkok less than an hour later, the actual process of evacuation to Australia commenced. Again, senior government officials took charge and almost immediately several unexpected problems became apparent.

There had been an understanding that 215 orphaned children plus a number of carers would be flown from Bangkok to Australia. Instead, the aircraft would carry almost one hundred more passengers, including medical staff, around eighty Australian Embassy officials and their families who were also being evacuated from Saigon, and the official and unofficial escorts and carers. As the preparations for boarding the aircraft were being completed, officials learned that not all the escorts and carers were Australian nationals – there were three Americans, one British and two New Zealand nationals accompanying the orphans. However, common sense prevailed and, due to the realisation that they would need all the assistance they could garner, all foreign nationals were allowed to travel.

Assistant Minister Morrison also adopted a hands-on approach. When the Qantas 747 touched down in Bangkok, he and a small group of senior Australian officials who had travelled with him exited the aircraft and were directed to the orphans' transit lounge within the main terminal. There, they met with diplomats from the Australian Embassy in Bangkok and, soon after, directed that loading commence for the 747's return flight. This was done in an orderly fashion – the smallest babies were boarded first, followed by infants and toddlers, with the older children led aboard before adults made their way onto the aircraft. During embarkation, medical staff briefly examined the orphans so they could then warn Sydney of their human cargo's broad health parameters. They found that the children's ages ranged from one week to fourteen years, that most were suffering from dehydration and malnutrition, and that some were in a serious but not critical condition.

The final passengers boarded QF 180 at 3.30 a.m. local time, but there was still a lot of organising to do in the main cabin before all those on the aircraft would be secured for take-off. The 747 finally departed for its nonstop flight to Sydney at 4.30 a.m. Some time before that take-off, someone aboard – a politician perhaps or someone with an eye to either posterity or publicity – decided that 'QF 180' was too simple, too bland for what they were doing. The aircraft and the flight would now be referred to as the Angel of Mercy.

•

For the older children at least, the direct flight from Bangkok to Sydney was a far longer, but far more pleasant, experience than the shuttle flight from Saigon. There were challenges and fears to be faced but they would be done while sitting in comfortable seats and without the buffeting and screaming engines that had made the short hop from Saigon to Bangkok such a terrifying ordeal for them all. There was the constant background hubbub of small children and babies, crying, screaming and squalling, but those children were now someone else's problem and the older children could relax – at least a little.

For just about everyone else, the flight was a far-from-pleasant experience. The pilot, Captain Bert Smithwell, left the flight deck after they had reached cruising altitude for a look around his aircraft. It was, he would later tell reporters, something that reminded him very much of a flying nursery. There were crying babies everywhere, nappies were being changed all over the main cabin and he had to tread carefully because the floor was littered with feeding bottles. Smithwell could have been forgiven for remaining in the cockpit for the remainder of the flight. Although part of the 747 had been converted into a small clinic, the sheer scale of the problems encountered overwhelmed the medical staff onboard. More than half of the orphans had quite serious medical conditions that required almost constant monitoring and regular treatments. And that was on top of the constant feeding and changing that even the healthy babies needed.

If that wasn't enough for the overworked staff, there were also several administrative tasks to be completed. Realising that there would be a need for both immediate and ongoing treatment for many – if not most – of the orphans, Spike Langsford directed that medical reports be prepared for all children based on complete medical examinations, plus all relevant clinical notes that others had made. These would be handed over to the medical teams waiting in Sydney. This in turn necessitated collecting and collating any records either the children or the carers had brought with them plus the preparation of a nominal roll. Although incomplete, a set of documents was brought together at around 3 p.m. on Saturday afternoon. Ten minutes later, Bert Smithwell advised passengers and crew to prepare for landing.

●

After landing, the aircraft was met by a fleet of ambulances accompanied by a crowd of doctors and nurses. Eighty children aboard the Angel of Mercy were placed in ambulances and taken directly to the Royal Alexandra Hospital for admission and urgent treatment. The hospital would later that day issue a statement reporting that no child was seriously ill and that all those suffering from minor ailments were responding well to treatment. Dr Barry Springthorpe, responsible for the children's hospital care, did say that ten children were in a worse state than the others but that none were in any great danger.[8] That was a bit of a sideshow, though, with the main show taking place in front of the cameras on the tarmac.

In keeping with the script, the media were out in force to document the occasion. They filmed orphans exiting the aircraft, one at a time, either led or carried by a nurse or carer to one of the waiting ambulances for transport to the hospital or to one of the waiting buses for carriage to the North Head Quarantine Station. There were interviews, too. Minister Bill Morrison had tears rolling down his cheeks as he described the evacuation flight, adding that he would now personally do anything he could to remove such children from harm's way. Bert Smithwell continued the melancholy tone, declaring QF 180's return to Australia as 'the saddest flight I've ever experienced. I think every person on the flight was moved. I think they'd have to be.'[9]

Half an hour after the Angel of Mercy touched down, they were all gone: orphans and carers to Quarantine Station or to hospital, officials to their next official function, and reporters to their newsrooms. Cleaners swarmed over the aircraft – this one would take a lot longer than usual to get ready for its next flight and it was already growing dark.

●

Even though they were expecting them, the arrival of 120 Vietnamese orphans at Quarantine Station that afternoon was an overwhelming event. Additional staff, medical personnel from state and federal health departments, and immigration officials were on hand but at times their presence only seemed to add to the chaos. The orphans' health remained at the forefront of all the welfare activities and so all were given another full medical check when they arrived at the facility. Twenty were found to be so ill that ambulances were called and they were transferred immediately to the Royal Alexandra Hospital. Again, medical checks confirmed that all the children were malnourished, dehydrated and in a debilitated condition. A significant number were diagnosed with bronchitis, pneumonia and gastroenteritis. One child had congenital syphilis, three were blind and a number were suffering from the after-effects of polio. These were the 'healthy' children.[10]

The doctors were both appalled and confronted by what they found. As most had little, if any, experience with either tropical or Third World medicine, they were constantly challenged professionally by what they found in their patients. The dentists in the medical team were equally confronted. At least one child, Hoa Stone, had such poor dental hygiene that a dentist removed all his baby teeth and he struggled with solid food until his second teeth came through. While a few children were almost well enough to be discharged immediately, most would require days, and some weeks, of treatment. In an ideal world, this would not be a problem, but these were orphans with adoptive families waiting for them all over Australia. Those families wanted their new children as soon as possible. This would be problematic – no one seemed to know exactly who all the children were.

One hundred and eighteen of the orphans were linked to adoptive parents before they boarded the aircraft.[11] Because the documentation that accompanied the children was so limited, however, it would prove difficult to match those children with either adoptive parents or actual documents at Quarantine Station or the hospital. While almost all the children started their journey in Saigon wearing or carrying some form of documentation – a wristband, a small pouch around their neck – that included their name and their destination, very few ended the day with it. Some material had simply been lost in transit while some had been removed to wash the children or change their clothes. The process was also complicated by the Australian lack of familiarity with Vietnamese names and the repetitiveness of some of those names. There were, for example, seven Nguyen Van Hungs among the orphans.

When it became obvious that it would be a struggle to correctly identify all orphans using the available documentation, the various adoption agencies, mostly ignored in the process to date, were called back into it. Phone calls between Sydney and Saigon resolved some misidentifications, but it would take until 23 April, more than two weeks after the children had arrived in Sydney, and involve state and federal agencies as well as several volunteer organisations for all 194 orphans aboard the Angel of Mercy to be identified. That figure, 194, was also the final, agreed figure. The higher numbers reported during the evacuation process were due in part to deliberate attempts to rort the system, attempts that had the potential to derail the entire evacuation operation.

As the QF 180 operation was being assessed by Immigration Department officials, it became obvious that not all the children aboard the flight were entitled to be there. Béla Venczel, one of the main players in the Saigon orphanage network and his wife, Caroline Vung, apparently used the movement of the Sancta Maria orphans to cover evacuation of several of Caroline's nephews aboard two of the RAAF flights. The Australian Embassy had previously denied the boys Australian entry visas. In a subsequent immigration interview, Venczel claimed that the children, aged three to seventeen years, mingled with the orphanage children on the tarmac at Tan Son Nhut as they waited to be evacuated. The younger ones were assumed to be part of the group being evacuated while the older boys carried them onto the aircraft and were assumed to be carers.

The incident was not disastrous but indicated the lengths to which South Vietnamese parents would go to save their children from a life under communism. It was, though, clearly against the spirit of Operation Babylift and if it became widely known would add to the fire then being stoked by those opposed to the whole concept of Babylift, a group whose numbers were beginning to grow.

•

Later that evening at the North Head Quarantine Station, the staff served the children a dinner they had spent a large part of the afternoon preparing. Guessing correctly that the children would be very hungry, they didn't scrimp on portion sizes. It was a meal that would long live in the older children's memories. There seemed to be food of every kind, including many dishes that none of them had ever seen before. As they wolfed down their food, the catering and welfare staff stood back and watched the scene with some satisfaction. Unfortunately, the children had come from eating the simplest foods in Saigon orphanages, or had been living a hand-to-mouth existence just a few days earlier, and the sudden exposure to this protein- and dairy-rich Western diet was to have several predictable results in the coming hours.

The first outcome became apparent when it was time to put the children to bed. Almost without exception, the older children had hidden food items somewhere on their persons. Many of them had spent a large part of their lives uncertain about where their next meal would be coming from, and in those circumstances putting a little food away for later made eminent sense. A second outcome was not long in coming. Unused to such rich food, the children's bodies revolted and before morning many were suffering from stomach aches and diarrhoea, conditions that would lessen and then disappear as they became used to their new circumstances.

•

There was a special event at Quarantine Station the next day, Sunday 6 April. A convoy of cars wound its way around the harbour to the station, where it disgorged a host of media types plus the prime minister of Australia, Gough Whitlam, and his wife, Margaret. The Whitlams were given a brief tour of the facility, while they talked to staff about their work and the orphans, were photographed looking at and listening to them, and finally posed for a series of photographs while the prime minister held a small Vietnamese orphan girl. The convoy left almost immediately afterwards and, ten minutes later, it was as if they had never really been there at all.

13

AFTERMATH

SAIGON, 4 APRIL 1975

Those not at Tan Son Nhut when the C-5A took off that afternoon assumed that everything must have gone pretty much
according to plan, while recognising that there actually had been
some hitches along the way. Wende Grant remained at Rathaven
after the staff escorts and children departed, catching up on
the paperwork that had several times threatened to derail their
planning. She was there when Joe Ruoff, a senior USAID official
in Saigon, telephoned to inform her that, apart from Margaret
Moses, none of the designated FFAC escorts had valid South
Vietnamese exit visas. As most would be returning to Saigon
almost immediately, he didn't think it would be a major issue,
but he wanted Wende to be aware of it.

It was now after 4 p.m. and, guessing that Rosemary would
probably be back at Newhaven, Wende telephoned the nursery.
The two women spoke briefly, agreeing that the lack of exit
visas shouldn't be a problem that day, but might become one
in the future, so they would need to do a bit more paperwork
for future evacuation convoys.

Shortly after 4.30 p.m., Ruoff phoned Wende at Rathaven a second time. This time, he sounded different and opened the conversation by asking Wende how she felt. Almost before she finished answering the question, Ruoff blurted that he had something to tell her. The plane had crashed, he said, adding that it had gone down just the other side of Tan Son Nhut. Ruoff continued that the news was still sketchy but that he had been told that there were survivors. The best advice he could now offer was for Wende to collect her best people and their emergency supplies and get out to the airport as soon as possible.

After she hung up, Wende ran to tell the other staff at Rathaven what had happened. She knew she had to keep moving, that doing something would act as an antidote to the dread that was growing inside her. If she stopped to think about what might have happened, she believed that she might not be able to go on. The first two people she saw after hanging up were the German Ilse Ewald and the Canadian Naomi Bronstein.[1] While Wende informed the staff of what she had learned and what she and the other two were now doing, Ilse put together an emergency medical kit and Naomi went to collect the nursery's ambulance. Two minutes later, the three women were in the ambulance, driving away from Rathaven. En route to the airport, they decided they would probably be of greater use at the Adventist Hospital, where most of the survivors were sure to be taken.[2] As they parked near the hospital's emergency department, another ambulance pulled up and its rear doors were thrown open. The first person to emerge from its interior was Christie Leiverman.

•

Susan McDonald had remained at Newhaven, helping to rearrange the house and look after several sick children, while Rosemary and several others accompanied the Newhaven orphans to Tan Son Nhut to see them aboard the giant cargo plane there. After Rosemary had returned to Newhaven from the airport she sat with Susan to share her concerns about the evacuation aircraft. She was concerned about its suitability as an evacuation vehicle for a substantial number of babies and small children. Rosemary doubted that the cargo compartment that housed most of the accommodation could be made either safe or secure for their children. She was also concerned about the troop compartment where their smallest babies had been squeezed in and where it seemed, when Rosemary left, that just Merrit Stark and Christie Leiverman would be responsible for the health and wellbeing of seventy-five babies.

As the conversation ended, the telephone rang. It was USAID – probably Joe Ruoff – and the caller informed Susan that there had been an accident and that many of their children were currently being rushed to the Adventist Hospital, several of them suffering injuries. The hospital was seeking assistance from childcare workers and could they please send some? Susan hung up and quickly explained to Rosemary the contents of the telephone call before the two women grabbed some personal items and rushed out into the street to flag down the first taxi they saw. Urging the driver to speed, they too arrived at the Adventist emergency department in time to see a mud-spattered Christie Leiverman disappear inside the hospital.

•

Christie Leiverman was in shock, living a nightmare that wouldn't go away. When the rescue helicopter dropped her and one of the C-5A crewmen at the Air America lines at Tan Son Nhut, there was an ambulance waiting to take them to the Adventist

Hospital. As they walked across to the ambulance Christie asked the crewman about how the children they hadn't found were likely to be, and he just answered, 'Fine.'[3] It was a trite answer, and one she continued to mull over during the ride in the ambulance and as she walked from the ambulance to the emergency department at the Adventist Hospital. Just short of that point she was stopped and embraced by Wende Grant, who asked her what had happened. Christie couldn't help herself, anger and frustration breaking through as she answered in harsh terms, 'The whole goddamned back of the plane blew out, that's what happened!'[4] Calmer now, when Wende then asked about Dolly, Birgit, Lee and Margaret, Christie said she had no news; they had been on the lower deck, she said, and she had been on the upper, so she didn't know.[5]

Seeing Christie alive gave Wende, Ilse and Naomi hope. If she had survived, surely some of the others had as well. As Christie was being directed into the emergency department, Wende went over in her head what she would say to the others, before walking with Ilse and Naomi across to where more ambulances were now pulling in to the hospital. Most of them seemed to be disgorging stretchers carrying babies, sometimes three or four to each. All appeared to be covered in mud but otherwise unharmed. The mud would certainly make it difficult to recognise anyone they knew – adult or child – and the three women tried to recall what their friends had been wearing when they last saw them. Remembering, they began looking for Margaret's navy-blue dress, Birgit's yellow slacks or Dolly's white pantsuit whenever an ambulance or taxi pulled up.

They split up, and for five minutes covered all the vehicles that arrived and all the people already inside the emergency department, including those lying on stretchers, whether they were conscious or not. When they came together again, the women found that they had not recognised a single person they knew apart from Christie. On this basis, Wende decided to speak to a flight crew member who was also waiting nearby, apparently uninjured and helping to unload the ambulances as they arrived. When Wende asked him what had happened to all those who had not yet been brought to the hospital, especially those from the lower deck, he answered that God knew and cared for all of those who had been in the cargo compartment. As the import of what he had said sunk in, Wende staggered outside, almost into the arms of Rosemary Taylor and Susan McDonald. The look on their faces said that they, too, now comprehended what they had lost.

•

When they first arrived at the Adventist Hospital and paid off the taxi driver, Rosemary and Susan had rushed towards the crowds gathered at the front of the hospital, seeing Christie in the distance entering the emergency department. They paused to watch several ambulances arrive and unload their patients, mainly babies and small children on stretchers as well as several adults, none of whom they recognised. Several minutes later, having forced their way through the crowd, they were confronted by a teary-eyed Wende Grant, accompanied by Ilse Ewald, clearly in shock, and Naomi Bronstein. Wende confirmed what they had just realised, that the accident was a bad one and that some of their children and friends were dead, but gave them to understand that it was even worse than they imagined and that no one in the lower part of the aircraft had survived.

•

Inside the emergency department, Christie Leiverman had her details taken and was given a glass of water and directed to a bench seat overlooking the entryway. There, she sat and watched and tried to unwind. She saw ambulances from other hospitals arrive, only to be redirected to the airport. She saw survivors from the crash arrive and noticed that, as the stretchers were carried from the ambulances and into the emergency department, it was almost impossible to tell whether the little mud-covered bodies were alive or dead. Then she could see that in one section, nurses would simply pass the children under a running shower and pass them on to someone else, saying, 'This one's alive, this one's dead.'[6]

Trapped inside a real-life horror movie, Christie watched the ambulances come and go, their movements and their occupants now scarcely registering in her consciousness. After a while – five minutes, fifty minutes? – she noticed that some movements had changed and that some Air America flight crew were carrying uninjured children out to cars and jeeps parked near the entrance, directing their drivers to take the children back to their home orphanages. She noted, too, that many of the children were seemingly incapable of movement, lying limply in the arms of big, brawny men. Most of them were still wearing wristbands and Christie imagined she could read 'New York', 'New Jersey' and other place names on them. They were going back to their orphanages or nurseries and Christie thought that perhaps she should, too. She asked to see a doctor, who took her pulse and blood pressure and then agreed that she was well enough to leave. She stood up and walked out and didn't look back.

•

The emergency department was being overrun. First it was the survivors, the children and adults, escorted and assisted by volunteers and servicemen to and then into the hospital. They were followed closely by doctors, nurses and medical orderlies from the Adventist Hospital itself and also from other hospitals and clinics, and even off-duty medical practitioners who learned of the disaster and believed that they might be able to help in some way. They were followed in turn by friends and relatives of those who shared some association, some affiliation with those directly involved in the unfolding events. Finally, there were two groups whose presence was barely tolerated and often actively discouraged – the press and that group of people who inevitably turn up wherever and whenever something newsworthy takes place, the ubiquitous stickybeaks.

The area went from crowded to overcrowded, at which point the senior medical staff made the wise decision to move all children in emergency upstairs to the paediatric ward, Ward 6. It soon also became crowded and then overcrowded, but at least it was with people who had a legitimate right to be there. Ward 6 also attracted Rosemary Taylor and Susan McDonald in their search for either children or staff, and both found the situation there very confronting. There were children everywhere, but little rhyme or reason in how those children were reacting to their situation. While some were crying, others were strangely silent. Where some were wearing wet and muddy clothes, others were completely naked. As Rosemary began to identify children from the FFAC nurseries, Susan began organising their transportation back to their most recent home.

When they had finished upstairs, the two women returned to the emergency department, again looking closely at all the adults either being treated or awaiting treatment; they saw no one they recognised. Outside, they spoke and came to the same conclusion: all their friends on the aircraft, with the exception of

Christie Leiverman, had most probably perished in the crash. At that point a truck arrived, and two stretchers were passed down from it. There were nine children on them and all were dead. Looking around further, they realised that all the ambulances, trucks and jeeps now arriving were bringing bodies rather than survivors, and that those bodies were being taken to the make-shift morgue that had been established in a fenced-off area in the car park.[7]

Looking across to the morgue, Rosemary and Susan saw Ilse Ewald at the fence looking in and moved across to comfort her. There were several body bags already inside the fenced-off area, laid out as if for inspection, but the guard on the gate refused the women access when they first approached him. After explaining who they were and why they were there, the guard relented and let Rosemary and Susan inside while Ilse preferred to remain on the other side of the fence. Immediately inside the entrance gate, three stretchers lay on the ground, each with a green adult body bag lying on top. Susan unzipped the first bag, and they looked down at the naked body of a woman with very white skin and long dark hair. Her skull had been crushed. Susan zipped the bag back up. The two women looked at each other briefly and then left the morgue, and the hospital, taking Ilse with them as they departed. Like Christie Leiverman, they didn't look back.

•

Dorothy Stark, Merrit's wife and Laurie's mother, learned about the C-5A crash while waiting in line at the post office at Tan Son Nhut. Her name was called out and when she identified herself she was escorted by one of the post office staff across the base to the Air America terminal. There was obviously a major rescue and recovery mission underway, as helicopters continued to arrive and depart as she walked to the terminal and while she waited inside. When the helicopters landed, volunteers would rush out and help to unload the often very small children. Some were so small, in fact, that the volunteers would lay them sideways on the stretcher with their heads to one side and their feet to the other.

That was just one of the little details Dorothy noticed as she sat and waited for news of her husband and daughter. Another was how the helicopters' constant comings and goings had created a permanent, thin veil of dust in the air that gave the sky in front of her a faint golden glow in the late afternoon sun.

The number and frequency of helicopter movements decreased, and when there was still no sign of either Merrit or Laurie, Dorothy was driven to the nearby Adventist Hospital. There, she recognised several of the survivors, either sitting on chairs and benches or lying on stretchers in the emergency department. She asked everyone she knew, and several she didn't, about her family, but no one could recall seeing either one of them after the aircraft went down. Eventually, though, she was paged and walked to the nearest telephone, which she picked up, identifying herself to the switchboard. After a second, a male voice she didn't recognise said simply, 'Merrit's at the apartment.'[8] That was a relief, but it was followed by the awful realisation that there was no mention of Laurie, and that Merrit would never leave Laurie by herself.

•

Not all the orphanage administrators went to the airport or the hospital. FCVN's Cherie Clark drove out to the crash site when she learned of the accident, parked her car nearby and got out to see what she could of the place where the aircraft had gone down. There were still columns of black smoke rising into the sky and, in the paddy field below, what appeared to be dozens of soldiers crisscrossing from one side to the other in a search pattern. She thought she saw tears on the cheeks of several soldiers closest to her. She also saw the thoroughness with which they looked: some walked closely together in lines along the scar in the field where the plane had skidded, while others waded through water-filled ditches searching for both survivors and bodies. In the distance, some way back across the paddy field, Cherie could see clothes fluttering in the light breeze that was now starting to spring up, clothes released from suitcases and bags that had burst open, scattering their owners' possessions across the muddy landscape.[9]

Among the soldiers Cherie watched were eight US marines. Those marines, US Embassy guards, had been off duty and relaxing at the Marine House when they were ordered to report to Tan Son Nhut, in camouflage and without weapons, to assist in the C-5A recovery operation. On arriving at the airport, the detachment was met by a Red Cross representative who briefed them on what had occurred and their role in the recovery before they were helicoptered out to the crash site. It was still daylight but because they expected to be onsite for several hours, all were carrying large, heavy-duty torches that could be handheld or placed on the ground to illuminate a work area.[10]

High above the wreckage, an English reporter named Julian Manyon looked down on the scene from a helicopter he had hired, making notes about what he saw. He noted that the C-5A had broken up as it skidded across the rice paddy and that the parts now most widely separated were the nose and the tail. Both remained clearly recognisable but between them other pieces of wreckage spread over hundreds of metres. Some of the pieces he looked down upon were still smouldering. As Manyon watched and wrote, a platoon of South Vietnamese soldiers arrived and, walking almost shoulder to shoulder, began wading through the mud and water looking for victims. Twice he saw soldiers bend down to lift the body of a small child from the paddy field, the corpse reminding Manyon from that distance of a drowned rabbit. Elsewhere, at the field's edge, American and South Vietnamese helicopters collected the bodies and ferried them back to Tan Son Nhut. It was, Manyon decided, almost like some kind of production line.[11]

The marines would be in that muddy field for the rest of the day and into the night. Although they could hear other searchers calling out that they had found a survivor, the marines would find only bodies and body parts. There was no rhyme or reason to the way the passengers had been treated by death. Take the clothes they had been wearing, for instance. Some bodies were fully clothed. On some, one side was fully clothed – half a shirt and half a pair of pants, say – while the other half was naked. One marine found a little girl, her dead face looking wide eyed up at the sky; the rest of her body was front first in the mud. Under a piece of aircraft debris he moved out of the way, another marine found a baby's arm protruding from the mud. It came up easily as he pulled because it was not attached to any other body part. They saw things that would make a grown man cry, and they did.[12]

•

There were others who were witnesses to the tragedy – locals, mostly peasant farmers; to them it was another interruption to the life cycle of an area that had remained largely unchanged for centuries. Wars came and went but the seasons were eternal. One of those witnesses was a young wife when the C-5A crashed and was a relatively old woman when she recalled the event for a journalist four decades later. 'I heard a big noise and slowly bits of plane started falling from the sky,' she recollected.[13] Still living in the house she occupied that day, not far from where the aircraft's nose came to rest, she said her husband wanted to rush straight to the wreckage but she demurred, berating him for wanting to see people who were dead or dying. Because there was so much human misery and sudden death in the paddy field, she believed the area was inhabited by the spirits of those whose lives ended that day, in that place.[14]

●

There was more than enough grief to go around. The DAO's Becky Martin, helping staff and survivors at the Air America terminal, realised that she had lost a lot of friends and colleagues that day. While most of the passengers brought alive or dead back to the terminal were children, there was a significant number of adults in both groups. As she rushed over to a helicopter carrying several child survivors – she would carry them from the helicopter to one of the waiting ambulances – Becky noted that the helicopter was also carrying the body of an adult, one of her work colleagues. The woman's name was Barbara and she had worked near Becky in the DAO's main office. What made her death even more tragic was that her daughter, who had been sitting alongside her, survived the crash.

Becky looked closely at her friend. Barbara's nose and mouth were full of mud, which also covered most of her clothes, but other than that there did not seem to be a mark on her. They would later speculate that she had been scared to death and that she suffered a massive heart attack as the C-5A came down. Another helicopter landed as Barbara's body was carried away, which brought with it the body of one of the aircraft's crew. This time, the cause of death was clear. The man's head had been crushed – he would have died instantly. Then another landed alongside it, carrying several body bags. Suddenly, Becky had seen enough and done enough. She simply turned around and walked away. She would go home now.

•

In some ways, the experience was worse for the Americans. The CIA station within the US Embassy had an office with secure communications out at Tan Son Nhut, and as more escorts' bodies were brought back to the airport and identified, those identifications were forwarded over the CIA's communications system – the 'Diamond' network – then distributed to the embassy and the several DAO offices. It was like a drip feed of disaster, which seemed to go on through the late afternoon and well into the evening.[15] With the accident, and the loss of all but one of the DAO evacuees, the American military establishment in South Vietnam took a hit from which it would never really recover. The ongoing North Vietnamese military successes had been both a setback and a challenge, but many in the DAO still believed some sort of negotiated settlement might still be possible, especially if President Ford could be persuaded to unleash the B-52s again. The C-5A crash took a lot of wind out of a lot of sails. DAO staff reported for work on 5 April, but their hearts were no longer in the work, or the fight, or the country.

•

Although there was a passenger manifest for the adults who flew out of Tan Son Nhut aboard Bud Traynor's C-5A, no such document existed for the orphans, so the final death toll must always have an element of conjecture about it. The figure that is most commonly quoted is 144, deduced from the confirmed deaths of thirty-five DAO escorts, five air crew, three medevac crew, seven FFAC escorts or relatives, two combat photographers and at least eighty-nine orphans. To that total can be added the three South Vietnamese militiamen killed on the ground when the C-5A touched down for the second time after skimming across the Saigon River.[16]

Most of those killed were travelling in the cargo compartment – one hundred and forty-one fatalities came from there, while just three came from upstairs in the troop compartment. FFAC was particularly hard hit in the disaster. Seventy-eight of their orphans were killed, a figure that included almost all the Allambie children, eighteen from To Am and several from Newhaven. Most of the orphans who survived, a figure of just over fifty, were babies from Newhaven and Phu My. Among those killed were Ilse Ewald's adoptee, Monique, and Birgit Blank's son, Sven. Christie Leiverman was the only FFAC staff member to survive. Killed along with the children they loved so dearly were Margaret Moses, Lee Makk, Birgit Blank, Sister Ursula Lee and Dolly Bui, alongside her daughter Tina and sons David and Michou. Laurie Stark also died in that muddy field.

•

When it was clear that no more survivors would be brought in from the crash site, Wende and Rosemary arranged for the surviving children to be returned to the nurseries they had left that morning. Several staff, Wende and Rosemary included, returned to Rathaven to personally break the news to Marina Bui that her mother, sister and brothers had been killed in the accident. Shortly after delivering this awful news, Bui Van To,

Dolly's husband, also arrived at Rathaven, having learned of the accident. He, too, was told of his family's fate.

There were also the survivors to consider. Ten of the orphans had sustained injuries serious enough to require hospitalisation. Of those, three were assessed as being seriously injured, requiring an extended period of hospitalisation. All those injured would eventually be medevaced out for treatment overseas. The orphans returned to their nurseries would also need to be cleaned up and comforted before being prepared once more for evacuation to the United States. The C-5A crash was undoubtedly a disaster for all those involved, but in the larger picture, it was a setback to rather than the ending of Operation Babylift. Other aircraft were already en route to Tan Son Nhut to continue the evacuations.

One of those aircraft's first mission was more sombre. All the recovered children's bodies and body parts were flown to the US military's Central Identification Laboratory and mortuary at a US military base in Thailand where, after a month of intensive forensic work, forty-five of the seventy-eight remains were eventually identified. All remains were eventually cremated at a Buddhist wat and the ashes interred at a Catholic cemetery at Pattaya in Thailand. US military personnel who had worked at the identification laboratory and mortuary contributed to pay for a headstone there.[17]

•

At Rathaven, Rosemary knew that news of the C-5A crash and the deaths of Margaret Moses and Lee Makk had to be sent to Australia. She and Susan McDonald called for a mission warden car and went to the home of an Australian Embassy secretary who they both knew and who said they would arrange for Canberra to be notified immediately by cable. Later that evening a telex was prepared at the embassy and sent to Canberra shortly after midnight. It read, in part:

Information received to date indicates plane had trouble in left wing, tried to circle and crashed in very marshy area. There appear to have been about 60 adults and from 250–300 children on board. To this time (0020 hours 5 April) some 20 adults and 50 children are reported as survivors.

According to Rosemary Taylor who visited hospital, Miss Margaret Veronica Moses and Miss Lee Makk, social workers in the Friends for All Children, were among those who perished in that they were not brought into the Seventh Day Adventist Hospital in Saigon. As search was called off at dusk, it is very remotely possible that there could be other survivors.

Miss Moses' mother was an attendant on one of the C-130s taking orphans to Bangkok and at this time it is not known whether she is aware of the crash. Rosemary Taylor has asked Sister Monica Marks, Convent of Mercy . . . to keep trying to telephone Taylor in Saigon. She would also like Marks to reassure her parents that Rosemary was not in aircraft.

Assume you will take appropriate steps to communicate with Mrs. Moses and other members of her family who are probably not known to Sister Marks in Adelaide. Will advise further information as available.[18]

By the time the cable arrived in Canberra, press reports from the major international news agencies had reached all Australian media outlets and the story was already front-page news. The main newspaper in Rosemary and Margaret's hometown of Adelaide reported that, 'A giant American C-5A Galaxy transport plane carrying 294 people, including 243 South Vietnamese orphans, crashed today near Saigon, killing between 120 and

140 on board. Some of the 43 escorts on the plane were reported to be Australian.' The article included an interview with one survivor: 'Some of us got out through a chute from the top of the plane,' said a mud-stained young American woman who had been one of the babies' escorts on the flight, 'but the children at the bottom of the plane did not have a chance.'[19]

The report did not mention the Adelaide connection through Margaret Moses and Lee Makk – it was too early for it to be made. Nor did it allude to the tragedy that was unfolding for the victims' families and friends. Those two threads came together the next morning in suburban Adelaide. Lee Makk's fourteen-year-old brother Jules opened the front door of his family's home and was immediately confronted by a phalanx of reporters, cameras and microphones: Why was his sister in South Vietnam? How long had she been there? Did she know of the dangers? How was the family taking the news? They wanted answers, but what they got was a heartbroken boy grieving his sister.

14

LAST RITES

SAIGON, 5–8 APRIL

At Rathaven and the other nurseries, there was no time for mourning. The pain Rosemary and Wende, the volunteers and the local staff were feeling was deep and profound, but they still had well over three hundred children in their nurseries and their focus must now be on them. There would be time enough for grieving later. In the wake of the C-5A crash, USAID had chartered a Pan Am 747, and early in the morning of 5 April FFAC was informed that the remaining and surviving FFAC children would be flown out from Tan Son Nhut that afternoon. That meant the staff needed to prepare all their children for international travel; supplies would have to be collected and prepared, and new documentation for each orphan put together in just a few hours.[1]

The death of their staff the previous afternoon meant the remaining volunteers had to work hard and start early on Saturday morning. Later that day they were joined by Mary Cusack, who had returned from Butterworth, and Sister Doreen Beckett, the Hy Vong administrator who had been absent escorting an orphan convoy to Europe. By the time the buses started arriving at the various nurseries around the middle of the afternoon, the volunteers had put together basic identification documents for the departing orphans. The final passenger list contained 324 names, representing most but not all of their children as neither Wende nor Rosemary was prepared to authorise the movement of orphans they considered too unwell to travel. They would be accompanied by eleven FFAC escorts, including Ilse Ewald and Wende, both of whom would return immediately after delivering the children to the West Coast, plus Pat Zirk and several other recently arrived American volunteers.

The buses from the FFAC nurseries arrived at Tan Son Nhut shortly after 4 p.m., but it was a very different Tan Son Nhut to the previous day. Airport security had been increased in the twenty-four hours since the crash because of the continuing speculation about its cause. A detachment from the US Air Force's Third Security Police Group based at Clark Air Base had flown in and would now search all aircraft and baggage before their departure as well as providing an onboard security presence. Concerns that a bomb might have been smuggled aboard the C-5A had also led to an edict that no Vietnamese nationals, except those actually being evacuated, were allowed to board any of the Babylift aircraft.

And so, for two hours from 4.30 p.m., a procession of passenger buses and vans pulled up on the tarmac near the stairs leading to the front and rear doors of a Pan Am 747 parked on the apron in the international departures area of Tan Son Nhut. Young Vietnamese women either carried or led the orphans to the foot of the stairs, where they handed the children over to an FFAC escort or to one of the Pan Am flight attendants who would then take each child into the aircraft. The Vietnamese and the escorts would then repeat the process until it was 6.30 p.m. and all children were aboard. There were then over one hundred young Vietnamese women in a half-circle facing the aircraft, weeping silently, and half a dozen young European women in the aircraft's doorways looking silently back at them. The Europeans disappeared into the aircraft and the Vietnamese returned to the buses, and at 7 p.m. the 747 moved along the taxiway to the main runway and five minutes later disappeared into the night sky.

•

Almost fifteen hundred orphans were evacuated from Saigon that weekend. An hour before the FFAC Babylift flight departed, another Pan Am 747 had taken off, this one chartered by Holt International and carrying 409 children and escorts from various orphanages and agencies in Saigon. Holt had declined an offer from the US government to fly out its orphans, instead chartering one of the Pan Am aircraft that was on the ground at Hong Kong. It proved quite a complicated and costly charter. Due to the rapidly deteriorating military situation in South Vietnam, Pan Am insisted that Holt purchase security insurance for the aircraft. The only company prepared to provide the requisite insurance was Lloyd's of London, and it charged Holt US$50 000 for every hour the plane would be on the ground in Saigon, with the total cost of the charter eventually reaching US$185 000. It was expensive but not as expensive as the FFAC flight, for which Pan Am charged the American government US$230 000.

Over the weekend, five MAC C-141s delivered military supplies for the South Vietnamese forces and departed Tan Son Nhut carrying almost four hundred orphans for examination and on-movement from Clark Air Base. Previously organised flights also departed – a British evacuation flight included 150 refugees, many of them small orphans, while the Canadian evacuation flight also carried quite a few orphans, including the remaining Cambodian orphans from Canada House in Phnom Penh. More would soon be on the way, too, as the C-5A crash and the loss of so many of the orphans it carried produced a massive wave of sympathy in the United States after calls for additional government action and efforts by numerous individual citizens and agencies to offer assistance. None would match the efforts of businessman Robert Macauley, who mortgaged his home to charter a Boeing 747 to fly three hundred orphans to the United States.

•

The Holt International evacuation flight landed at Seattle International Airport shortly after midnight on 6 April. It was met by a team of doctors and nurses, and a fleet of buses and ambulances. Among the people waiting on the tarmac and in the terminal were officials and volunteers from the Holt organisation, US border and immigration officials, and a sprinkling of reporters who stayed a fair distance back from the orphans and their carers. It was a low-key affair treated with dignity and respect, with a clear focus on the children and their wellbeing. The same could not be said for the arrival of the FFAC flight in San Francisco.

•

The second attempt to evacuate the FFAC orphans was different from the first in several respects. The doomed flight had carried the healthiest babies and children, but the 5 April flight carried all those capable of travelling, including those judged unsuitable thirty-six hours earlier, and those who, though traumatised, had survived the crash. Christie Leiverman, who would play an important nursing role on the plane, buried herself in preparations for the flight because so many of the children had special needs. The carers were required to carry at least five varieties of baby formula while special foods were prepared for children with cleft palates, nutritional diseases and general malnutrition. There was a risk in sending many of the children off on international travel but Wende and Rosemary agreed that it was a risk worth taking.[2]

Very little was left to chance on this journey. When FFAC's 747 touched down at Honolulu International Airport later that night, the US Air Force and Hawaiian state authorities had a contingency plan in place, which had been activated even before the aircraft landed, triggered by the governor of Hawaii declaring a state emergency. Air Force personnel were at their action stations when the aircraft touched down; security police and Safety Office personnel formed a cordon between the 747's stairs and along the walkways leading to an area in the main terminal specifically equipped for receiving the orphans. In that area, there was food and drink for the orphans and carers; there were doctors, nurses and orderlies to check the health of them all; and there were literally hundreds of volunteers to bathe, change and hold the children while ground staff cleaned and reprovisioned the aircraft. Three hours after they arrived, they were all back in the air.

The 747 touched down at the Presidio military base on the shores of San Francisco Bay, and in the hours before its arrival quite a crowd built up in the terminal. The crowd grew to several hundred and would include at least three hundred members of the media – reporters, and sound and cameramen – plus military and local police, volunteers, airline officials, Dr George Carnie, chairman of FFAC board, and President Gerald Ford, all waiting in the late evening darkness. Carnie spoke to the president who, he would later report, was 'very, very concerned about getting more children out of Vietnam'[3] and indicated that USAID would pay all costs associated with the airlift. Further conversation was cut short by the arrival of the Babylift flight.

The 747 had touched down on the Presidio's airfield a few minutes earlier, but now moved slowly onto the floodlit tarmac in front of the terminal. It came to a halt and sat there, with nothing happening, as tension among the onlookers continued to build. Stairs were pushed into place at the front door and, when that door was opened, a medical team climbed the stairs and entered the aircraft. A few minutes later, a second set of stairs was wheeled to the rear door and when it was opened Christie Leiverman and several other carers emerged, each one carrying an infant attached to an intravenous drip. The children were carried to waiting ambulances and the young women returned to the aircraft to collect other children. Eventually some forty-seven children were admitted to hospital.[4]

The ambulances at the rear stairs were a sideshow, though, and the main show remained at the front. After an appropriate interval, President Ford and his entourage climbed the stairs and entered the aircraft. A few minutes later, into the glare of dozens of arc lights, Ford emerged carrying a small Vietnamese girl in his arms. She looked a little apprehensive and he grinned broadly as he whispered words of welcome into her ear.

•

Rosemary was shattered by the crash of the C-5A and grieved for every life that was lost that day. She especially felt the loss of her schoolgirl friend Margaret Moses, more so because she felt personally responsible for bringing Margaret to Saigon. In her own words, Rosemary was 'numbed beyond the possibility of emotion . . . the living still had to be cared for; there was no time to dwell on the tragedy'.[5] And so, once the main tranche of FFAC children had flown out on the evening of 5 April, Rosemary Taylor again threw herself into her work.

There were several tasks she believed had to be completed before she herself could consider evacuation. There were still more than two dozen orphans in her nurseries, most of them in Hy Vong, with several others in hospital but expected to be discharged in the near future. To assist her in closing down their operations, Ilse Ewald and Doreen Beckett agreed to stay behind with Rosemary, and they were assisted by two other volunteers expected back from Europe after escorting an orphan convoy. Susan McDonald would also remain in Saigon as long as possible, but Wende Grant would return to the United States to take care of the logistics there.

The women had a lot of work to do and no one was certain just how much time they would have to complete the self-imposed tasks. By the beginning of the second week of April, all in Saigon knew that the fall of South Vietnam was now just a matter of days away, although exactly how many days was anybody's guess. The US Embassy was trying to have all US citizens evacuated and approached Susan McDonald, urging her to leave immediately. Susan said that she wasn't prepared to leave the children behind and that she would consider evacuation when transportation had been arranged for all the orphans as well. Similar approaches to the Australians by Australian authorities prompted an identical response.

To begin with, they shut down Hy Vong. All but the very sickest babies had been evacuated and those who remained were either sent to hospital or billeted out at Phu My. All Hy Vong's equipment, furniture and food supplies were also transferred to Phu My. While overseeing this, Rosemary organised caretakers for all of their nurseries and wrote letters of recommendation for all their local staff and arranged for their final wages to be paid. Unfortunately, it was all in vain. As Rosemary and the others prepared to close To Am, Newhaven and Rathaven, they were again almost overwhelmed by a wave of refugee orphans. As towns and villages in the Mekong Delta either fell or were abandoned to communist forces, orphanages – most of them run by religious orders – were evacuated, the sisters bringing their charges to Saigon, naturally gravitating to the FFAC nurseries they knew so well. Some of the orphans they brought had already been identified for possible transnational adoption.

As the days passed, To Am, Newhaven and Allambie gradually began to fill up again. Local staff who had been on the brink of departure were asked to remain and the volunteers who had left for other countries or been killed in the 4 April crash were replaced by volunteers from the orphanages that had been abandoned. Among the volunteers was a familiar face. Father Joe Turner, the US Army chaplain who had helped Rosemary and Elaine Moir back in 1971, had returned to Saigon but as a civilian rather than as an army officer. He had travelled there at his own expense, determined to continue the work he had started many years earlier. Rosemary found him a place to stay at Rathaven.

While the nurseries filled up and the volunteers and staff worked their long shifts with their new children, Rosemary buried herself in work. Day after day, she processed travel documentation for as many of their new arrivals as she could, organising to have them flown out on either Pan Am or Air France, the only two airlines now willing to operate flights out of Tan Son Nhut. With assistance from both Doreen and Ilse, Rosemary put together duplicates of as many of the documents that had been lost in the crash as possible. When there was time, the women would also meet with South Vietnamese bureaucrats and volunteers who thought they would be able to use the FFAC facilities after the overseas volunteers had departed.

•

Those trying to organise the evacuation of orphans from Saigon didn't need distractions, but there were distractions aplenty. The first was an about turn by the South Vietnamese government on those evacuations. On Sunday 6 April, out of the blue, a government spokesman announced that all future flights had been suspended. The reason given for the suspension was that the quota for evacuations had been met by flights over the last forty-eight hours with the implication that, should the quota be revisited and revised, the flights would be allowed to resume. At the same time, the spokesman announced that there would be no more mass authorisations of exit visas.

Although the spokesman made no reference to it, the fact was that Operation Babylift had attracted criticism from the time it was first mooted. The most immediate and trenchant criticism came from the South Vietnamese government's most committed opponents, the communist parties at home and abroad. Within hours of the first evacuation flight, the unauthorised departure of Ed Daly's World Airlines cargo jet, the Vietcong issued a statement through the North Vietnamese News Agency criticising the evacuation operation. The statement claimed that the operation not only violated the children's ultimate right to self-determination but was aimed at sowing division among the Vietnamese people. It further claimed that there were almost one million orphans in South Vietnam, with twenty thousand of them fathered by American soldiers. It said, as well, that those children were currently wasting away in orphanages set up by the United States and the Thieu regime and ended with the question, 'Are these humanitarian acts of the US imperialists?'[6]

It was criticism shared by the communist government of East Germany, which condemned the US airlift of orphans as baby snatching designed to wash away US guilt over the war. This criticism was directed towards Australia as well. Despite the explanatory note delivered to North Vietnamese authorities before the first Australian contribution to Operation Babylift, those very same authorities immediately accused Australia of taking part not in humanitarian operations, but rather in some kind of 'American plot'.[7] The Communist Party of Australia soon joined the chorus, its newspaper posing and answering the rhetorical question, 'When does a kidnapper become a national hero? When you are president of World Airlines [sic] and take fifty-five war orphans on an unsafe plane to be dumped in the United States.'[8]

The criticism would continue for at least as long as the airlift itself, and that was set to last for several more days. Under considerable pressure from a number of governments, including those of the United States, Canada and Australia, the South Vietnamese government issued a second statement several hours after it had released the first. This one was short and to the point, saying that the humanitarian evacuation of South Vietnamese war orphans would resume.

•

Gough Whitlam and those close to him believed that the 5 April Angel of Mercy orphan flight was a success – at least from the perspective of lessening the negative publicity the prime minister had been receiving – so much so that a decision was made to follow it up with a second airlift of orphans to Australia, one that was to take place as soon as possible. While conceding that there had been many and quite serious problems with the Angel of Mercy flight, Whitlam and his advisers believed that the political positives more than outweighed the medical, economic, social and even political costs attached to the operation. For the second mission, though, the prime minister would stand back a little further from the mechanics of the airlift. Senior bureaucrats in the relevant agencies and departments took over and ran the operation as well as they could. It was then that Australia's most famous nurse came to be involved.

•

Those senior bureaucrats had commissioned several after-action reports into the first Babylift flight and based their planning for the second partly on what they had learned from the first. Among the changes they insisted upon was a new destination for the orphans, in part because the North Head Quarantine Station was now at capacity. It was clear after the first flight that future evacuated orphans would almost certainly bring with them a range of health and hygiene problems, and that a proportion – perhaps as high as 50 per cent – would require hospitalisation upon their arrival. The most obvious solution to these two issues was to bring the orphans back to a specialist facility where their medical problems could be treated as part of their reception. There was such a facility, and it was available.

The Fairfield Infectious Diseases Hospital in inner suburban Melbourne had been established just after the turn of the twentieth century and was now the country's premier institution of its type. The hospital's staff were recognised internationally for their work and would bring the requisite experience and expertise to any problems the orphans may present. Finally, since 1959, the hospital's matron had been a nurse known to everyone in the country: Vivian Bullwinkel.

•

Matron Bullwinkel was uniquely qualified for the position. Not only was she a very experienced and competent administrator, but early in her nursing career Vivian had herself contracted many of the diseases that were routinely referred to her hospital. In 1941, she had been one of the youngest nurses sent abroad with the Australian Army Nursing Service, sailing to Singapore in August of that year to serve in one of the Army general hospitals attached to the Australian Imperial Force's 8th Division. The Australians had been dispatched to Singapore and Malaya to deter the Japanese from attacking any British colonies or other interests in the area.

The deterrent didn't work. On 8 December 1941, Japanese troops stormed ashore in northern Malaya and Japanese bombs rained down on Singapore. Just over ten weeks later, over ninety thousand Allied troops were surrendered to a Japanese force barely one-third that size. Vivian Bullwinkel and the other 129 Australian Army nurses were not among that number, having been evacuated by sea in the days before the surrender. Vivian was, however, one of sixty-five nurses aboard a cargo vessel, the *Vyner Brooke*, sunk by Japanese aircraft two days after fleeing Singapore. Vivian survived the sinking and, after several hours in a lifeboat, was washed up on a beach on Banka Island.[9]

On Monday 16 February 1942, Vivian was at the end of a line of twenty-two Australian nurses ordered to march into the sea by a Japanese officer in charge of a patrol of sixteen soldiers who were supposed to accept the surrender of a large group of nurses and civilians. She was the only nurse to survive when that officer ordered his men to march the women into the sea and kill them all. Vivian subsequently survived three and a half years in a series of prison camps, living through bouts of tropical diseases and near-starvation to be one of just twenty-four of the *Vyner Brooke* nurses to return to Australia. Remaining in nursing as a civilian after the war, Vivian rose steadily through the ranks of her profession and, aged sixty in 1975, was regarded as one of the finest nurses and medical administrators in Australia.

Late in the evening of 5 April, Matron Bullwinkel received a telephone call in her quarters in the grounds of the Fairfield Infectious Diseases Hospital from the hospital's medical superintendent, Dr John Forbes. He was calling to ask Vivian if she could put together a team of around fifteen nurses to travel to South Vietnam almost immediately. Forbes informed Vivian that two hundred South Vietnamese war orphans were being evacuated from Saigon by the Australian government and were flying to Melbourne, where they would be admitted to Fairfield for observation and treatment. Forbes himself would lead the mission and would be accompanied by two other doctors from Fairfield, Sandilands and Lucas. With barely a pause, Vivian assured Forbes that a nursing team would be available the next morning and that she would lead it.

As she began her planning Vivian realised that she did not have enough nurses at Fairfield to both meet John Forbes's request and keep staffing levels at the hospital at their required levels. Phone calls to matrons at other hospitals, including the nearby Heidelberg Repatriation Hospital, soon produced the additional nurses Vivian needed. Enquiries with hospital administration also confirmed that two new wards at Fairfield, numbers 9 and 15, could be opened and staffed as admissions areas for the Vietnamese orphans. Finally, needing someone to test and validate her plans, Vivian spoke to Val Seeger, her close friend and that night's charge sister, about what she hoped to do. The two experienced nurses agreed that it should work.

Furious activity the following morning saw all the necessary medical kit and nursing supplies packed and the nurses' party briefed by 9.30 a.m. The doctors and nurses then boarded a bus and, proceeding via the Heidelberg Repatriation Hospital to collect additional nurses, continued up the Hume Highway to Sydney. There, they were to board a commercial flight to Bangkok the next day to meet a RAAF C-130 that would be waiting for them. That aircraft would carry them to Saigon to collect the orphans before returning with them, via Bangkok and on a commercial airliner, to Melbourne and the Fairfield Hospital. All obvious steps to make the evacuation flight a success had been taken – all who required them were given cholera vaccinations that morning – and the bus trip to Sydney was useful for talking through various medical and logistic scenarios.

The evacuation team arrived at Sydney's Kingsford Smith Airport in the late afternoon and were taken to a lounge in the terminal. They were told there at 7 p.m. that their mission had been cancelled. Their only consolation was that they would now be flown back to Melbourne rather than having to repeat the road trip. Back at Fairfield the following day, Vivian received another call informing her that the flight had been cancelled because of a breakdown in negotiations between the Australian and South Vietnamese governments. Those negotiations were continuing, though, and Vivian and her staff should remain prepared to fly to Saigon at very short notice.

•

Public appetite, expectation and pressure to do something continued to build in Australia. On 5 April, the Victorian Social Welfare Department announced that it could not handle any more applications to adopt South Vietnamese orphans. Two days later, the Western Australian Department of Community Welfare announced that it, too, would be closing its adoption books. In just a few days, eight hundred Western Australian families had lodged applications with the department for the adoption of Vietnamese orphans.[10] The department noted that it normally received about nine hundred applications a year.

•

If there was pressure on the Australian government, there was usually pressure on Geoffrey Price and this time was no exception. Again, it started with an Immediate cable from Canberra arriving on his desk on 6 April, opening with the sentence, 'The Prime Minister has decided a second flight to evacuate a further group of orphans should take place as soon as possible . . ,'[11] That flight was put on hold by the South Vietnamese government's suspension of all evacuation flights later the same day. By the time the suspension was reversed, Price had already begun working on a second Babylift flight, and the next day sent an interim report to Canberra.

In that report, the Australian ambassador said it was very difficult to find the number of orphans that Canberra had requested – an initial figure of two hundred had been bandied about – and that the deadlines Canberra was suggesting were increasingly unrealistic given the circumstances on the ground in Saigon. Price detailed how the number of children available for adoption in Saigon had rapidly and suddenly declined in recent days with many of the major adoption agencies being literally cleaned out. This meant that the embassy now had to deal directly with local orphanages if it was to find enough children to justify a second RAAF airlift to Australia.

Preparing his report during the morning of 7 April, Price informed Canberra that by late the previous evening he had nothing more than vague promises of up to one hundred orphans being made available for repatriation to Australia. Unfortunately, very few of that number had the necessary paperwork completed. Price concluded that 'the competition for orphans had now become very intense . . .'[12] The sentence does not appear to have been written with any deliberate irony.

•

This would probably have been surprising news to Rosemary Taylor and her few remaining volunteers. Some time in those confused days, Rosemary had read a report in the *Saigon Post* that suggested the Australian government had agreed to take an unlimited number of South Vietnamese orphans provided those orphans were going to Australian parents. Knowing that hundreds of prospective parents had applied to welfare departments across the country and knowing that her friends and supporters had set up temporary facilities in Australia to receive and house orphans, she believed that common sense dictated that those facilities should be used to hold orphans who had been removed from harm's way until the hundreds of prospective parents had been approved. It would probably turn out that there were more parents than children but, if the opposite was the case, the extra children could be transferred to FFAC facilities in North America.

Several times in several days, Rosemary approached the Australian Embassy to check on the veracity of the *Saigon Post* article and to float the idea of housing FFAC orphans in Australia. Each time she was rebuffed. Australia could and would accept South Vietnamese orphans and had aircraft and personnel on standby to do just that. However, the only orphans they would evacuate would be those who had identified and approved adoptive parents waiting for them in Australia. There would be no space made available for orphans who 'might' find Australian parents or who were in transit to parents in other countries. There would be no exceptions to the rule and no appeals against the rule.

So Rosemary became something of a spectator during the last days of the life of the Republic of South Vietnam. The temporary suspension of the second Australian Babylift operation would give planners and organisers in Canberra, Melbourne and Saigon additional time to address some of the problems that had emerged during the Angel of Mercy operation, and that was a good thing. However, it would also give the NVA and Vietcong forces now closing in on Saigon the additional time they might need to capture the city. In the end, on all sides, it looked very much like a race against time.

15

GHOSTS IN THE FOG

Tullamarine, 18 April

Despite public utterances about success on all levels, those closest to the Angel of Mercy evacuation flight knew how haphazard the whole operation had been and how close the Australian government had come to flying into Sydney an aircraft carrying significant numbers of dead, dying and extremely distressed children. The temporary suspension of the second Australian orphan evacuation flight provided an opportunity, albeit brief, to quickly review what had gone wrong with the first flight's planning and organisation to attempt to ensure that the very same issues did not affect the second. The Immigration Department took the lead in this.

Several key issues were quickly identified and documented, and most were not apparent until shortly before the Qantas 747 touched down in Sydney. For instance, the exact number of orphans the aircraft was carrying was not known until after it had landed and the children were counted by immigration officials. Those same officers were not informed until twenty-five minutes before the aircraft landed that there were a number of children aboard who would require immediate hospitalisation and, even then, they were only told there would be ten or twelve orphans involved. However, when the Commonwealth's Chief Medical Officer boarded the aircraft to briefly examine the orphans, he immediately increased this number to seventy. It was the correct assessment, but it would cause transportation and other problems downstream.

Not only were the numbers of those children a mystery for those waiting in Sydney, so were their details. The age range proved to be wider than expected, with some children in their teens, one just a few days old and most seeming to be around three. After landing and a final examination by local medical staff, authorities found that most children aboard the Angel of Mercy needed medical attention. All were dehydrated and all needed food and water. Their dehydration levels were such that they were immediately rehydrated, irrespective of whether they were being taken to the North Head Quarantine Station or directly to hospital.

Transportation was also a problem. Because most children were very young and very small, putting them on individual bus seats to Quarantine Station was completely unsuitable. If future orphan convoys were to be carried aboard buses, each child would need to be accompanied by an adult and would need to be sitting on that escort's lap. Those escorts would need to be fresh. The escorts and carers who had travelled with the children aboard the Angel of Mercy were physically, psychologically and emotionally drained by the time they arrived in Sydney and were simply unable to give any more than they had already given.

Finally, all involved in that first Australian Babylift flight agreed that it would have been far better to have too many escorts and carers in the air and on the ground than to have too few. It had been a stress and a strain for all involved in Saigon, Bangkok and on the flight, and more staff – many more staff – would have made it easier for all involved. The report also suggested removing most agency volunteers from the process, as they tended to interfere and have strong opinions of their own.[1]

•

Things just didn't seem to be getting any better for Geoffrey Price and his reduced staff at the Australian Embassy. Amid the scramble to maintain diplomatic and consular services (and appearances) the federal Coalition opposition decided to send a 'fact-finding mission' to Saigon. Led by prominent Coalition figures Ian Sinclair and Andrew Peacock, the group had little to see and less to do, but they did require a degree of briefing and a modicum of escorting to official meetings, and so diverted resources from dozens of other things Price thought would be a better use of his staff's time and energy. One of those things was finding orphans for the second Australian Babylift.

On 9 April, another Immediate cable landed on Price's desk. Again it was from DFA in Canberra and again it opened with the ominous words, 'The Prime Minister has confirmed that we should go ahead with a second uplift of orphans from Saigon, staging through Bangkok.'[2] This time, too, conditions were clearly delineated around each and every child selected for evacuation. Canberra now insisted that for each orphan put aboard the aircraft, the embassy held authenticated proof that both parents were either deceased or irrevocably lost to the child. If either parent was still alive, the embassy must hold a genuine certificate stating that the parent had agreed that the child should be adopted.[3] Such documentation would counter claims that the children being evacuated were not genuine orphans, but it was also an additional impost on an already overtaxed embassy staff.

Finding enough orphans to fill a passenger jet proved to be more difficult than even Price had suspected it might be. There were still thousands of children in Saigon's orphanages and nurseries, with hundreds more arriving weekly as part of the refugee stream from the provinces. The problem was the conditions the Australian government had placed upon the selection process for eligible evacuees. The conditions specified in the 9 April cable would take months to complete in normal times and April 1975 in Saigon was certainly far from normal. In Australia, the process for approving suitable adopting families had been overwhelmed by the sheer numbers seeking that approval, while Whitlam's insistence that Australia would not ever be used as a transit point further shrank the potential pool of evacuees.

By 14 April, Price and his team had been able to identify just sixty-four potentially suitable orphans. They identified another five children with Vietnamese mothers and expatriate Australian fathers who could – at a stretch – also be included in the airlift. They had further identified several other Vietnamese mothers whose children had quite solid claims to repatriation, but it was proving almost impossible to source the numbers that Canberra was suggesting.

A lifeline of sorts appeared from a most unusual source. Eric Nicholls, a Methodist minister from Adelaide, arrived in Saigon at the same time as Geoffrey Price's team was trying to source orphans. Nicholls was president of the South Australian branch of the Australian Society for Inter-Country Aid to Children (ASIAC), a charity committed to helping at-risk children through sponsorship, the provision of food, medical supplies and clothes, and adoption. Nicholls was also a hard worker and he and his wife had already adopted two Cambodian and two Vietnamese children, so he knew his way through and around the various adoption protocols at home and in South Vietnam. He also had several ASIAC members back in Adelaide who had been approved as adoptive parents. Each day in Saigon, he would source a few orphans here and there and take them back to Newhaven where Susan McDonald would help look after them. With Eric Nicholls's assistance, Geoffrey Price thought he might be able to meet the numbers Canberra had set.

With that in mind, Price drafted and sent a cable to Canberra outlining his hopes of finding a suitable contingent of orphans. Included in the cable were some of his own suggestions based on what he and his team had learned from the first Australian Babylift flight. Price estimated that at least twenty of the children being sent back to Australia were less than twelve months old and would need closer monitoring than the older children they would dispatch. For this flight, he therefore believed that a ratio of one attendant for every four orphans would be appropriate.[4] He also very strongly suggested that the RAAF C-130s not be considered for any leg of the evacuation flight. They were not suitable for carrying children and Price believed that using them would put the orphans' health at risk.

•

Price's cable may have passed another somewhere in the ether as a cable arrived from Canberra addressing some of the issues he had raised soon after his own cable had been sent from Saigon.[5] The inward cable informed Price of the arrangements put in place for the second Babylift flight. The chartered Qantas Boeing 707 would depart Sydney at 11 a.m. on 16 April and fly to Melbourne to collect the evacuation party. That party would comprise both a medical component and an official component, consisting of officials from the relevant government departments and agencies to be responsible for immigration protocols for the orphans and carers. After boarding the evacuation party and its equipment and supplies, the aircraft would depart for Bangkok, arriving at 7.50 p.m. local time. The medical staff and officials would then proceed to Saigon at a time nominated by Saigon, probably the next day.

For the return flight, Qantas wanted to depart Bangkok at 6.35 p.m. on 17 April. This direct flight to Melbourne would be met by a fleet of buses and ambulances to transport the children directly to the Fairfield Infectious Diseases Hospital. Price was informed that the senior official in the party would again be the Commonwealth Health Department's Dr W. A. 'Spike' Langsford and that the medical party would include Dr John Forbes from Fairfield Hospital, other medical specialists, two translators and a team of thirty nurses led by Vivian Bullwinkel.[6]

•

At around the same time as Geoffrey Price received the operational plan's outline in Saigon, Vivian Bullwinkel received a similar notification at Fairfield. Hers contained some additional and different detail. Now, only around eighty orphans were to be airlifted back to Australia, a sharp reduction from the two hundred suggested ten days earlier, and the medical and support staff would be reduced in size accordingly. Thirty staff would now be taken, twenty-two nurses and medical orderlies from the Heidelberg Repatriation Hospital, and eight from Fairfield Hospital. Those eight would include John Forbes, another doctor, Val Seeger and four other nurses plus Vivian, again acting as matron for the flight.

Vivian immediately drew up a list of supplies and equipment she believed would be essential. Starting her list she included plenty of disposable nappies, a variety of milk products, but especially milk with a low fat content, and plenty of feeding bottles to distribute it. They would need the usual baby and toddler food plus normal meals for the older children. Medically, there were anti-diarrhoeal medicines, saline solution – and a way of introducing it to babies suffering from dehydration – plus glucose and oral electrolyte fluids. Finally, they would need several carry cots, if they could be sourced in time.[7]

•

As the second Australian Babylift flight drew closer, there were ongoing complications at the Saigon end. There, South Vietnamese authorities now also insisted that any orphans nominated for evacuation be matched with adoptive parents in Australia. (As it turned out, two unmatched children would travel, but their status as genuine orphans was irrelevant.) The general unavailability of orphans for Australian adoption also resulted in the target figure being successively reduced, with eighty becoming aspirational and only seventy-five more or less confirmed on the eve of the chartered aircraft leaving Australia.

There was a solution to this problem, but Rosemary Taylor and her orphans were never going to be allowed to be anything but bit players in the Australian Babylift operations. They were approached again in those last few days and asked whether any of their children – new or old, healthy or ill – had confirmed adoptive parents in Australia. They had children in all four of those categories but only two of those children had been assigned to Australian families. Both were offered places on the forthcoming evacuation flight, an offer Rosemary accepted.

Children with assigned parents in other countries were not considered but, in the last two days before the flight, Australian authorities agreed to evacuate urgent medical cases for treatment in Australia; presumably, they would be repatriated when that treatment had been completed. It was too little, too late, though. With the South Vietnamese government collapsing there was no one to approve their exit visas and the children remained in Saigon.

•

The best-laid plans often go astray, and so it would be with the second Australian Babylift operation. Rather than waiting for an aircraft at Tullamarine, the medical team again travelled to Sydney by coach, and at 1.45 p.m. on Thursday 17 April boarded a Qantas 707 for the nine-hour flight to Bangkok. Vivian used that flight time to prepare her nursing contingent for what was to come. She began by dividing them into two teams and assigning several specific tasks to each team. Team One would transfer to an RAAF C-130 at Bangkok and fly the short hop to Saigon. (Despite the C-130's shortfalls on the first Australian Babylift mission, and Geoffrey Price's forceful recommendations, C-130s would be used for the evacuation's Saigon–Bangkok leg, probably because of the prohibitive cost of insuring civil aircraft flying into Saigon.) In Saigon, Team One would sort the orphans into broad categories based on their age and the level of care and support they would need on the return flight to Australia.

The remaining nurses, now officially designated Team Two, remained in Bangkok and were responsible for converting the Qantas 707 into the type of mobile hospital and nursery that Vivian believed they would need. The aircraft's interior was segmented, with each area configured to support a specific function. The aircraft's rear section was set up for the babies and for older children presenting symptoms of serious illnesses. The central section was configured for those needing normal care and monitoring while the forward section, normally reserved for first-class passengers, would be used as a staff meals and rest area.

A misunderstanding with Thai authorities about clearance checks meant that all the Australians had to stay overnight in Bangkok. Team One, led by Vivian, departed for Saigon aboard an RAAF C-130 early the next morning.[8] After the relative luxury of the Qantas 707, the C-130 was very obviously a workhorse of the air. Seating along either side of the main cabin comprised side-mounted, drop-down aluminium seats with webbing back supports. Apart from a cleared walkway down the middle of that cabin, all the aircraft's cargo space was stacked floor to ceiling with packing cases. At the front of the aircraft, the flight deck and the flight crew sat high above this mass of people and cargo.

There was no air conditioning aboard the C-130, and the interior became as hot and humid as a sauna when all the doors were closed. Those conditions were alleviated somewhat at a higher altitude but any relief was more than cancelled out by the engine noise, an assault on the eardrums that made any form of conversation virtually impossible. Fortunately, the flight was a short hop rather than a long haul, and two hours after boarding, everyone lined up to disembark. The C-130 made its final approach to Tan Son Nhut low and fast to avoid possible ground fire, and as soon as it rolled to a stop the cargo ramp was lowered and Vivian, the doctors and nurses exited quickly.

Not far away across the tarmac, a small group of uniformed Australian airmen waited, and the medical team followed a loadmaster to meet them. After introductions, one of the men in uniform, the senior officer present, pointed out another two

C-130s parked on the tarmac a short distance away. Both had their engines running and both had their cargo ramp doors down. Vivian and her nurses were addressed by another officer who explained that the orphans had already been loaded onto the aircraft directly from the buses that had brought them to the airport, while the Australians were en route from Bangkok. Working with their carers, RAAF nurses and loadmasters had placed all the babies on one aircraft and the toddlers and small children on the other. Vivian quickly divided her team between the two C-130s, where there was a quick handover and a teary farewell from the carers. Vivian was the last to board the babies' flight and soon after the ramps were raised and within minutes both aircraft were in the air.

When her aircraft levelled off at its cruising altitude, Vivian unbuckled her seatbelt and went to inspect the cargo for which she and her nurses had now assumed responsibility. After a cursory check of the babies, Vivian realised that there were several serious shortcomings in the carrying arrangements. The babies had been placed in the cardboard boxes prepared at Butterworth two weeks earlier, with some containing one, others containing two and one even containing three babies. Most of those were distressed and crying, all were sweaty and grimy and, to Vivian, far too many showed obvious signs of malnourishment. One baby, whose name tag declared they were eighteen months old, was later found to be a badly undernourished three-year-old.

During the flight back to Bangkok, doctors and nurses on both aircraft examined the orphans to determine what ailments they had and to assess what kind of specialised treatment each might require on the long-haul flight back to Australia. What they found was like a catalogue of tropical and Third World medical problems. Among the conditions were a range of internal infections including shigella, an intestinal disease caused by parasites, while most of the children were believed to be infested by a range of other parasites. There were a series of skin infections and diseases, boils, abscesses and scabies – infections caused by lice and by poor nutrition and hygiene.

Several children appeared to be suffering from more serious and communicable diseases, among them chickenpox, whooping cough and salmonella. Several were assessed as having respiratory infections, some with suspected tuberculosis, while all, without exception, were judged to be malnourished to a greater or lesser degree. During these examinations and initial treatments, one orphan on Vivian's aircraft, an eight-month-old boy, died.[9]

At Bangkok, the transfer of the orphans from the RAAF aircraft to the Qantas 707 was completed quickly and without any of the histrionics that had accompanied the first Babylift flight. Thai authorities provided both assistance and support, and within just over an hour they were all back in the air. For Vivian, it was especially pleasing to see what her Team Two had achieved in her absence. The Qantas 707 had been converted from a passenger aircraft into a flying children's hospital and nursery. The orphans also noted the change, with some falling asleep shortly after take-off and others immediately wolfing down the food they were offered.

It would be a long night for both medical staff and cabin crew aboard the 707. They were carrying seventy-four children whose ages ranged from a few weeks to several years, children who had never travelled on an aircraft before and most of whom were tired and ill. The night was a constant blur of action – changing nappies, feeding babies with formula and older children with foods they might never have eaten before, while monitoring the health and wellbeing of them all. It proved to be a complete team effort, both flight attendants and nurses acknowledging that neither could have done it without the other.

After a nine-hour flight through the night, the second Babylift flight landed at Melbourne's Tullamarine Airport in the early morning light of Friday 18 April. It touched down amid patches of fog and taxied across the tarmac, not to the main terminal but to a long line of waiting ambulances. As it did so, it almost disappeared into several thicker fog patches only to emerge into the open again. To one of the few reporters sent out to cover the event, the orphans of Babylift Two seemed to arrive in Melbourne like ghosts in the mist.[10]

Two children did not board those ambulances. Upon their arrival, one was released into the care of her natural mother while a second was handed over to his father and almost immediately left on another flight to Western Australia. The remaining seventy-two were placed in either the ambulances or in one of three small buses there for the medical team.[11] When they arrived at Fairfield Hospital the two new wards were ready for them, but Vivian noticed a distinct wariness among the older children. Part of it was no doubt due to all the changes they had been through in recent days and part of it may have been due to the weather being far cooler than anything they had previously experienced. But, she thought, a lot of their discomfort probably came from recognising that they were in an institution that was staffed by people in uniforms.

At Fairfield, the facilities allowed for more detailed medical examinations, which confirmed much of what the evacuation aircraft's medical team had found or suspected. Malnourishment remained the most common affliction, but tests revealed several more serious underlying issues. Fifteen orphans were carrying hepatitis B, four were carrying salmonella and one had been born with congenital syphilis. Pneumonia was also identified in several children. Those who required immediate and ongoing treatment remained in hospital until they were well enough to be placed in the care of their adoptive parents, and all children were moved on as soon as they were fit to travel.

In the meantime, Vivian and her nurses were given several stark reminders of what the orphans' previous lives had been like. They observed how many overate when food was served and were also surprised at how many hoarded food against the possibility that there might not be any more to come. For the first week, too, there were problems with getting the older children to sleep. Several became very distressed if they found their bed was near a door or a window, and several would crawl under their bed or cot and sleep there. Eventually, in the older children's ward, the nursing sisters found a solution. A number of beds were pushed together in the centre of the room and several lights in the ward were left on overnight.

Despite Fairfield staff's best efforts, for some children a complete physical recovery would take a long time, and not all would make it. The week after the orphans arrived at Fairfield, late in the evening of Tuesday 23 April, one of the babies – a four-month-old boy – died. John Forbes attributed the death to 'generalised sepsis associated with malnutrition',[12] and stated that two other babies were struggling and remained in intensive care. A second baby, also a four-month-old boy, died at Fairfield in early May, the cause of death again being an infection complicated by malnutrition. Shortly afterwards, on 8 May, Forbes revealed that forty-four orphans remained at Fairfield receiving medical treatment, but that thirteen others had been released to their adoptive parents the previous day.

There would be two more tragedies before the last of the orphans left Fairfield. Another baby, just four months of age, died at Melbourne's Royal Children's Hospital on 29 May from pneumonia complicated by severe malnutrition. The final death, another four-month-old child, occurred on 17 June, again at the Royal Children's Hospital, caused by a combination of a bowel infection and pneumonia. By then, all but a handful of the Fairfield children were living with their new families.

•

The children's physical recovery was remarkable and after just a few days they were running around and playing their children's games in the wards, corridors and grounds of Fairfield Hospital. Their mental and emotional recovery was harder to determine, but Vivian and her nurses were pleasantly surprised by the ease with which the children formed strong bonds with the other children and with the staff, particularly the nurses assigned to their wards. Against this backdrop, bureaucrats were working steadily at both state and federal levels, checking documents and matching children with adoptive parents, then double-checking everything because any mistakes would be disastrous. With pressure to begin uniting children and families, within a week of their arrival Vivian was advised that the healthy older children should be prepared for adoption. The first four children to be adopted were transferred to South Australia on 30 April.[13]

Shortly after the children began leaving to join their new families, the letters started arriving. Most were addressed to Vivian, some were addressed to individual nurses and a few were addressed to the hospital itself. The letters were from the Babylift children's adoptive parents expressing profound feelings of appreciation and gratitude for the love and care that their new sons or daughters had been shown from the time they had been collected in Saigon. The letters continued to arrive in the coming weeks, months and even years. They, and the children's lives that each one represented, would become one of Vivian's most cherished memories as she moved from a career in nursing to a new life in retirement. In a lifetime of service to others, Vivian would sometimes think that caring for the Babylift orphans might just have been the most important service of all.[14]

16

SUNSET

SAIGON/CANBERRA, APRIL TO JUNE 1975

Operation Babylift continued throughout April, although at a much lower level than was seen during the first four days of its operation. Planning for the ongoing operation by American agencies, such as it was, appears to have been haphazard and was clearly impacted by external events, particularly the vicissitudes of the collapsing South Vietnamese war effort and the parallel collapse of the South Vietnamese government and its institutions. The original USAID evacuation program had envisioned thirty evacuation flights, with babies and small children being the priority evacuees. Both proved to be aspirational targets in many respects.

All up, there were more than thirty evacuation flights, but many of them were unauthorised and therefore not part of Operation Babylift. Ed Daly's World Airways made two more refugee evacuation flights from Tan Son Nhut despite being formally banned from doing so, while a number of chartered aircraft flew out refugees, including orphans, again operating outside the formal Operation Babylift framework. Finally, commercial carriers continued to fly scheduled services into Saigon until the middle of April. There were only two carriers involved – Air France and Pan Am – and their flights were few and far between, but both evacuated significant numbers of orphans as well as large numbers of expatriates and government officials fleeing the country. It was elements of this unofficial evacuation that continued to give rise to rumours of corruption and malfeasance.

Removing orphans from South Vietnam, irrespective of how it was posited in humanitarian terms, was always going to attract criticism, not least because the whole saga of the war in Vietnam had polarised opinion around the world. While there might have been legitimate concerns about the motives and attitudes of some of the prospective foster and adoptive parents who volunteered when South Vietnam was collapsing, far more damage was done to public confidence by a spate of stories that questioned the underlying morality of what Babylift was attempting to achieve. The stories ranged from legitimate concerns about what the airlift was actually saving the babies from to suggestions that there was no legitimate reason to believe that the orphans would be any worse off under a communist government than they had been under a capitalist government, and perhaps might even be better off. Other stories that circulated, though, were pure sensationalism.

Among those that did the rounds was a story suggesting that prospective parents in Country X – the location changed with the story – were shopping around the adoption agencies asking in particular for 'a light-skinned baby with not too-slanty eyes'.[1] In other reports, there were breathless exclusives that Eurasian babies in Saigon were being sold as 'passports', living talismans that guaranteed the owner/parent passage through all the security checkpoints at Tan Son Nhut. While such reports should have been seen as the fantasies they were, they were accepted at face value by those opposed to both the war and the Babylift operation.

More concerns would be raised, and would linger for years afterwards, by those stories based on fact rather than fantasy. In all countries involved in the evacuations – including Australia – a number of the 'orphans' airlifted out were found to not be orphans at all, but rather the children or other relatives of South Vietnamese officials or South Vietnamese with privileged access. There were also reports coming out of Saigon that the Babylift operation was extremely unpopular with the South Vietnamese themselves, who were upset and angry that the Americans chose to fly out planeloads of children who would probably be safe under a communist regime, while displaying little apparent concern about the fate of people who had fought for and worked with them.[2] It was a vexing time for many.

•

It was a more than vexing time for Rosemary Taylor and the other volunteers who had remained in Saigon. There were only a handful of them now – Wende Grant and several others had flown back to the United States on the third official Babylift flight – but again they were in danger of being overwhelmed by numbers. By 24 April, their once almost-empty nurseries were rapidly filling up again, with numbers growing from just over twenty to more than 250. There had been promises – many promises – of an aircraft to evacuate the bulk of them to North America, but during the previous week there had been no concrete action behind those promises. That changed when USAID informed Rosemary that a C-141 transport aircraft would arrive at Tan Son Nhut on 26 April and could evacuate around two hundred of her orphans. Susan McDonald volunteered to supervise the operation for FFAC.

Early on 26 April, the scenes from three weeks before were repeated at Tan Son Nhut. A convoy of buses had proceeded from Allambie to the airport carrying two hundred and fifty orphans from the remaining FFAC nurseries; around twenty children considered unfit to travel remained behind. At the airport the orphans' carers either carried or led the children out to the aircraft, where they were handed over to other carers or air force nurses. Several babies – the youngest, mainly – were carried in the cardboard boxes that had carefully been prepared for them. Inside the aircraft, the older children were strapped into the canvas seats attached to the sides of the fuselage, two to a seat, and strapped in place with a single seatbelt. The crew were able to seat seventy-five of the older children that way.

The babies, if not already in their cardboard boxes, were placed in woven baskets specially carried for that purpose. The boxes and baskets were then placed securely at the aircraft's rear while all the other children were placed on blankets that were spread across the cargo area's floor. Susan and the other nurses and escorts were scattered throughout the aircraft, which would initially fly them to Clark Air Base. The loading was quick and efficient, and almost before anyone was ready for it, goodbyes were spoken and the C-141 was taxiing towards the runway. Rosemary watched it go: 'As the plane moved away, I felt an immediate sense of relief and freedom, such as I'd never before experienced. The burden of all those children for so many years had been weighing intolerably. Now we were alone and the children in other hands.'[3]

•

Although Operation Babylift would officially run for another week, Susan McDonald's C-141 flight on Saturday 26 April was the last orphan evacuation flight from Saigon. She and 250 babies and small children flew from Tan Son Nhut to Clark Air Base, a journey made more interesting than expected when they ran out of fresh water an hour after take-off. At Clark, the evacuees spent their first night in the gymnasium and the next several days waiting to fly to the United States. There was only a single flight out each day, but that flight would carry each child in their own special seat and there would be one escort for every two children.

Susan was eventually flown back to America aboard one of these flights, later saying that landing in the United States was like landing in heaven, with a line-up of ambulances, doctors and prospective parents there to welcome them. She was especially happy to be back in a place where all babies were expected to live and where she wouldn't have to bury one of her precious children before they had been given a fair chance at life.

•

There were no Australian officials at Tan Son Nhut to see Operation Babylift's last flight take off that day because, by 26 April, there were no Australian officials left in South Vietnam. All remaining officials, including any associated with Detachment S operations in humanitarian support and orphan evacuation, had been withdrawn the previous day.

Earlier that month, the deteriorating security situation in Saigon saw the flight elements of Detachment S withdrawn from that city and relocated to Bangkok. From there, the detachment would fly several relief missions each day, departing early in the morning and returning late in the evening. Its principal task was always the same and entailed flying to An Thoi on Phu Quoc island, the site of what had been a notorious prisoner-of-war camp. Now, though, it was a temporary refuge for some forty thousand civilians who had fled just a few weeks earlier from the northern cities of Hue and Da Nang, just ahead of the communists and aboard a convoy of ten very overcrowded freighters. Each day, the C-130s of Detachment S would fly to the island carrying up to 13 500 kilograms of rice or other items such as powdered milk, bread, meat, fuel and canvas for making shelters.[4] All that came to an end on 24 April when the unit was ordered to evacuate the remaining Australian official presence in South Vietnam the next day.

Geoffrey Price continued to be frustrated in his attempts to run the evacuation in the way he believed most appropriate and would later – again – blame the prime minister for micro-managing and in doing so preventing Price from discharging his responsibilities as Australia's Ambassador to South Vietnam. He was particularly keen to arrange passage to Australia for his locally engaged staff, fearing that they would be subjected to some form of retribution if they were still there when the communists took over. His wishes in this area were frustrated from the start. While Price was not aware of Whitlam's instructions about the admission of adult Vietnamese to Australia, he soon became aware of delays in the paperwork for his staff's visa approvals. Price always believed that these delays were deliberate.

This time the sticking point was Canberra's insistence that all South Vietnamese nationals hoping to be evacuated to Australia had to hold valid exit visas from their government. Probably acting on advice, the South Vietnamese working at the Australian Embassy had delayed applying for exit visas until the last possible moment and, when they did, found there was no longer a functioning bureaucracy able to approve those applications. Price could plead for special circumstances all he liked, but those pleas fell upon deaf ears. It was Rosemary Taylor and the orphans all over again, and once more the outcome was depressingly familiar. Some 130 South Vietnamese who Price believed should have been airlifted to Australia were left behind to face an uncertain future.

There were two scheduled RAAF evacuation flights from Tan Son Nhut that day, and between them they would carry seventy-eight South Vietnamese nationals on the first leg of their journey into exile in Australia. However, of that number only six were locally engaged staff. The others included two more orphans, eleven Australian diplomatic staff and a party of thirty-four nuns from the order of the Congregation of Mary the Great, included at the request of 'a member of the Roman Catholic hierarchy', who was not subsequently identified.[5]

The first of the day's two flights carried all the South Vietnamese nuns and the two orphans; the second, the Australian Embassy staff, nine Australian journalists, the six approved South Vietnamese staff and a very full load of personal belongings. The second flight was a lot later in the day and was a slower, more confronting and more emotional departure than the first. The emotion was generated by Geoffrey Price and his diplomatic staff's farewells to the Vietnamese who had worked for and supported the Australians through some very trying times in recent months. Price made certain that all those travelling were driven to Tan Son Nhut in the embassy's official cars and, once there, he handed over the keys to all the cars to the Vietnamese staff remaining in Saigon. Then he and all the other Australians took whatever Vietnamese and American currency they were carrying and passed that to their former staff members as well.

It was emotional for everyone when the Vietnamese left to face whatever fate had in store for them, but the Australians were brought back to earth with a thud. When it came time to load the C-130, the loadmaster found that the ambassador's party had far more baggage than had been estimated.[6] Protocol dictated that the ambassador, his staff and their baggage had priority, so four RAAF security guards were left behind, much to their mortification,[7] when the ambassador's C-130 took off shortly after 7 p.m. Fortunately, a second C-130 had been circling off the coast in case of an emergency. It was called in to pick up the four airmen, plus some baggage that wouldn't fit on the previous flight. There was a bit of light-hearted pushing and shoving at the aircraft's ramp and, when it was over, the last Australian serviceman departed Vietnam sixty years to the day after the first Australian serviceman had splashed ashore at Gallipoli.

•

On 22 April, a US Army major told Rosemary that she would have to be evacuated 'very soon'. She replied that she would not be leaving while the children she was responsible for had not been evacuated themselves.[8] That evacuation occurred on 26 April, and Rosemary knew that if she, Ilse Ewald and Doreen Beckett were again told they were to be evacuated, they would go. Until then, Rosemary would tie up any loose ends she found. One was financial. She realised that the orphanages would need money for at least twelve months after their children were placed in case the placement failed, so tried to cash in what assets she could while also giving away others to staff and other orphanages like Phu My, which would still be operating after they left.

After several more warnings about an imminent evacu-ation, Rosemary, Ilse and Doreen were finally summoned to the

US Embassy on 29 April where, after waiting several hours, they climbed up a stairway to the embassy roof to be evacuated in one of the last helicopters to carry evacuees away from Saigon. After a short flight, the three women were put down on the deck of the USS *Blue Ridge*, sitting off the coast as a transit point for evacuees. The next day, North Vietnamese forces smashed into Saigon.

•

At 11.30 a.m. on 5 May, a telegram was delivered to the prime minister's office in Canberra. Sent from the SS *Greenport* the previous day, it read:

> Australian citizens Doreen Beckett Rosemary Taylor arriving Subic Bay Philippines Sunday 4 aboard Vietnam evacuation ship Greenport bound Guam. Wish desperately to disembark Philippines and continue commercial airlines. Have financial wherewithal but no Philippine visa please intercede with Philippine authority to grant transit visa on arrival and transfer to airport. Impossible without your intervention help us please; conditions aboard unspeakable.

A marginal note was added to the telegram: 'Advised by Miss J. Crawford (DFA) that Miss Taylor was seen by Consul official on Saturday – she will have to continue on to Guam as Philippines authorities will not allow evacuees to be off-loaded and trans-ship. Commercial flight from Guam will be possible.'[9]

•

The Whitlam government would subsequently be widely criticised for the small number of South Vietnamese refugees it allowed into Australia both before and after the fall of the country to communist forces. Rather than a confusion of competing priorities, that outcome was the result of specific policies, of hurdles that were deliberately put in place.[10] On 14 April, Prime Minister Whitlam told the Immigration Department to suspend processing Vietnamese migrant applications for those who would be eligible for consideration 'within the normal guidelines of Australian immigration policy'.[11] Eight days later, he announced that Australia would only accept applications from spouses and children of Australian citizens and of Vietnamese students living in Australia. Additionally, and on a case-by-case basis, Australia would consider applications from Vietnamese with 'long and close associations with the Australian presence in Vietnam and whose lives would be in danger'.[12] The prime minister would confirm these criteria several times in the coming weeks while, as a final impediment, he insisted that any Vietnamese approved should only be granted temporary rather than permanent resident status.

The restrictions Whitlam insisted upon created a degree of unrest in the bureaucracy and in Cabinet. Senior officers in DFA pointed out that the criteria now being applied meant that the Immigration Department was refusing the entry into Australia of people who normally would be approved if they were any other nationality but Vietnamese. It became a political point of difference, too, with Opposition Leader Malcolm Fraser pointing out that the prime minister appeared to be narrowing the immigration criteria for just a single nationality. Foreign Minister Don Willesee, increasingly isolated, opposed this restrictive approach and tried to change Whitlam's mind, but Whitlam had the support of other senior ministers. Clyde Cameron, for example, 'could see no reason why we should take the risk of opening our doors to war criminals'.[13]

Two things forced Whitlam to adopt a slightly different approach to Vietnamese refugees. The first was public opinion.

In early May, DFA reported to Cabinet that it was receiving letters – hundreds of them – running thirty to one in favour of admitting more Vietnamese refugees. The second, related to the first, was the government's continuing fear that its stance vis-à-vis Vietnamese immigration, be that by orphans or refugees, was becoming an electoral liability. The outcome was the announcement of some concrete steps to address the issue. In June 1975, a team of immigration officials was sent to Hong Kong to select 201 refugees from the camps there for resettlement in Australia. The next month, a second team was sent to Singapore and Malaysia to select another three hundred refugees.

Again, there were many who argued, both then and in the many years since, that this was another case of the government offering far too little far too late. The United Nations estimated that by early June 1975 more than 140 000 South Vietnamese had fled their homeland; by the end of September just a few more than 1100 had been approved for entry to Australia as refugees. Soon there was a change of government and a change of policy that would continue under both conservative and progressive administrations. Between 1976 and 1986, more than 94 000 Vietnamese refugees were accepted for resettlement in Australia, including more than two thousand who arrived by boat. Those refugees, their children and grandchildren have made a deep and lasting contribution to the fabric of the multicultural society that Australia is today.

EPILOGUE
PICTURES OF CHILDREN

The exact number of children airlifted out of Saigon in the last
weeks of the war will never be known because record-keeping
took second place behind the joint winners in Operation Babylift:
political expediency and urgency. Around 2900 children were
flown to North America, primarily Vietnamese orphans but
also Cambodian children destined for adoptive families in the
United States and Canada. Another thousand or so were sent
to the United States as a transit point on a journey to another
destination, most probably in Western Europe. Some 150 orphans
were flown directly to the United Kingdom and perhaps the same
number directly to other European nations. Australia accepted
266 orphans, 194 from the first Angel of Mercy flight to Sydney
and seventy-two on the subsequent flight to Melbourne. All have
interesting and important stories to tell.

•

The very first Operation Babylift flight ended in disaster in a
muddy rice paddy on the outskirts of Saigon. Today at the crash
site, in one corner of a field, there is a homemade memorial

to those who perished in the accident. It comprises a number of religious symbols on and around a piece of the C-5A's tail-plane, and over the years it has attracted a growing number of visitors. If those visitors talk to the locals, they will hear any one of a number of stories that have grown up around what happened there.

Some will hear that the memorial is not really a memorial at all, but rather a shrine built to appease the restless spirits of those who had died so violently there. One of the elderly women from a nearby village may explain how the ghosts of babies and children haunt the area and that the spirits of those who died remain trapped at the spot where they died. Others may tell of a second altar that Westerners do not know about or visit; it is for the spirits of the South Vietnamese militia and several Vietcong fighters who were also killed when the giant aircraft crashed down. They will tell of passers-by who had sometimes seen the ghosts and how some of the other villagers, never them, are frightened that the ghosts might try to steal their children.[1]

Most older villagers are always willing to recount their stories about what happened on that Friday all those years ago, even if those memories are sometimes at odds with what others recalled about the incident. The area where the C-5A came down, An Phu Dong, is a lot more developed now than it was then, but old Mrs Tram has lived there all her life and has no intention of leaving. She still recalls how 'the plane couldn't fly . . . it made a whirring sound. It exploded into pieces, you know, and crashed on my brother's land.'[2] That brother was one of many villagers who rushed to the scene to find there was nothing they could do to help. He saw children lying dead in the mud and he saw scattered body parts, but he also saw survivors. Mrs Tram did not accompany the other villagers to the site because she was afraid of ghosts and knew they would be starting to gather there.[3]

•

The efforts to provide a hopeful future for at least some of South Vietnam's orphans, efforts that culminated in Operation Babylift in April 1975, exposed some villains but also threw up a lot of heroes. One of the latter was US Army chaplain Father Joe Turner. Turner returned to Saigon during the last weeks of the war, in his own time and at his own expense, and in two weeks there was able to find adoptive homes in the United States for twelve orphans, also organising their evacuation to their new homes. In peacetime, the army could not find a place for him. Passed over for promotion several times, possibly because of his advocacy on behalf of enlisted men, Father Joe returned to his home town of Philadelphia, where he spent the rest of his life engaged in street work and social activism. Falling victim to cancer, Father Joe Turner died in the Philadelphia Veterans' Affairs Hospital in July 2001. Aged seventy-three, and an orphan himself, Joe Turner had no known relatives.

Ed Daly, a hero to some and a villain to others, was always a larger-than-life figure. An English reporter based in Saigon at the time provided a pen picture of the March/April 1975 Ed Daly.

> Daly is a slow-talking, sharp-brained business tycoon who, if his airline business ever fails, should have no trouble getting bit parts in gangster movies. His face is craggy and deep-lined, his voice is gravelly and he has a taste for large doses of Bourbon whiskey which slow him down but rarely knock him out.[4]

Despite what appeared to be an absolute ban, Ed Daly and his World Airways remained involved in Operation Babylift and would eventually be directly responsible for the evacuation of 1090 orphans from South Vietnam. Daly would also subsequently be fined US$243 000 by the US Immigration Service for his unauthorised flights and would himself estimate that the various refugee and orphan flights cost World Airways around $2 million, an amount he paid out of his own funds. Times were tough for World Airways in the early 1980s when pre-existing financial difficulties were exacerbated by the deregulation of the airline industry. Ed Daly steered the company through the bad times but wasn't there for the good times he was convinced would follow. He died suddenly in 1984. World Airways would continue operating for another thirty years before going into receivership in March 2014.

Dennis 'Bud' Traynor and his co-pilot, Tilford Harp, were both subsequently awarded the Air Force Cross for their herculean efforts in almost saving their aircraft and those aboard that day. In all, some thirty-seven gallantry medals would be awarded to the C-5A crew members, or their next of kin, for a whole series of selfless acts during and after the crash. Traynor went on to a long and distinguished air force career and, in retirement, his thoughts returned to that day in April 1975. He started a Facebook group for survivors and relatives of those who were on his aircraft that day, a group that soon had two hundred members and organised an annual reunion that continues to this day.

Wende Grant continued her involvement in FFAC and orphan welfare, formally and informally, for the rest of her life. Wende and her husband, Duane, eventually adopted nine children, including six Vietnamese and two Cambodian children. Wende Steinorth Grant died in October 2010, a week before her one hundredth birthday. Wende's friend and fellow enthusiast for child welfare, the Canadian Naomi Bronstein, died just two months later in December 2010. Naomi died in Guatemala, aged sixty-five, and was still working when she suffered a massive and fatal heart attack. For some time previously, Naomi had been running a mobile health clinic for impoverished rural children.

Dr Merrit and Dorothy Stark returned to the United States and a decade later were living in a small southern city where Merrit, then almost seventy, was the medical director at a state hospital for the mentally disabled. Merrit's medical deputy on the doomed C-5A flight, Lieutenant Regina Aune, made an almost complete recovery from the severe injuries she suffered in the crash. Regina went on to raise a family with her husband, Bjorn, and have a successful air force career as well. Joining academia after that career, and after losing her husband, Regina Aune lives in semi-retirement in San Antonio, Texas.

Sister Susan McDonald's life was changed irrevocably by her experiences in Vietnam. After travelling back to the United States with the orphans of the last Babylift flight, she continued to Europe with subsequent convoys taking orphans to their new adoptive families. She escorted children to England and to France, staying briefly with the surviving members of Dolly Bui's family before escorting other children to Germany, where she visited Ilse Ewald. In the years to come, Susan lived and worked in Dacca, Bangladesh, alongside Mother Teresa's Missionaries of Charity in orphanages and refugee camps. Later, she worked in Guatemala following an earthquake there, nursed in Nicaragua, and lived and worked among the poor in Haiti.

Since 1998, Susan has been running Vietnamese Adoptee Services, a charitable organisation that assists the thousands of orphans that FFAC and other organisations managed to bring out of South-East Asia. The organisation operates from a home in Crestwood, part of greater St Louis in Missouri, and while the service is not directly affiliated with the Sisters of Loretto, Susan's order, they do provide the financial support that allows her to continue to operate. Part of what she has done and continues to do is establish both formal and informal networks that allow the former orphans to meet and exchange stories and hints about how to approach the common problems they all face.

Soon after she left Vietnam, Susan began having a recurring dream, one that would return at intervals long into the years ahead. In the dream, a friend comes to Susan and tells her that the C-5A has crashed and that the children were on it. Then she is at the crash site and she runs towards the broken and burning aircraft. As she gets closer she notices there are small pieces of paper floating and drifting in the air, first a few but then dozens as she draws closer to the plane, floating like snowflakes across the scene. The closer she approaches, the more there are, and she pauses to pluck one from the air. It is not an ordinary piece of paper, though – it is a photograph, a photograph of one of her orphans. And she turns and calls out to the others now gathering at the crash site: 'It's alright! There weren't any children on the plane. They were just pictures. Pictures of children.'[5]

•

Elaine Moir, dubbed 'The Waif Smuggler' by the Melbourne press for her achievements in 1972, continued her work on behalf of the orphaned and underprivileged for as long as she was able. In 2004, she was hard at work organising entry and exit visas for a group of seven Vietnamese children deemed suitable for corneal transplants at Australian hospitals. Later in life, Elaine was struck down by motor neurone disease and passed away at her Glen Iris home on 6 August 2012. The Waif Smuggler at home and the Dragon Lady in Saigon, this remarkable Australian passed her collection of notes, books and pamphlets on adoption reform in Australia and intercountry adoption to the National Library of Australia in Canberra, where they will remain an important resource for anyone interested in either area.

Rena Huxley (Briand), too, continued to follow her two passions: orphan welfare and writing. After two books on orphans in South Vietnam, she published a third on opal miners at Coober Pedy before again travelling overseas to become involved in intercountry adoptions, this time in Sri Lanka.

•

Geoffrey Price continued in the diplomatic service after the fall of South Vietnam and in December 1977 was appointed High Commissioner to Singapore, with subsequent postings as Ambassador to The Netherlands, Pakistan and Turkey before his retirement in 1994. A trenchant critic of Gough Whitlam's changing priorities and interference during the last days of South Vietnam's existence, Geoffrey Price died suddenly on 1 January 1999.

•

The mother superior of one of FFAC's feeder orphanages, possibly the orphanage at Vinh Long, wrote to the Makk family in Adelaide in the days following Lee's death. She had been with Lee on that final day, she wrote, and had travelled with her on the bus from Allambie to Tan Son Nhut. On that trip, Lee had sung gentle songs to the children in a language the mother superior did not recognise. It was certainly not Vietnamese, but nor was it English or French as the mother superior knew both those languages. Lee's family knew she would have been singing in Hungarian and singing the folk songs and lullabies she had learned when she was around the same age as the children she would die alongside.[6]

Gyoparka (Lee) Makk died on the day of her thirtieth birthday. Her ashes now rest with those of her parents at a cemetery in Brisbane, while a ward in a psychiatric unit in an Adelaide hospital commemorates her work.

●

During her time in Vietnam, Margaret Moses became a prolific writer of letters and poems in which she set down her thoughts about what she saw going on around her. Posthumously, some of her poems were published in an anthology entitled *Turn My Eyes Away*. There was a recurrent theme in much of what she wrote: 'I never got over the horror of children who had never lived, dying.' Margaret Moses senior used some of the settlement money she received (see Appendix) to establish the Margaret Moses Memorial Fund to help mothers in Vietnam, Thailand and Cambodia to raise their own children. Margaret Veronica Moses's ashes are buried at the Enfield Memorial Park in Adelaide's northern suburbs.

●

Rosemary Taylor made it to Guam, and from there flew to Denver, Colorado, where she joined the other volunteers to organise placements for the hundreds of orphans she had helped find new lives in the West. Once all the work had been done, she flew back to Adelaide to spend time with family and friends, to grieve for lost loved ones and to recharge her dangerously low batteries. She was at home on Australia Day, 26 January 1976, when her name was listed among others who had been awarded Australia Day honours she was made a Member of the Order of Australia. The accompanying citation stated that the award was 'for service to the community in the field of international relations.'

For most of the two years following the fall of South Vietnam, Rosemary Taylor was on the move, travelling around the world to assist with the placement of FFAC's orphans, provide after-placement advice and assistance when necessary, and take part in the process of determining the post-Vietnam direction that FFAC would follow. All the time, she could feel the pressure starting to build. Her advice was constantly sought, and she found that her opinions sometimes carried a weight she wasn't certain they deserved. Rosemary felt the weight of expectations and it wasn't a weight that she was comfortable carrying. In 1977, she visited a second-hand bookshop in London, bought dozens of books and took them to a remote farmhouse in France. For the next eighteen months she read and studied theology and philosophy, rebuilt her strength and commitment, and slowly regained her capacity to engage with the world.

Towards the end of 1979, Rosemary returned to South-East Asia. FFAC had resumed operations in the region from a new headquarters it had established in Bangkok. That was where Rosemary relocated to and where she immediately threw herself back into working with handicapped and deprived children living in camps scattered across the country. This time was a bit different, too – Rosemary was a worker, able to devote her time and energy to those who needed it, rather than to administrative tasks and meetings, endless meetings. She would gradually involve herself in other projects but for fifteen years she worked for and with others, and that was all she had ever really wanted to do.

In 2013, Rosemary returned home to Adelaide and slipped into a quiet and uncomplicated retirement. If she was asked to look back over her life and assess what she had achieved in fifty years of service to others, she would most probably respond by brushing off the question as irrelevant, but here is what could be said. After working in Alaska and experiencing the harsh realities of life and death in fringe communities, Rosemary travelled to Vietnam, where she and a small group of like-minded young women – Elaine Moir, Margaret Moses and Lee Makk among them – worked to break down the barriers to intercountry adoption in Australia and elsewhere in the world. She, and they, believed that it was better to live to be an adult in another country than to be a dead baby or child in your own, and they acted on that belief. Between 1967 and 1975, some four thousand orphans passed through their nurseries on their way to new lives somewhere else, a figure that represented more than 80 per cent of all intercountry adoptions from Vietnam.

They did all this in a country that was at war and in a place that was a long way from home. Their health, both physical and mental, suffered because of the conditions in which they lived and worked, and because of how much of themselves they gave so willingly. Two of them would die in the last, desperate days of South Vietnam's existence and all would carry scars from their time in Saigon. If any of those remarkable young women were asked to define their legacy, they would point to the orphans' lives they saved. That is both true and admirable but is just a part of their wider legacy. As individuals, and as part of a team, they made a difference and that is something about which they – and we – should all be very proud.

APPENDIX

FIGHTING DRAGONS

Washington's immediate response to the C-5A crash involved a barrage of requests and demands from a range of departments and agencies asking for answers to questions that simply could not be answered because of a paucity of information about what had actually caused the aircraft to go down. Enemy action appeared to be the most likely explanation, with possible indications of either a small bomb being placed aboard the aircraft or some other form of sabotage. US Air Force security police were immediately dispatched from Clark Air Base to Tan Son Nhut with instructions to screen all baggage taken aboard US military flights and prevent any attempts to hijack aircraft by placing armed guards on all flights.

There were two other responses. One was fear that if they couldn't get the first evacuation to work properly, what hope did they have of making the rest of Operation Babylift successful? The second was the framing of another question: What if nothing was done to the aircraft but, rather, something was *wrong* with the aircraft? That was a chance that no one was prepared to take – no more C-5As would be used in the operation.

•

Finding out precisely what had happened to Bud Traynor's aircraft was always going to be difficult. When Traynor himself returned to the crash site the following morning, he found South Vietnamese soldiers 'guarding' the site, although most seemed to be studiously avoiding looking at the civilians who were searching for anything they could use among the debris. The local province chief had supplied the troops but Traynor was convinced – and evidence later showed – that numbers of those troops looted the aircraft and its cargo.[1] Prime targets appear to have included avionics and communications equipment from the cockpit.

An accident investigation team flew in from Clark Air Base the day after the crash and its members were briefed at Tan Son Nhut by a DAO staff member. He assured them that local authorities had secured the site from Vietcong interference, so they would all be safe. Unfortunately, he continued, they had not been able to secure it from pilferage, so he wasn't certain how much could be salvaged from the wreckage. The short answer to that was not a lot, as most of what they were looking for, in particular the flight recorder, was gone before they arrived. They had played this game before, though, and let it be known that they would pay and pay well for any instruments that were brought in. Aircraft parts soon began to arrive.[2]

The navy came to the air force's assistance. The most vital piece of evidence in the investigation was the rear cargo door that blew out, which was now somewhere on the bottom of the South China Sea. The precise location of the mid-air explosion was not known, but several US Navy vessels began searching what was considered the most likely location. It was a search that would be successful in just a few days. First recovered was the body of the loadmaster who had been blown out of the aircraft along with the door, and later that day the door itself was recovered from the bottom of the sea. Taken first to Subic Bay for a preliminary investigation and then to the United States, the door would be at the centre of a number of investigations and at the heart of a number of court cases.

The investigations led to a conclusive explanation of what had happened to the C-5A as it passed through 23 000 feet shortly after crossing the coast above Vung Tau. Three of the ten locks that held the right aft cargo door in position failed, all three being replacement locks rather than original components. The failure of those three locks put so much pressure on the remaining seven that they, too, failed almost immediately and simultaneously. The considerable pressure differential between the aircraft's interior and exterior blew the cargo door out and triggered a catastrophic decompression. In blowing out, the cargo door destroyed the aircraft's right pressure door, the clamshell door, and it was this object that sliced into the tailplane assembly, severing control cables and hydraulic lines. The aircraft and most of its passengers would have survived the decompression but the loss of aeronautical controls guaranteed that the C-5A would crash.

One key finding related to the locking mechanisms that failed in the cargo door. Investigators believed that the three door locks were replaced with either used or otherwise inferior substitutes, cannibalised for use on other aircraft without any record of the substitution being kept. All the theories about sabotage and the possibility of a bomb on board were now irrelevant. Mechanical failure was clearly the primary cause of the crash and there were serious implications from that. Other investigations revealed that the disaster could quite easily have been worse. When all the flight recorder data was crunched using flight simulators, an interesting outcome was found. Traynor, it emerged, had put his aircraft down in the best possible location. Had the C-5A made it back to Tan Son Nhut and landed on the main runway, it would not have been able to stop and would have run off the end of the runway at a speed of 250 kilometres an hour. It was unlikely that anyone aboard would have survived.

•

After the door blew out of the aircraft, one of its loadmasters tried to reassure a very concerned Christie Leiverman that she would be alright because C-5As had suffered similar problems before and had landed safely. Some days after the crash, US Ambassador Graham Martin was berating a junior staff at the embassy in a very public way for what he considered defeatist reporting. As he finished his tirade, Martin added, '. . . and if Washington had checked with me before using the C-5A, I wouldn't have given authorisation. Those kids would still be alive.'[3] All along, it seems, the senior American official in South Vietnam had doubts about the suitability of the C-5A for evacuation operations.

•

In the aftermath of the crash, questions about both the C-5A's suitability and its airworthiness began to circulate. They were especially prevalent in Washington and were given a sinister element when titbits of information were leaked to the press. The original USAID proposal, it was suggested, was for the orphans to be flown out aboard Nightingales, the specially equipped C-141s that were already on the ground at Clark Air Base and that Rosemary was told would be utilised. Late in the planning, a C-5A was substituted to undertake the initial Operation Babylift flight. The substitution was made because the C-5A, the largest cargo aircraft in the world, was a symbol of America's strength and ingenuity, and could carry hundreds of orphans across the Pacific to California to be met and welcomed to the United States by President Ford. And so a substitution was made.

There was more to it than that, though. After the crash, Dick Cheney, then the White House Chief of Staff, set out to discover how the C-5A had been substituted for more suitable aircraft. What Cheney and several other investigators would learn was that the directive to make that substitution came from a joint State Department–Defence Department coordination group. In the coming months and years, the reasons why that directive was given would become clear. They were, in summary, because the Lockheed Corporation had a problem with the C-5As – it had a number of design and operational faults that affected its performance and reliability, preventing it from becoming the flagship of both the company and the Military Airlift Command.

Fixing all the issues would be a very, very expensive exercise, one that Lockheed had neither the money nor the inclination to undertake by itself. For the corporation, the obvious backer for the rehabilitation and upgrade program was the US government, appropriating the necessary money through Congress. To give that idea every chance of succeeding, a large and public display of the aircraft's capabilities and potential was needed. None of this would ever be documented in those terms but just as Lockheed, and certain of its supporters in Congress and government service, were looking for an opportunity to showcase the aircraft, along came Operation Babylift.[4]

•

Even without this background, responsibility for the death of almost 150 people was always going to be contested in a courtroom. The lawsuits began at the end of the northern summer of 1975 and soon fell into a pattern that became depressingly familiar to the plaintiffs in the coming decade. Lockheed, the principal defendant, would deny any liability for the accident and, when claims for compensation were lodged, would insist on contesting every claim individually rather than as part of a class action. Only when it had lost several individual cases, and any subsequent appeals, did it consider admitting any liability and begin to pay out claims. It appeared to believe, with some justification, that the longer it dragged out the process, the less it would ultimately be required to pay.

The first cases brought before the courts were over the deaths of the adults aboard the C-5A. Expert witnesses appeared for the plaintiffs, detailing the various aeronautical and safety issues associated with the aircraft. The defendants would disclaim corporate knowledge of most of this and the jury would retire only to return a short time later with a finding in favour of the plaintiffs. After several cases had resulted in damages payments of up to $1 million (all figures are in US dollars) being awarded, the US government stepped in and negotiated a settlement for the outstanding cases. In that settlement, the government assumed 65 per cent of the liability and Lockheed the remaining 35 per cent. The judge awarded the plaintiffs a total of $8.755 million, which came to around $300 000 for each adult who died, less attorneys' fees and expenses.

That was the quick case, taking just over a year to conclude from the time the first papers were lodged with the courts.

However, even though the amount and schedule of payments was agreed to in 1976, it would take until the mid-1980s for all the monies to be disbursed.[5]

•

FFAC and Margaret Moses senior decided to use part of the damages payment to put in place some kind of living memorial to Margaret, Lee and all the others who had served, and those who had died, in South Vietnam. With some of the money, they established the Margaret Moses Memorial Fund with the specific objective of supporting deprived children, especially the handicapped and orphaned in the developing world.

•

The second cluster of cases was fought on behalf of the children who had survived the crash. FFAC and the children's adoptive families argued that all had suffered shock and psychological trauma in the accident as well as physical injuries, including varying degrees of brain damage caused by the sudden decompression and lack of oxygen. In response, Lockheed's lawyers argued that no surviving child had suffered 'significant' damage because of the crash. FFAC closed its submissions by asking that the surviving children be awarded enough money to cover the ongoing medical and remedial education expenses that their adoptive families would incur.[6]

The intricate legal battles from the earlier hearings were repeated. Cases were dealt with on an individual basis, with Lockheed contesting each as well as individual points within individual cases. Again, it was all to no avail as jury after jury found in favour of the plaintiffs and a succession of judges awarded payments that ranged from $37 000 to almost $1 million. In 1982 alone, several cases were settled for an average of $325 000 while others were settled out of court and on the eve of the trial for similar amounts. Eventually, in 1984, the US government again stepped in to facilitate a group settlement for all outstanding cases. At a total cost of $13 million plus, Lockheed agreed to pay all surviving children a lump sum of $125 000 and to set up a trust fund of $2.25 million to cover their ongoing medical expenses.

Similar scenes and similar outcomes were also recorded on the other side of the Atlantic. In Europe, in the first case involving a surviving orphan bound for adoption, Lockheed's lawyers again tried a series of discrediting and delaying tactics, but they were no more successful there than they had been in the United States. When the first child was awarded damages in excess of $1 million, Lockheed opted to settle all the other cases as a class action and out of court. They would pay the remaining children $17.8 million and set up a trust fund containing $2.9 million for future medical expenses.[7]

•

The last tranche of proceedings commenced in April 1986 to determine the compensation payable to the prospective parents of adoptee orphans who had been killed in the crash. The class action suit started with lawyers for Lockheed offering a $10 million settlement. The trial judge almost immediately suggested to the FFAC counsel that the organisation prepare a submission outlining how it would disburse their portion of the settlement money if the Lockheed proposal was approved. He also made the point that he would like to see any proposal FFAC put forward include a provision that at least part of the money be set aside to support orphan services in the United

States as American citizens would be funding a large part of it. Proceedings were then complicated by a court-appointed adviser recommending that the money go to another charity, the Edna McConnell Clark Foundation, which had no obvious connection with the FFAC operation.

In the end, the judge went his own way, dividing most of the Lockheed settlement offer among the adoptive families who had taken part in the case. Each family was granted $85 671 for the child they had lost, with three families who were each adopting two children given double that amount. The monies for the nine families who did not take part in the class action suit would revert to Lockheed while the sixteen orphans who had not yet been assigned when they were killed were not included in the findings. In the settlement, FFAC was awarded $500 000. The judge also made the point that $39 000 of the final figure awarded to the plaintiffs was punitive damages, and he urged all plaintiffs to donate that part of the amount to a charitable organisation.

If the judge actually thought that was going to happen, he would be disappointed, but there was more than enough disappointment to go around. FFAC shared in that disappointment, reckoning that one-twentieth of the final sum did not reflect either its commitment or its loss. The decision to award damages at a fixed rate was also puzzling to many. While some of the adoptive parents had known of, and even provided support to, the children they were in the process of adopting, others had not even received their adoptee's name before that adoptee was killed.

FFAC chose to follow through with the judge's recommendation to donate the punitive damages to charity. Rosemary and one of the recipient families drafted and signed a letter to all the other recipient families asking them to consider donating part of their settlement money to the Margaret Moses Memorial Fund. The responses were unusual. One family donated $10 000 to the fund, while another thanked FFAC for the eleven years of legal work they had put in to achieve the settlement. Another cheerfully described the European holiday their family could now afford while two-thirds of the recipients simply didn't reply at all.

In the end, though, it didn't really matter. Rosemary and FFAC had more important things to do than worry about money. Somewhere out there were children in need.

ACKNOWLEDGEMENTS

Like all stories that make it to print, *Operation Babylift* is made up of contributions from many people, although any errors or omissions are mine alone. At Hachette (Australia), Sophie Hamley and Matthew Kelly supported and encouraged me from the start to tell this story, whose final form owed much to the editorial skills of Brigid Mullane.

The staff at three great Australian cultural institutions, the National Library of Australia, the National Archives of Australia and the Australian War Memorial continue to maintain standards of professionalism that make the life of a writer a lot easier than it might otherwise be.

A number of people with a direct interest in the story also helped me to tell it. They included Gyoparka (Lee) Makk's brother Jules and sister Maria, Kim and Mali Moir, who I thank for their enthusiasm and the information they shared about their mother Elaine, Chantal and several other Babylift orphans who preferred to not be identified, and Rosemary Taylor, who found time to talk to me and who is, almost literally, the mother of a thousand children.

My wife, the ever-supportive Pam, three children and their partners and eight grandchildren have displayed a winning mix of support and forebearance. Unfortunately for them, I have yet to run out of stories.

In the background, the South Australian Women's Memorial Playing Fields Trust, through its support of women's sport and women's contributions to Australia's overseas involvements, continues to be a source of both inspiration and satisfaction to me.

Finally, there was someone who was there at the start of the journey that is this book who is not here for the finish. A close friend and a close relative, one of the bravest people I have ever known and one whose selflessness is mirrored by those I have written about in *Operation Babylift*, this book is dedicated to my sister, Laraine Delia Talbot, nee Shaw (1947–2018).

ENDNOTES

Prologue: Da Nang, Friday 28 March 1975 (pp. ix–xx)

1 By 1975, World Airways had 150 flight crew and 300 cabin crew flying fourteen modern jet aircraft, both passenger and freight, and one luxury prop-driven passenger aircraft. Daly was the best-placed of all Western carriers to meet such a requirement.

2 Larry Engelmann, *Tears Before the Rain,* Dec Capo Press, New York, 1997, p. 12.

3 Larry Engelmann, *Homesick Angel: Last flight from Da Nang*, Vietnam Magazine, 24 March, 2017, www.historynet.com/homesick-angel-last-flight-da-nang.htm, accessed 24 March 2017.

4 David Butler, *The Fall of Saigon*, Simon and Schuster, New York, 1985, p. 137.

5 Ken Healy begun his aviation career flying refugees out of China, just ahead of the communist takeover there in the late 1940s.

6 Engelmann, *Homesick Angel*.

7 Ibid. The cameras kept rolling as the incident unfolded and much of the footage is now available on the internet. Tom Aspell survived and would later be picked up by a rescue helicopter.

8 Engelmann, *Tears Before the Rain*, p. 5.

9 Engelmann, *Homesick Angel*.

10 Healy assumed the sluggish control was caused by the damage his aircraft had sustained. The wheel wells of the 727 were full of people hanging

onto control cables for dear life. It was their weight that was causing the resistance in the controls.

1 Building a warm nest (pp. 3–27)

1   Personal: Mount Barker, *Albany Advertiser*, 9 October 1941, p.3. Ted Moir was one of at least a dozen Moirs from the district who would enlist in the army during the war.

2   National Archives of Australia (NAA), Edward George Moir, Ref: B833, WX15905. Ted Moir was buried in the camp cemetery. In 1946, his remains were reinterred in the main Commonwealth War Cemetery at Kanchanaburi in Thailand.

3   Money, Lawrence, 'Viet orphan airlift crusader a "saint"', *Sydney Morning Herald*, 20 August 2012, Online, accessed 22 March 2018.

4   Rosemary Taylor, *Orphans of War*, Collins, London, 1988, p. 227.

5   This may or may not have been his real name. At one time, Jean-Henri told Rena that he had taken the name of one of his friends to escape his past as a German collaborator in World War II. Whoever he was, Briand seems to have been something of a Walter Mitty.

6   Rena Briand, 'A Bunny turns war reporter in Vietnam', *Maclean's Magazine*, vol. 80, no. 4, April 1967, p. 30.

7   Ibid.

8   Rena's husband's real name was most likely Bernard Jacobs, she later learned, and he most likely did some work for the CIA. She believed that he was subsequently deported to France.

9   Rena Briand, *The Waifs*, Phuong-Huang Press, Melbourne, 1973, p. 8.

10   St Vincent's College, founded by the Sisters of Charity in 1858, is the oldest Catholic girls' school in New South Wales and the oldest registered girls' school in Australia.

11   'Around the churches', *Canberra Times*, 28 January 1967, p. 15. See also the *Women's Weekly* article from early 1967.

12   Taylor, *Orphans of War*, p. 2.

13   Almost three hundred years old, the order was founded in France to specifically address the needs of the poor and orphans, the elderly and the mentally ill.

14   Alister Brass, *Bleeding Earth*, Alpha Books, Sydney, 1969, p. 18. In mid-April 1967, the South Vietnamese Ministry of Health released a number of statistics, including details about the country's medical establishment. Of the 859 registered doctors in the country, all but 158 were either serving in the army or were in administrative posts or teaching positions, or had retired. The system was at breaking point.

15 Richard Beckett, 'The children of war', *Canberra Times*, 28 March 1967, p. 4.

16 Taylor, *Orphans of War*, p. 226.

17 Joshua Forkert, 'Refugees, orphans and a basket of cats', *Journal of Australian Studies*, vol. 36, no. 4, 2012, p. 92.

18 The Good Shepherd convents and schools had been working in Vietnam since 1871, run by the Sisters of Charity of St Vincent de Paul. At that time, the convent school had an enrolment of one hundred girls aged from nine to sixteen. As well as the mother superior, there were eight nuns present there at the time – five Irish, two Vietnamese and one Malaysian. The orphanage at Vinh Long was set up in 1958 under the direction of the Malaysian nun, Sister Ursula Lee.

19 This incident is detailed in Yen Phan, *Family Ties: Operation Babylift, Transnational adoption and the sentimentalism of US and Vietnam relations, 1967–2002,* Senior Thesis, Haverford, 2012, p. 25.

2 Warm nest to Allambie (pp. 28–51)

1 Dana Sachs, *The Life We Were Given*, Beacon Press, Boston, 2010, p. 7.

2 Taylor, *Orphans of War*, p. 92. The little girl recovered completely in hospital and was later adopted by a family in Belgium.

3 Ibid., p. 84. At one time, the overflow of babies spread into other diplomatic homes. The British Ambassador and his wife once housed six babies in their residency and ultimately twenty-four orphans would pass through their home.

4 This was necessarily far more than they would have liked. There always seemed to be a disproportionate number of orphans with cleft palates and they presented a set of particular problems. If the children weren't fed slowly and carefully, they were prone to developing respiratory complaints.

5 Just one child would ever be sent to an adoptive family in New Zealand, in 1969, and the process proved to be a bureaucratic nightmare.

6 Taylor, p. 44. During the next four years, nearly all the rooms would be converted for the use of the children and would also be upgraded extensively.

7 Geoffrey Ward and Ken Burns, *The Vietnam War*, Ebury Press, London, 2017, p. 477.

8 'War waif has home here', *Canberra Times*, 20 January 1971, p. 1.

9 The White Australia Policy was a series of administrative barriers, introduced at the time of Federation, designed specifically to exclude non-white migration to Australia.

10 Joshua Forkert, *Orphans of Vietnam: A history of intercountry adoption policy and practice in Australia*, 1968–1975, PhD thesis, University of Adelaide, p. 54. In answer to a question in parliament in 1967, the then Immigration Minister Billy Snedden said non-European adoptees would be admitted if all the necessary enquiries had been completed in Australia and overseas, again deflecting national policy decisions to state agencies and departments.

11 'Australia should admit South Vietnamese orphans', *Canberra Times*, 6 September 1967, p. 3.

12 Rena Briand, 'The Waifs', p. 123.

13 Both girls were two years old and had spent all but a few weeks of their lives in orphanages. Both were adopted in Saigon by proxy, and their adoptions were arranged by Anne Forder of the Catholic Relief Services Office in Saigon. Forder also accompanied them to Australia. Her office sent a dossier on ten orphans to the head of Australian Catholic Relief, Monsignor Crennan, at his office in Sydney. The two girls were selected from this dossier.

14 Taylor, *Orphans of War*, p. 47. To Am's operating model was so successful that World Vision based its model on it when it opened its own orphanage/nursery in Saigon in 1971.

15 Sachs, *The Life We Were Given*, p. 38.

16 NAA, Ref: B 925, V1978/60196: Immigration Department – Vietnamese Orphans.

17 Over thirty years after the event, Elaine was still reluctant to discuss how she evaded immigration authorities in Saigon and Singapore to avoid embarrassing those involved. See Forkert, *Orphans of Vietnam*, p. 120.

18 By way of comparison, the Catholic charity Caritas had placed a few orphans in 1971/72, while International Social Services placed twenty-six orphans between 1968 and 1972. There were also a small number of privately organised adoptions. See Taylor, Orphans of War, p. 71.

3 From Newhaven to Rathaven (pp. 52–70)

1 For instance, a 1972 report to a US Senate committee suggested that there were eight million children under fourteen years of age in South Vietnam requiring some form of assistance and that 25 000 of these children were living in institutions. See Forkert, *Orphans of Vietnam*, p. 92.

2 Nancy Cato, 'Orphans a way to make money in Vietnam', *Canberra Times*, 23 August, 1972, p. 19.

3   Marion Quartly, Shurlee Swain and Denise Cuthbert, *The Market in Babies*, Monash University Publications, Melbourne, 2013.

4   'Sister Susan is a CNN Hero', www.laraprice.com, accessed 22 March 2018.

5   Ibid. See also Engelmann, *Tears Before the Rain*, p. 19.

6   Air France let Susan have a ticket for return travel to Saigon in exchange for agreeing to escort five orphans out of Vietnam when she returned. The date of that return was left open. She flew from Kentucky, where she was still working, to New York and then on to Paris where she spent a few days with friends before continuing to Saigon. See Engelmann, *Tears Before the Rain*, p. 19.

7   NAA, Ref: B 925: V 1978/60194, Memo No. 1522/73 dated 25 May 1973.

8   Ibid.

9   Robert Strobridge (Ed.), *Turn My Eyes Away*, FFAC, Boulder, CO, 1976, p. 17.

10 Taylor, *Orphans of War*, p. 76.

11 Strobridge (ed.), *Turn My Eyes Away*.

12 Taylor, *Orphans of War*, p. 81.

13 Linda Boris, *Every Sparrow That Falls*, self-published, New York, 2017, p. 28.

14 'Mary Nelle Gage and the orphan evacuation from Saigon', 7 December 2012, Ide421.blogspot.com, accessed 26 April 2018.

15 Taylor, *Orphans of War*, p. 110.

16 Sachs, *The Life We Were Given*, p. 7.

17 Taylor, *Orphans of War*, p. 110.

18 'Sister Susan is a CNN hero'.

19 Engelmann, *Tears Before the Rain*, p. 19.

20 Taylor, *Orphans of War*, p. 11.

4 Endgame (pp. 71–87)

1   Taylor, *Orphans of War*, p. 136.

2   Elements of some units would still be struggling to reach the coast two weeks later.

3   Ty Andre, *On My Brother's Shoulders*, Wakefield Press, Adelaide, 1997, p. 254.

4   Andre, *On My Brother's Shoulders*, p. 255.

5   Much of this section is based on the official report prepared by Wende and Rosemary for an FFAC newsletter they subsequently published.

6   Sachs, *The Life We Were Given*, p. 5.

7   Geoffrey Price was familiar with both Vietnam and Saigon. His first posting with the Department of Foreign Affairs had been as Third

Secretary in the Australian Legation in Saigon between 1955 and 1957.
At the age of forty-four, he returned to Saigon as Australia's ambassador
in 1974.

8   NAA, Vietnam – Situation Reports, Ref: A1209, 1974/7556.

9   NAA, Ref: A 1209, 1974/7556. The Sitrep was based on official sources
within the South Vietnamese government, who briefed Western diplomats
on a regular basis – sometimes daily, sometimes weekly.

10 It would never be possible to tally the number of people aboard when Ken
Healy's 727 took off from Da Nang airport. The estimate of 250 was for
passengers in the main cabin and there may have been up to eighty more in
the cargo hold. Some twenty-four crowded into the wheel wells but all bar
seven had fallen out by the time they landed. When flight and cabin crew,
journalists and camera crew were added in, the total was around 360, or
three times the recommended payload. See Engelmann, *Homesick Angel.*

5 Looking for an exit (pp. 88–102)

1   The message would be encoded in a weather report, which gave a
maximum temperature and the likelihood of rain. It would be proceeded
by playing Bing Crosby's 'White Christmas'. Taylor, *Orphans of War*,
p. 152.

2   Jenny Hocking, *Gough Whitlam: His time*, vol. 2, Miegunyah Press,
Melbourne, 2012, p. 219.

3   Editorial, *The Advertiser*, 1 January 1975, p. 8.

4   Peter Edwards, *The Fall of Saigon* [booklet], National Archives of
Australia, Canberra, 2006, p. 15.

5   By early 1975, Australia had opened a diplomatic mission in Hanoi while
also maintaining an embassy in Saigon. In March, Graeme Lewis, the
chargé d'affaires in Hanoi, flew to Vientiane in Laos to meet David Wilson,
who was about to become the first ambassador to Hanoi. Lewis then
took an Air Vietnam flight to Saigon, passing over Pleiku in the central
highlands. Below, the NVA had just commenced an assault on the town.
What happened next is unclear, but it appears that the civilian aircraft was
mistaken, by one side or the other, for an enemy aircraft and was hit by an
anti-aircraft missile. The aircraft and all aboard disappeared.

6   Clyde Cameron, *China, Communism and Coca-Cola*, Hill of Content,
Melbourne, 1980, p. 230.

7   'Speed up adoptions or babies will die', *Canberra Times*, 2 April 1975, p. 1.

8   This section is based on Chris Coulthard-Clark's official history of the
RAAF in Vietnam, *The RAAF in Vietnam,* Allen & Unwin, Sydney, 1995,
pp. 320–31.

9   One original proposal saw them being sent to Da Nang to evacuate refugees. Da Nang fell to the NVA on Easter Saturday, removing that from their task sheet.

10 Graham Martin was also particularly sensitive to the plight of orphans, having once served as a State Department coordinator for a United Nations refugee program. Frank Snepp, *Decent Interval*, Penguin, New York, p. 236.

11 Like Ed Daly, Gerald Ford was an orphan.

12 NAA, Ref: B 925, V1978/60196.

13 Charles Henderson, *Goodnight Saigon*, Berkley Calibre, New York, 2005, pp. 232–4; see also Snepp, *Decent Interval*, p. 236.

14 Email, Maria Makk to author, 25 March 2018.

15 FFAC Newsletter/1975.

16 NAA, Ref: A1209, 1974/7556.

17 Klaus, Neumann, *Across the Seas: Australia's response to refugees'*, p. 243.

18 Joshua Forkert details this in both his works: *Orphans of Vietnam*, p. 167 and 'Refugees, orphans and a basket of cats', p. 431.

19 Holt International was formed by Oregon farmer Harry Holt who, with no help from anyone but family members, founded an orphanage in South Korea during the Korean War and would subsequently place more than four thousand orphans of mixed race with families in the United States, a number that included the eight he and his wife adopted.

20 Henderson, *Goodnight Saigon*, p. 262.

6 The noose tightens (pp. 103–112)

1   Forkert, *Orphans of Vietnam*, p. 162.

2   Ibid., p. 167.

3   When she left, Anne Stark told her parents that she would return as soon as she could. They told her to stay in Denver, as they thought they too would soon be evacuated.

4   Daly's comments over that week would be reported in a number of newspapers. See, for instance, the *Canberra Times*, 3 April 1975.

5   Forkert, *Orphans of Vietnam*, p. 168.

6   Item 11, Elaine Moir collection, NLA. Elaine's children, Kim and Mali, donated a collection of their mother's material related to adoption to the National Library of Australia. The collection contains books and booklets, handwritten notes and other ephemera related to the adoption of Vietnamese orphans by Australian families.

7   In fact, fewer than 20 per cent of the children were believed to be of mixed-race parentage, and a far lesser proportion of those were fathered by US soldiers.

8   In one of his more florid moments, Whitlam yelled at Foreign Minister
     Don Willesee, 'I'm not having hundreds of fucking Vietnamese Balts
     coming into this country with their religious and political hatreds against
     us!' Cameron, *China, Communism and Coca-Cola*, p. 230.
9   'Speed up adoptions or refugee babies will die', p. 1.
10   Coy Cross, *MAC and Operation Babylift*, Scott Air Force Base, IL, 1989, p. 1.

7 A partial implosion (pp. 113–27)

1   NAA, Adoption of Vietnamese orphans – Uplift flight, Ref: A1209,
     1975/657.
2   Clyde Cameron later offered a different perspective on the incident.
     Angered by what he believed was an ill-considered public rebuke, he gave
     up all responsibility for the orphans issue and told Whitlam to 'shove the
     Vietnamese exercise up his backside'. See Cameron, *China Communism
     and Coca-Cola*, p. 229, I; and Forkert, *Orphans of Vietnam*, p. 170.
3   NAA: Ref: M522: Whitlam/Personal Papers.
4   National Archives of Australia, Prime Minister and Cabinet – Adoption
     Vietnamese orphans, Ref: A1209, 1975/456.
5   Coulthard-Clark, *The RAAF in Vietnam*, provides a detailed account of the
     incident and response.
6   Forkert, *Orphans of Vietnam*, p. 176.
7   NAA, Ref: A1838: 3014/10/15/6 Part 1.
8   Edward Zigler, *The Vietnamese Children's Airlift: Too little, too late*,
     American Psychological Association, Chicago, 1975, p. 9.
9   Both Healy and Daly would subsequently claim that they did not hear the
     air traffic controllers ordering them to abort the take-off and return to their
     terminal; Healy argued that it would have been far too late for that anyway.
     The controllers themselves claimed that they extinguished the runway
     lights, which they weren't supposed to do, in anticipation of a predicted
     Vietcong attack. See Cross, *MAC and Operation Babylift*, p. 45.
10   NAA, Department of Prime Minister and Cabinet, Ref: A1209, 1975/546.
11   The full story is told in some detail in Sachs, *The Life We Were Given*.
12   The full speech and notes can be found online at www.fordlibrarymuseum.
     gov/LIBRARY/document/0067/1563032.pdf.

8 Last-minute nerves (pp. 131–42)

1   'Saigon – a city of despair', *The Advertiser*, 3 April 1975, p. 2.
2   The documentation around this set of exchanges can be found at: National
     Archives of Australia, Ref: A1209, 1975/546, PM&C: Adoption of
     Vietnamese Orphans.

3   NAA, Ref: A1209, 1975/546.

4   Ibid.

5   Ibid.

6   Forkert, *Orphans of Vietnam*, p. 173.

7   NAA, Adoption of Vietnamese orphans-Uplift flight, Ref: A1209, 1975/657, Cable O.CHI95835, 3 April 1975. [Typo corrected.]

8   Forkert, *Orphans of Vietnam*, p. 221.

9   Qantas could/would not fly to Saigon because of the danger and the prohibitive cost of insuring that aircraft if they had actually wanted to do so.

10 Forkert, *Orphans of Vietnam*, p. 177.

11 NAA, Uplift flight to Sydney, Ref: A1209, 1975/658.

9 Tan Son Nhut (pp. 143–58)

1   Engelmann, *Tears Before the Rain*, p. 80.

2   Ibid., p. 37.

3   FFAC Newsletter/1975.

4   Andre, *On My Brother's Shoulders*, pp. 258–61.

5   Ibid.

6   Not all trips through the city were that dramatic. Hoa Stone, from the Sancta Maria Orphanage farm, was one of a small group collected by a van and driven without incident to Tan Son Nhut.

7   Taylor, *Orphans of War*, p. 160.

8   The use of the C-5A was to be a one-off operation with subsequent evacuation flights using C-130s and C-141s.

9   As a child, Traynor was referred to as 'Little Buddy' by his family. Shortened to 'Bud', it was a nickname he would carry for the rest of his life.

10 Traynor, Dennis, 'Twelve minutes out', *Airlift/Tanker Quarterly*, Spring 2005, p. 8.

11 Tom Archdeacon, 'Fateful flight carried a lifetime of bonds', *Dayton Daily News*, 7 June 2015, http://www.pressreader.com, accessed 13 May 2018.

10 American babylift (pp. 159–70)

1   When a South Vietnamese official learned that Lee did not have her passport, he began to make a fuss. Intervention by Dolly and a telephone call to Rathaven cleared up the matter and Lee continued to the C-5A with the Allambie children.

2   If he knew – and he may not have – Bob King also neglected to mention that this was the first time a C-5A had been used for a medical evacuation mission.

3   Cross, *MAC and Operation Babylift*, p. 34.

4   Taylor, *Orphans of War*, p. 162.
5   It was extremely emotional for Birgit, who had also become very close to a young Vietnamese girl working as a helper at Birgit's nursery. When Birgit was about to board the C-5A, the young Vietnamese embraced her and both burst into tears. Birgit promised to return one day. See, Boris, p. 240.

11 Catastrophic decompression (pp. 171–90)

1   Sachs, *The Life We Were Given*, p. 74.
2   Tom Archdeacon, 'Fateful flight carried a lifetime of bonds', *Dayton Daily News*, 6 June 2014.
3   Henderson, *Goodnight Saigon*, p. 265.
4   Ian Thompson, 'Operation Babylift crash brings tragedy, hope', *Solona Daily Republic*, 31 January 2014.
5   Sachs, *The Life We Were Given*, p. 75
6   Shortly after the aircraft came to a halt and he stood up, Merrit Stark had been quite distressed to find that one of the babies near him was dead, strangled by the cord attached to the pouch around its neck.
7   It was later discovered that, as well as lacerations and bruises, Regina had sustained broken bones in both feet and a fractured back. She ended the day in the Adventist Hospital.
8   Merrit Stark was mistaken in that belief. The baby who became Landon Carnie, and his twin sister, Lorie, were en route to join their adoptive family in Washington state and were officially reported dead when they weren't found in the wreckage. More than twenty-four hours after the crash, they were found by a farmer huddled together at the edge of the rice paddy. Initially in the cargo compartment, they had been taken upstairs shortly after take-off. Their rescuer had placed them some distance from the other children and they were subsequently overlooked.

12 Australian uplift (pp. 191–205)

1   Marion Quartly, Swain and Cuthbert, *The Market in Babies*, Monash University Publications, Melbourne, 2013, p. 109.
2   Forkert, *Orphans of Vietnam*, p. 212.
3   Hoa Van Stone, *Heart of Stone*, self-published, Glenelg, 2007, p. 17.
4   Andre, *On My Brother's Shoulders*, p. 18.
5   Forkert, *Orphans of Vietnam*, p. 212.
6   Taylor, *Orphans of War*, p. 173.
7   Formed in London in 1856 by James Brooke, the first Rajah of Sarawak, by 1975 the Borneo Company had become a large, diversified general trading company.

8 Forkert, *Orphans of Vietnam*, p. 214.

9 Peter George, 'Orphans ticketed to a new life', *Canberra Times*, 7 April 1975, p. 1.

10 NAA: Ref: A 1209, 1975/658 – Uplift Flight to Sydney. After the first Babylift operation, the Immigration Department conducted an internal assessment of the operation. That assessment is held in this file.

11 Forkert, *Orphans of Vietnam*, p. 211.

13 Aftermath (pp. 206–22)

1 Naomi Bronstein was a wife and mother from Montreal who, with her husband Herb, was a leading light in the movement for transnational adoption in Canada. In March 1975 she left Herb and their eleven children – most of them adopted – in Montreal to travel to South-East Asia to help Wende close down Canada House in Phnom Penh and take its orphans back to Canada.

2 The Adventist Hospital in Saigon agreed to take over and run what had been the US 3rd Field Army Hospital when the Americans pulled out after the Paris Peace Accords in early 1973. Located adjacent to Tan Son Nhut airport, the hospital retained two or three wards for the remaining Americans with the rest of the hospital for the South Vietnamese.

3 Taylor, *Orphans of War*, pp. 171–72.

4 Ibid.

5 Taylor, *Orphans of War*, p. 165.

6 Boris, *Every Sparrow that Falls*, p. 145.

7 Taylor, *Orphans of War*, p. 165.

8 Sachs, *The Life We Were Given*, p. 76.

9 Boris, *Every Sparrow that Falls*, p. 151.

10 Young, Roger, 'Operation Babylift', www.northwestvets.com, accessed 9 April 2018.

11 Julian Manyon, *The Fall of Saigon*, Rex Collings, London, 1975, pp. 56–57.

12 Henderson, *Goodnight Saigon*, p. 231.

13 Simon Parry, 'Still rootless: The child refugees of Vietnam war's final chaotic days', *Post Magazine*, *South China Morning Post*, 11 April 2015.

14 Ibid.

15 Snepp, *Decent Interval*, p. 274.

16 See, for example: Roger Young, 'Operation Babylift', at northwestvets.com, accessed 9 April 18, and Coy Cross, *MAC and Operation Babylift,'* p. 38.

17 Sachs, *The Life We Were Given*, p. 77.

18 NAA, Ref: A1209, 1975/546.

19 AAP, 'War orphans jet crash', *The Advertiser*, 5 April 1975, p. 1.

14 Last rites (pp.223–39)

1   The master files for all the FFAC children had been in the suitcase
Margaret Moses took aboard the C-5A and were lost in the crash. The
staff now had to piece together the original documents for their travelling
children.

2   Sachs, *The Life We Were Given*, p. 67.

3   Zigler, *The Vietnamese Children's Airlift*, p. 16.

4   There would later be considerable criticism of authorities for allowing the
survivors of the C-5A crash to be flown out the following day. Doctors
and psychologists claimed that many of them needed more time to recover
physically or psychologically from the trauma they had suffered, and their
almost immediate evacuation actually aggravated their injuries.

5   Taylor, *Orphans of War*, p. 175.

6   'Babylift continues despite crash', *Canberra Times*, 7 April 1975, p. 5.

7   The Tribune, 8 April 1975.

8   'Hypocrisy on war orphans,', *Tribune*, 8 April 1975, p. 1.

9   I told the story of Vivian Bullwinkel and the *Vyner Brooke* nurses in *On
Radji Beach*, Pan Macmillan, Sydney, 2010.

10 'Orphans ready for adoption', *Canberra Times*, 9 April 1975, p. 8.

11 NAA: Ref: A 1209, 1975/456

12 National Archives of Australia, Ref: A1209, 1975/657.

15 Ghosts in the fog (pp. 240–54)

1   National Archives of Australia, Immigration Department – Vietnam,
Ref: B925, V1978/60194 contains the full report prepared by the
Immigration Department.

2   National Archives of Australia, E. G. Whitlam – Personal Papers,
Ref: M522, vol. 5.

3   Forkert, *Orphans of Vietnam*, p. 209.

4   NAA, Ref: M522, vol. 5.

5   NAA, Ref: A 1209, 1975/546.

6   NAA, Ref: A1209, 1975/657.

7   NAA, Ref: M522, vol. 5.

8   Despite recommendations against using the C-130, it became the only
method of air transportation to and from Saigon – partly because,
I suspect, Qantas's insurer would not cover that leg of the journey.

9   Norman Manners, *Bullwinkel*, Hesperian Press, Perth, 2000, p. 216.

10 *The Age*, Melbourne, 19 April 1975, quoted in Forkert, *Orphans of
Vietnam*, p. 192.

11   There was no need to complete customs and immigration formalities as all the relevant paperwork had been done en route by the departmental officials accompanying the flight.

12   NAA, Ref: A 1209, 1975/658.

13   One issue that did emerge from the second Babylift operation was the over-representation of South Australian adoptive families in the final resettlement of orphans, with fifty-eight of the seventy-two children joining South Australian families. Eric Nicholls had certainly done a good job in Saigon.

14   Manners, *Bullwinkel*, p. 219.

16 Sunset (pp. 255–65)

1   *Tribune*, 8 April 1975. Such stories were spread across the more extremist mouthpieces on both sides of politics.

2   Manyon, *The Fall of Saigon*, p. 62.

3   Taylor, *Orphans of War*, p. 208.

4   Coulthard-Clark, *The RAAF in Vietnam*, p. 326.

5   National Archives of Australia, M522, vol. 5.

6   Later, arguments would erupt over whether or not Price evacuated his family's pet cats, while Gough Whitlam would deny that his government prioritised filing cabinets over people.

7   Coulthard-Clark, *The RAAF in Vietnam*, p. 330.

8   Taylor, *Orphans of War*, p. 199.

9   NAA, Ref: M522, vol. 5.

10   Klaus Neumann, *Across the Seas: Australia's response to refugees*, Black Inc., Melbourne, 2015, p. 228.

11   Ibid. There are also references in the NAA's Whitlam Papers file.

12   Ibid. There are also references in the NAA's Whitlam Papers file.

13   Neumann, *Across the Seas*, p. 238. This show of support would not save Cameron. At a caucus meeting on 5 June, he was moved from Labour and Immigration to Science and Consumer Affairs.

Epilogue: Pictures of children (pp. 267–77)

1   Parry, 'Still rootless'.

2   Ibid.

3   Sachs, *The Life We Were Given*, p. 83. In Vietnam, the dead must receive a proper burial so their restless souls can find peace.

4   Manyon, *The Fall of Saigon*, p. 61.

5   Engelmann, *Tears Before the Rain*, p. 25.

6   Author's conversation with Maria Makk, Lee's sister.

Appendix: Fighting dragons (pp. 279–88)

1   Thomas Tobin, Arthur Laehr and John Hilgenberg, *Last Flight from Saigon*, US Government Printing Office, Washington, DC, 2002, p. 34. It was rumoured that one DAO employee/escort who was killed was carrying $10 000 worth of jewellery when she boarded the aircraft but nothing when her body was recovered.

2   Cross, *MAC and Operation Babylift*, p. 41.

3   Snepp, *Decent Interval*, p. 240. From the distance of forty-plus years, it is still difficult to understand Graham Martin's misreading of so much about the course of the last few months of the war. He had lost a son who was serving in the army during the American involvement several years earlier and this may provide a partial explanation.

4   See both Rachel Winslow, *The Best Possible Immigrants*, University of Pennsylvania Press, Philadelphia, PA, 2017, p. 202; and Taylor, *Orphans of War*, p. 246.

5   Winslow, *The Best Possible Immigrants*, p. 202.

6   See Taylor, *Orphans of War*, p. 240; Butler, *The Fall of Saigon*, p. 485; and Winslow, *The Best Possible Immigrants*, p. 202.

7   Butler, *The Fall of Saigon*, p. 485.

BIBLIOGRAPHY

Books

Andre, Ty, *On My Brother's Shoulders*, Wakefield Press, Adelaide, 1997.

Bassett, Jan, *Guns and Brooches*, Oxford University Press, Melbourne, 1997.

Boris, Linda, *Every Sparrow That Falls*, self-published, USA, 2017.

Brass, Alister, *Bleeding Earth*, Alpha Books, Sydney, 1969.

Briand, Rena, *The Waifs*, Phuong-Huang Press, Melbourne, 1973.

Briand, Rena, *Woman at War: No tears to flow*, Phuong-Hoang Press, Melbourne, 1971.

Butler, David, *The Fall of Saigon*, Simon and Schuster, New York, 1985.

Cameron, Clyde, *China, Communism and Coca-Cola*, Hill of Content, Melbourne, 1980.

Cameron, Clyde, *The Cameron Diaries*, Allen & Unwin, Sydney, 1990.

Cawthorn, Nigel, *Vietnam: A war lost and won*, Arcturus, Sydney, 2004.

Coulthard-Clark, Chris. *The RAAF in Vietnam*, Allen & Unwin, Sydney, 1995.

De Hartog, Jan, *The Children,* Hamish Hamilton, London, 1968.

Engelmann, Larry, *Tears Before the Rain*, De Capo Press, New York, 1997.

Ferguson, Barbara, *Rain in My Heart,* Lothian Books, Melbourne, 2006.

Forkert, Joshua, *Orphans of Vietnam: A history of intercountry adoption policy and practice in Australia 1968–1975*, PhD thesis, University of Adelaide.

Gladwin, Michael, *Captains of the Soul*, Big Sky Publishing, Sydney, 2013.

Henderson, Charles, *Goodnight Saigon*, Berkley Calibre, New York, 2005.

Hocking, Jenny, *Gough Whitlam: His time, volume 2*, Miegunyah Press, Melbourne, 2012.

Kelly, Paul, *The Unmaking of Gough*, Allen & Unwin, Sydney, 1994.

Manners, Norman. *Bullwinkel,* Hesperian Press, Perth, 2000.

Manyon, Julian, *The Fall of Saigon*, Rex Collings, London, 1975.

McHugh, Siobhan, *Minefields and Miniskirts*, Doubleday, Sydney, 1993.

Neumann, Klaus, *Across the Seas: Australia's response to refugees*, Black Inc., Melbourne, 2015.

Oakes, Laurie, *Crash Through or Crash*, Drummond, Melbourne, 1976.

O'Neill, Robert, Vietnam *Task,* Cassell, Melbourne, 1968.

Oppenheimer, Melanie, *Volunteering*, UNSW Press, Sydney, 2008.

Quartly, Marion, Swain, Shurlee and Cuthbert, Denise, *The Market in Babies*, Monash University Publications, Melbourne, 2013.

Reid, Alan, *The Whitlam Venture*, Hill of Content, Melbourne, 1976.

Sachs, Dana, *The Life We Were Given*, Beacon Press, Boston, 2010.

Shaw, Ian, *On Radji Beach*, Pan Macmillan, Sydney, 2010.

Snepp, Frank, *Decent Interval*, Penguin, New York, 1980.

Steinman, Ron, *Women in Vietnam*, TV Books, New York, 2000.

Stone, Hoa Van, *Heart of Stone*, self-published, Adelaide, 2007.

Strobridge, Robert (Ed.)*, Turn My Eyes Away*, Friends for All Children, Boulder, CO, 1976.

Taylor, Rosemary, *Orphans of War*, Collins, London, 1988.

Terry, Susan, *House of Love*, World Books, London, 1967.

Tobin, Thomas, Laehr, Arthur and Hilgenberg, John, *Last Flight from Saigon,* US Government Printing Office, Washington, DC, 2002.

Ward, Geoffrey; and Burns, Ken, *The Vietnam War*, Ebury Press, London, 2017.

Warner, Denis, *Not with Guns Alone*, Hutchinson, Melbourne, 1977.

Willbanks, James, *Vietnam War Almanac*, Facts on File, New York, 2009.

Winslow, Rachel, *The Best Possible Immigrants*, University of Pennsylvania Press, Philadelphia, 2017.

Monographs and Articles

Archdeacon, Tom, 'Fateful flight carried a lifetime of bonds', Dayton Daily News, 6 June 2015.

Baldwin, Suzy, 'A down-to-earth near-saint', *The Bulletin*, 1 March 1988.

Beckett, Richard, 'The children at war', *Canberra Times*, 28 March 1967.

Briand, Rena, 'A Bunny turns war reporter in Vietnam', *Maclean's Magazine*, vol. 80, no.4, April 1967.

Bullard, Steven, 'After the fall', *Wartime*, no. 53, 2011.

Cross, Coy, *MAC and Operation Babylift,* Scott Air Force Base, Illinois, 1989.

Edwards, Peter, *The Fall of Saigon* [booklet], National Archives of Australia, Canberra, 2006.

INDEX

hachette
AUSTRALIA

If you would like to find out more about Hachette Australia,
our authors, upcoming events and new releases you can visit
our website or our social media channels:

hachette.com.au

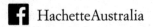 HachetteAustralia

 HachetteAus